FENG SHUI

—— FOR ——

辛卯 **2011**

THE YEAR OF THE METAL RABBIT

兔年運程下卷

The Year of the Metal Rabbit

Feng Shui for 2011

The author can be reached at:

Mastery Academy of Chinese Metaphysics Sdn. Bhd. (611143-A)

19-3, The Boulevard, Mid Valley City,

59200 Kuala Lumpur, Malaysia.

Tel   : +603-2284 8080

Fax   : +603-2284 1218

Email   : info@masteryacademy.com

Website : www.masteryacademy.com

DISCLAIMER :

Published by JY Books Sdn. Bhd. (659134-T)

INDEX

PREFACE

The Feng Shui Renaissance that has been taking place in the recent years has given rise to more and more interest in Classical Feng Shui, and a lot of enthusiasts and amateurs who are keen to dabble or try their hands at what I call 'F-I-Y' or Feng-Shui-It-Yourself. As a master trainer, teacher and practitioner of this classical field, I am of course always thrilled to see more people interested in Feng Shui, and its complementary fields, Chinese Astrology, Yi Jing and Face Reading.

This book has been produced in response to this increasing interest amongst members of the public for Feng Shui information and knowledge, and to cater to those who for reasons of time or perhaps, distance, are unable to attend my annual Feng Shui and Astrology seminars.

With this book, you will be well-informed on the Qi that will influence properties in 2011, and how best to utilise the energies of 2011 in your own home or office. In addition to the overall outlook for the year, based on the Flying Stars chart for 2011 and the Afflictions for 2011, there is the section on the Flying Stars for all 8 Houses in 2011.

It is this section, together with the monthly Flying Stars outlook for all 12 months of 2011, based on the Main Door and Bedroom locations, that will make it possible for you to gain a high level of personalised information about how the Qi of 2011 will affect you and your family, or your business. Don't worry if you're not familiar with how to plot a Flying Stars chart - just drop by my website **www.joeyyap.com** and make use of the Flying Stars calculator there.

As most of you will know, luck is divided into Man Luck, Earth Luck and Heaven Luck. Feng Shui is just one component in the Cosmic Trinity, so do not be overly concerned if there are negative stars at your Main Door or in the bedroom you are residing in. The full impact of the stars must also be viewed in light of the landforms in the area, which will trigger or activate the stars' negative or positive energies. If you would like to know more about how to do simple assessments of forms, you may want to look into my *Feng Shui for Homebuyers* series.

I always tell my clients and students that we should never be paranoid, nor should we let Feng Shui paralyse us into inaction. Remember, for every Yin there is a Yang and vice versa. Nothing is truly totally bad or totally good in Chinese Metaphysics. The most important thing is to understand what the Feng Shui influences are and prioritise your actions and make informed decisions.

I hope you find this book helpful, practical and most importantly, informative and I wish you all the best in the Year of the Metal Rabbit.

Warmest Regards,

Joey Yap

July, 2010

Author's personal website :
www.joeyyap.com

Academy websites :
www.masteryacademy.com I www.maelearning.com I www.baziprofilling.com

Joey Yap on Facebook :
www.facebook.com/joeyyapFB

MASTERY ACADEMY
OF CHINESE METAPHYSICS™

At **www.masteryacademy.com**, you will find some useful tools to ascertain key information about the Feng Shui of a property or for the study of Astrology.

The Joey Yap Flying Stars Calculator can be utilised to plot your home or office Flying Stars chart. To find out your personal best directions, use the 8 Mansions Calculator. To learn more about your personal Destiny, you can use the Joey Yap BaZi Ming Pan Calculator to plot your Four Pillars of Destiny – you just need to have your date of birth (day, month, year) and time of birth.

For more information about BaZi, Yi Jing, Date Selection, Xuan Kong or Flying Star Feng Shui, or if you wish to learn more about these subjects with Joey Yap, logon to the Mastery Academy of Chinese Metaphysics website at **www.masteryacademy.com**.

MASTERY ACADEMY
E-LEARNING CENTER
www.maelearning.com

www.maelearning.com

Bookmark this address on your computer, and visit this newly-launched website today. With the E-Learning Center, knowledge of Chinese Metaphysics is a mere 'click' away!

Our E-Learning Center consists of 3 distinct components.

1. Online Courses
These shall comprise of 3 Programs: our Online Feng Shui Program, Online BaZi Program, and Online Mian Xiang Program. Each lesson contains a video lecture, slide presentation and downloadable course notes.

2. MA Live!
With MA Live!, Joey Yap's workshops, tutorials, courses and seminars on various Chinese Metaphysics subjects broadcasted right to your computer screen. Better still, participants will not only get to see and hear Joey talk 'live', but also get to engage themselves directly in the event and more importantly, TALK to Joey via the MA Live! interface. All the benefits of a live class, minus the hassle of actually having to attend one!

3. Video-On-Demand (VOD)
Get immediate streaming-downloads of the Mastery Academy's wide range of educational DVDs, right on your computer screen. No more shipping costs and waiting time to be incurred!

Study at your own pace, and interact with your Instructor and fellow students worldwide...at your own convenience and privacy. With our E-Learning Center, knowledge of Chinese Metaphysics is brought DIRECTLY to you in all its clarity, with illustrated presentations and comprehensive notes expediting your learning curve!

Welcome to the Mastery Academy's E-LEARNING CENTER...YOUR virtual gateway to Chinese Metaphysics mastery!

Introduction

Introduction :

In order to fully utilise the information and material in this book, you need to have a basic understanding of how to derive certain information - for example, the location of your Main Door, the various directional sectors in your home and your personal Gua number.

How to ascertain the Location of your Main Door

In order to tap into the beneficial Qi of the year and the kind of Qi that will influence your home in 2011, it is important to be able to identify the various directional sectors of your home and also determine which sector your Main Door is located. This knowledge is particularly important for those who wish to make use of the information contained in the 8 Houses for 2011 chapter, which is based on the directional sector in which your house or office Main Door is found.

The first step is to divide your house into the 9 grids. To do this, you just need a simple scout's compass and a plan of your house. On the plan of your house, draw the 9 Grids as illustrated in Step 1 and Step 2.

Step 1

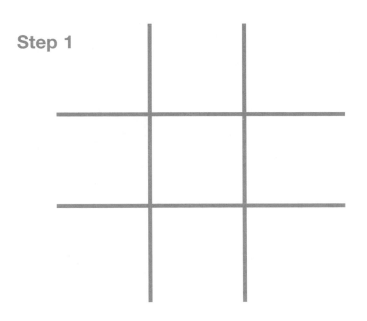

Step 2

Next, stand in the center point of your house and establish the North direction using the compass. On the plan of your house, mark out the sector in that direction as North and then identify all the other directions according to the directions of the compass.

Step 3

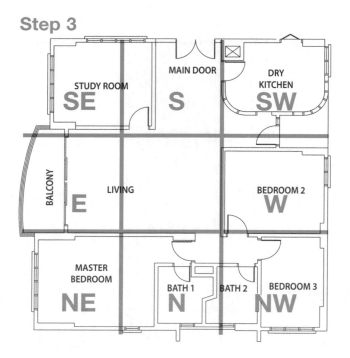

Using this simple 9 Grids, you will be able to identify the favourable and unfavourable sectors in your home and make less or more use of the corresponding rooms in the home. You will also be able to ascertain the location of your Main Door and from there, determine what kinds of energies will influence your home in 2011.

Personal Gua and Flying Star Feng Shui Chart

My personal website **www.joeyyap.com** has online calculators that will assist you in calculating your personal Gua and also the Flying Star Feng Shui chart of your house. For those of you with an interest in BaZi, you can also make use of my BaZi Ming Pan calculator to obtain your personal BaZi chart.

Find Your Gua Number and Animal Sign

Gua Number for 1912 - 2103 Years

Year of Birth		Gua Number for Male	Female	Year of Birth		Gua Number for Male	Female	Year of Birth		Gua Number for Male	Female	Year of Birth		Gua Number for Male	Female
1912	壬子 Ren Zi Water Rat	7	8	1936	丙子 Bing Zi Fire Rat	1	8	1960	庚子 Geng Zi Metal Rat	4	2	1984	甲子 Jia Zi Wood Rat	7	8
1913	癸丑 Gui Chou Water Ox	6	9	1937	丁丑 Ding Chou Fire Ox	9	6	1961	辛丑 Xin Chou Metal Ox	3	3	1985	乙丑 Yi Chou Wood Ox	6	9
1914	甲寅 Jia Yin Wood Tiger	2	1	1938	戊寅 Wu Yin Earth Tiger	8	7	1962	壬寅 Ren Yin Water Tiger	2	4	1986	丙寅 Bing Yin Fire Tiger	2	1
1915	乙卯 Yi Mao Wood Rabbit	4	2	1939	己卯 Ji Mao Earth Rabbit	7	8	1963	癸卯 Gui Mao Water Rabbit	1	8	1987	丁卯 Ding Mao Fire Rabbit	4	2
1916	丙辰 Bing Chen Fire Dragon	3	3	1940	庚辰 Geng Chen Metal Dragon	6	9	1964	甲辰 Jia Chen Wood Dragon	9	6	1988	戊辰 Wu Chen Earth Dragon	3	3
1917	丁巳 Ding Si Fire Snake	2	4	1941	辛巳 Xin Si Metal Snake	2	1	1965	乙巳 Yi Si Wood Snake	8	7	1989	己巳 Ji Si Earth Snake	2	4
1918	戊午 Wu Wu Earth Horse	1	8	1942	壬午 Ren Wu Water Horse	4	2	1966	丙午 Bing Wu Fire Horse	7	8	1990	庚午 Geng Wu Metal Horse	1	8
1919	己未 Ji Wei Earth Goat	9	6	1943	癸未 Gui Wei Water Goat	3	3	1967	丁未 Ding Wei Fire Goat	6	9	1991	辛未 Xin Wei Metal Goat	9	6
1920	庚申 Geng Shen Metal Monkey	8	7	1944	甲申 Jia Shen Wood Monkey	2	4	1968	戊申 Wu Shen Earth Monkey	2	1	1992	壬申 Ren Shen Water Monkey	8	7
1921	辛酉 Xin You Metal Rooster	7	8	1945	乙酉 Yi You Wood Rooster	1	8	1969	己酉 Ji You Earth Rooster	4	2	1993	癸酉 Gui You Water Rooster	7	8
1922	壬戌 Ren Xu Water Dog	6	9	1946	丙戌 Bing Xu Fire Dog	9	6	1970	庚戌 Geng Xu Metal Dog	3	3	1994	甲戌 Jia Xu Wood Dog	6	9
1923	癸亥 Gui Hai Water Pig	2	1	1947	丁亥 Ding Hai Fire Pig	8	7	1971	辛亥 Xin Hai Metal Pig	2	4	1995	乙亥 Yi Hai Wood Pig	2	1
1924	甲子 Jia Zi Wood Rat	4	2	1948	戊子 Wu Zi Earth Rat	7	8	1972	壬子 Ren Zi Water Rat	1	8	1996	丙子 Bing Zi Fire Rat	4	2
1925	乙丑 Yi Chou Wood Ox	3	3	1949	己丑 Ji Chou Earth Ox	6	9	1973	癸丑 Gui Chou Water Ox	9	6	1997	丁丑 Ding Chou Fire Ox	3	3
1926	丙寅 Bing Yin Fire Tiger	2	4	1950	庚寅 Geng Yin Metal Tiger	2	1	1974	甲寅 Jia Yin Wood Tiger	8	7	1998	戊寅 Wu Yin Earth Tiger	2	4
1927	丁卯 Ding Mao Fire Rabbit	1	8	1951	辛卯 Xin Mao Metal Rabbit	4	2	1975	乙卯 Yi Mao Wood Rabbit	7	8	1999	己卯 Ji Mao Earth Rabbit	1	8
1928	戊辰 Wu Chen Earth Dragon	9	6	1952	壬辰 Ren Chen Water Dragon	3	3	1976	丙辰 Bing Chen Fire Dragon	6	9	2000	庚辰 Geng Chen Metal Dragon	9	6
1929	己巳 Ji Si Earth Snake	8	7	1953	癸巳 Gui Si Water Snake	2	4	1977	丁巳 Ding Si Fire Snake	2	1	2001	辛巳 Xin Si Metal Snake	8	7
1930	庚午 Geng Wu Metal Horse	7	8	1954	甲午 Jia Wu Wood Horse	1	8	1978	戊午 Wu Wu Earth Horse	4	2	2002	壬午 Ren Wu Water Horse	7	8
1931	辛未 Xin Wei Metal Goat	6	9	1955	乙未 Yi Wei Wood Goat	9	6	1979	己未 Ji Wei Earth Goat	3	3	2003	癸未 Gui Wei Water Goat	6	9
1932	壬申 Ren Shen Water Monkey	2	1	1956	丙申 Bing Shen Fire Monkey	8	7	1980	庚申 Geng Shen Metal Monkey	2	4	2004	甲申 Jia Shen Wood Monkey	2	1
1933	癸酉 Gui You Water Rooster	4	2	1957	丁酉 Ding You Fire Rooster	7	8	1981	辛酉 Xin You Metal Rooster	1	8	2005	乙酉 Yi You Wood Rooster	4	2
1934	甲戌 Jia Xu Wood Dog	3	3	1958	戊戌 Wu Xu Earth Dog	6	9	1982	壬戌 Ren Xu Water Dog	9	6	2006	丙戌 Bing Xu Fire Dog	3	3
1935	乙亥 Yi Hai Wood Pig	2	4	1959	己亥 Ji Hai Earth Pig	2	1	1983	癸亥 Gui Hai Water Pig	8	7	2007	丁亥 Ding Hai Fire Pig	2	4

- Please note that the date for the Chinese Solar Year starts on Feb 4. This means that if you were born in Feb 2 of 2002, you belong to the previous year 2001.

Year of Birth			Gua Number for Male	Gua Number for Female	Year of Birth			Gua Number for Male	Gua Number for Female	Year of Birth			Gua Number for Male	Gua Number for Female	Year of Birth			Gua Number for Male	Gua Number for Female
2008	戊子 Wu Zi	Earth Rat	1	8	2032	壬子 Ren Zi	Water Rat	4	2	2056	丙子 Bing Zi	Fire Rat	7	8	2080	庚子 Geng Zi	Metal Rat	1	8
2009	己丑 Ji Chou	Earth Ox	9	6	2033	癸丑 Gui Chou	Water Ox	3	3	2057	丁丑 Ding Chou	Fire Ox	6	9	2081	辛丑 Xin Chou	Metal Ox	9	6
2010	庚寅 Geng Yin	Metal Tiger	8	7	2034	甲寅 Jia Yin	Wood Tiger	2	4	2058	戊寅 Wu Yin	Earth Tiger	2	1	2082	壬寅 Ren Yin	Water Tiger	8	7
2011	辛卯 Xin Mao	Metal Rabbit	7	8	2035	乙卯 Yi Mao	Wood Rabbit	1	8	2059	己卯 Ji Mao	Earth Rabbit	4	2	2083	癸卯 Gui Mao	Water Rabbit	7	8
2012	壬辰 Ren Chen	Water Dragon	6	9	2036	丙辰 Bing Chen	Fire Dragon	9	6	2060	庚辰 Geng Chen	Metal Dragon	3	3	2084	甲辰 Jia Chen	Wood Dragon	6	9
2013	癸巳 Gui Si	Water Snake	2	1	2037	丁巳 Ding Si	Fire Snake	8	7	2061	辛巳 Xin Si	Metal Snake	2	4	2085	乙巳 Yi Si	Wood Snake	2	1
2014	甲午 Jia Wu	Wood Horse	4	2	2038	戊午 Wu Wu	Earth Horse	7	8	2062	壬午 Ren Wu	Water Horse	1	8	2086	丙午 Bing Wu	Fire Horse	4	2
2015	乙未 Yi Wei	Wood Goat	3	3	2039	己未 Ji Wei	Earth Goat	6	9	2063	癸未 Gui Wei	Water Goat	9	6	2087	丁未 Ding Wei	Fire Goat	3	3
2016	丙申 Bing Shen	Fire Monkey	2	4	2040	庚申 Geng Shen	Metal Monkey	2	1	2064	甲申 Jia Shen	Wood Monkey	8	7	2088	戊申 Wu Shen	Earth Monkey	2	4
2017	丁酉 Ding You	Fire Rooster	1	8	2041	辛酉 Xin You	Metal Rooster	4	2	2065	乙酉 Yi You	Wood Rooster	7	8	2089	己酉 Ji You	Earth Rooster	1	8
2018	戊戌 Wu Xu	Earth Dog	9	6	2042	壬戌 Ren Xu	Water Dog	3	3	2066	丙戌 Bing Xu	Fire Dog	6	9	2090	庚戌 Geng Xu	Metal Dog	9	6
2019	己亥 Ji Hai	Earth Pig	8	7	2043	癸亥 Gui Hai	Water Pig	2	4	2067	丁亥 Ding Hai	Fire Pig	2	1	2091	辛亥 Xin Hai	Metal Pig	8	7
2020	庚子 Geng Zi	Metal Rat	7	8	2044	甲子 Jia Zi	Wood Rat	1	8	2068	戊子 Wu Zi	Earth Rat	4	2	2092	壬子 Ren Zi	Water Rat	7	8
2021	辛丑 Xin Chou	Metal Ox	6	9	2045	乙丑 Yi Chou	Wood Ox	9	6	2069	己丑 Ji Chou	Earth Ox	3	3	2093	癸丑 Gui Chou	Water Ox	6	9
2022	壬寅 Ren Yin	Water Tiger	2	1	2046	丙寅 Bing Yin	Fire Tiger	8	7	2070	庚寅 Geng Yin	Metal Tiger	2	1	2094	甲寅 Jia Yin	Wood Tiger	2	1
2023	癸卯 Gui Mao	Water Rabbit	4	2	2047	丁卯 Ding Mao	Fire Rabbit	7	8	2071	辛卯 Xin Mao	Metal Rabbit	1	8	2095	乙卯 Yi Mao	Wood Rabbit	4	2
2024	甲辰 Jia Chen	Wood Dragon	3	3	2048	戊辰 Wu Chen	Earth Dragon	6	9	2072	壬辰 Ren Chen	Water Dragon	9	6	2096	丙辰 Bing Chen	Fire Dragon	3	3
2025	乙巳 Yi Si	Wood Snake	2	4	2049	己巳 Ji Si	Earth Snake	2	1	2073	癸巳 Gui Si	Water Snake	8	7	2097	丁巳 Ding Si	Fire Snake	2	4
2026	丙午 Bing Wu	Fire Horse	1	8	2050	庚午 Geng Wu	Metal Horse	4	2	2074	甲午 Jia Wu	Wood Horse	7	8	2098	戊午 Wu Wu	Earth Horse	1	8
2027	丁未 Ding Wei	Fire Goat	9	6	2051	辛未 Xin Wei	Metal Goat	3	3	2075	乙未 Yi Wei	Wood Goat	6	9	2099	己未 Ji Wei	Earth Goat	9	6
2028	戊申 Wu Shen	Earth Monkey	8	7	2052	壬申 Ren Shen	Water Monkey	2	4	2076	丙申 Bing Shen	Fire Monkey	2	1	2100	庚申 Geng Shen	Metal Monkey	8	7
2029	己酉 Ji You	Earth Rooster	7	8	2053	癸酉 Gui You	Water Rooster	1	8	2077	丁酉 Ding You	Fire Rooster	4	2	2101	辛酉 Xin You	Metal Rooster	7	8
2030	庚戌 Geng Xu	Metal Dog	6	9	2054	甲戌 Jia Xu	Wood Dog	9	6	2078	戊戌 Wu Xu	Earth Dog	3	3	2102	壬戌 Ren Xu	Water Dog	6	9
2031	辛亥 Xin Hai	Metal Pig	2	1	2055	乙亥 Yi Hai	Wood Pig	8	7	2079	己亥 Ji Hai	Earth Pig	2	4	2103	癸亥 Gui Hai	Water Pig	2	1

• Please note that the date for the Chinese Solar Year starts on Feb 4. This means that if you were born in Feb 2 of 2002, you belong to the previous year 2001.

Using the 12 Month Outlook based on Bedroom Location Section

To use this section, you must know the location of your property's Main Door, and the location of your bedroom. Note that your bedroom may be located on the Ground Floor or 1st or 2nd floor.

1. Identify the location of your Main Door.

In the example below, the Main Door is located in the West. So turn to page 145, for the section on the 12 month outlook for all 8 bedrooms for a West Main Door House.

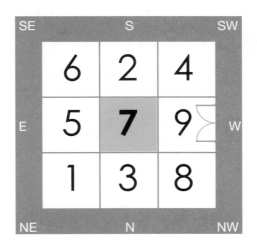

2. Identify the location of your bedroom.

In the example below, the Bedroom is located in the South. So turn to page 154, and you will find the 12 month outlook for your bedroom, located in a West Main Door house.

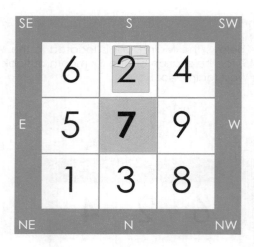

2011 Feng Shui Afflictions

2011 Feng Shui Afflictions

2011 Feng Shui Afflictions:

The Grand Duke (太歲) – EAST 2 82.6° - 97.5°

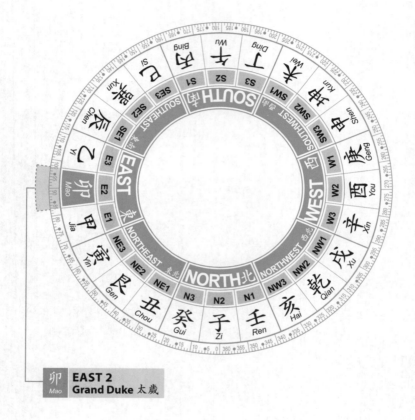

| 卯 Mao | **EAST 2** **Grand Duke** 太歲 |

The Grand Duke Star flies into the East 2 sector for the year, and therefore this sector should not be activated or disturbed. Aggravating the energies of the Grand Duke Star for the year sees the possibility of dangers, hazards, and mishaps. Health risks are also possible, with the Grand Duke causing some medical troubles and complications for the residents of the property. Where work is concerned, it is not good to face the East 2 sector as one is likely to be affected by the energies of the Grand Duke. It would be better to put your back to this direction, as this will help you command greater authority at work, as well as exert a better sense of control. It will also bode well towards decision-making at the workplace.

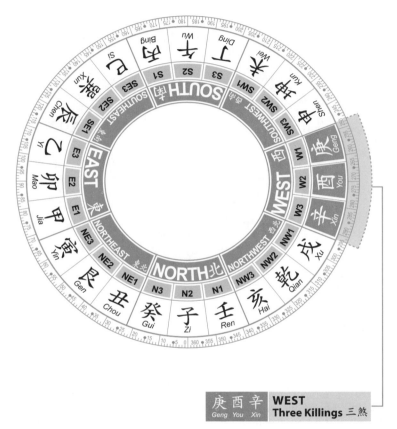

3 Killings (三煞) – WEST 247.6° - 292.5°

庚	酉	辛	**WEST**
Geng	You	Xin	**Three Killings** 三煞

The West sector of your property sees the presence of the Three Killings this year. You should carefully avoid disturbing the area, and particularly, avoid performing any groundbreaking or renovation in the area. The negative repercussions that can be brought about in this area include accidents, mishaps, and possible catastrophes. The chances of robberies and theft are also high. If the Three Killings is aggravated, possible medical troubles and complications are also possible for the inhabitants of the property.

The 5 Yellow Star (五黄) – EAST 67.6° - 112.5°

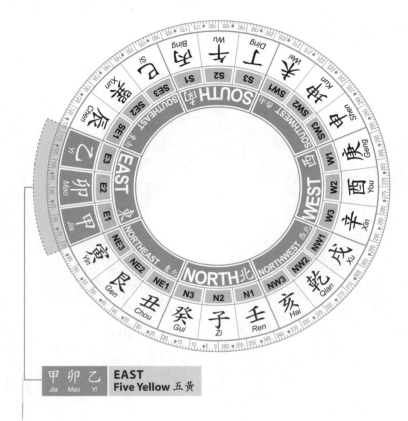

甲 卯 乙	**EAST**
Jia Mao Yi	**Five Yellow** 五黄

The #5 Yellow Star flies into the East sector for the year. As the #5 Yellow can have repercussions that are very negative, the East sector is thus considered to be the most negative one of the year and one that is best avoided. If the sector cannot be wholly avoided for some reason, then it would be best to pacify the energies of the #5 Yellow by using metal items made of brass, copper, or iron in the area. Renovation work in this sector must also be steadfastly avoided; if this is impossible, then any form of renovation work here should only be done after a good date has been carefully considered and selected.

The Year Breaker (歲破) – WEST 2 262.6° - 277.5°

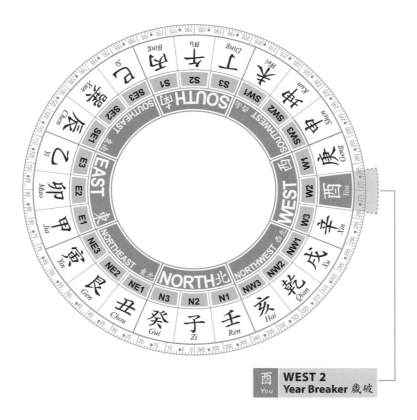

| 酉 You | **WEST 2** Year Breaker 歲破 |

The West 2 sector is afflicted with the presence of the Year Breaker for the year. This star, which also goes by the name 'Wrath of the Grand Duke,' brings about negative repercussions that should not be activated by renovations or groundbreaking in the area. This sector should thus be undisturbed, as otherwise the consequences could be quite negative. This star brings about negative effects that could be worse than the ones brought upon by the Grand Duke.

Flying Stars Feng Shui for 2011

Flying Stars Feng Shui for 2011

Overview

Wealth Sectors   : Northwest, West

Academic Sectors : Southwest, Northeast

Negative Sectors : North, South, East

2011 Flying Stars by Sectors :

Direction / Location	Annual Star	Forecast
西北 Northwest	八白 8 White	The Northwest sector is the Wealth location for 2011, as the Wealth Qi is ushered in from this direction. If your home or office Main Door is located in the Northwest sector, you can expect to enjoy good financial returns along with a strong potential for career advancement. Activate this sector, and use it as often as often as possible. Even if there is no door in the Northwest sector of your property, you can still derive the positive benefits of the #8 White Star's positive Qi by tapping into the direction. It can also be derived by placing a Yang-type object in the area. Some good examples include fans, clocks, and televisions.
西 West	九紫 9 Purple	Using the West door in your home or office may lead to promotions, new ventures, new beginnings and general happy events. Couples looking to tie the knot or trying to start a family will also benefit from using the West sector or their home. As the secondary wealth sector of the year, The presence of the #9 Purple Star makes the West sector in 2011 a good area for boosting income, particularly for starting a permanent job or endeavours of a long-term nature. If you have a West main door, wealth activities, such as investment or work that hinges on recognition or the limelight, will prosper.

Direction / Location	Annual Star	Forecast
東北 Northeast	一白 1 White	Scholars and academicians should actively use this area for the year 2011. Those who involved in philosophy, writing, research and literary pursuits may also want to conduct their activities in this sector for a more rewarding result. The #1 White is also beneficial for career and wealth related pursuits, though it may lead to some travelling for this purpose. Utilizing this sector may lead to your superiors recognizing your hard work and also the possibility of assistance from those around you.
東南 Southeast	六白 6 White	This year finds the #6 White Star in the Southeast sector, making it a great location for an office or a study. Spending more time here will help you move up the corporate ladder, increase support from bosses and improve your network of helpful work acquaintances. Having a main door in the Southeast sector will be a boon for you if you hold a corporate position and are in line for a promotion.

Direction / Location	Annual Star	Forecast
西南 Southwest	四綠 4 Green	The #4 Green Star enters the Southwest sector of your property in 2011. This star brings a favorable outlook for those who are involved in academic and scholarly pursuits as well as for those who make a living in the creative, artistic or literary fields. If you sit in the Southwest sector of your office or use the Southwest door often, you can also expect some travelling in the cards this year. There may also be potential for romantic interlude and better relationships for couples using this area of their home.
北 North	三碧 3 Jade	The #3 Jade Star has flown into the North sector for the year 2011. This area should be avoided for the most part. The negative influences of this star may bring result in constant arguments and bickering as well as heated disagreements. In extreme cases, the negative effects of the #3 Star may even lead to legal complications and lawsuits. The effects and be countered and weaken somewhat by placing an oil lamp or bright red items in this sector for 2011.

Direction / Location	Annual Star	Forecast
東 East	五 黃 5 Yellow	This is the most dangerous sector for 2011. Avoid undertaking important activities in this sector of your home and business. You should not renovate this sector of your property for the duration of this year, it is best to keep this area quiet and inactive. However, if you have no other choice and have to use this area, weaken the negative effects of the #5 Yellow Star by placing metal items made of brass, copper or iron in the East.
南 South	二 黑 2 Black	As the #2 Black Star has flown into the South this year, try to avoid using this area. The negative influence of this Star can cause occupants in the South sector this year to suffer from ill health that is far more serious than the usual cough-cold-fever. Where possible, pregnant women should completely avoid using this sector. However, it bodes well for gains and investment through property and real estate industries. Having metal objects made of copper, brass, bronze or pewter may weaken the negative Qi in this area but the best remedy would be to avoid the South sector altogether.

The 8 Types of Houses in 2011

Main Door in North Sector

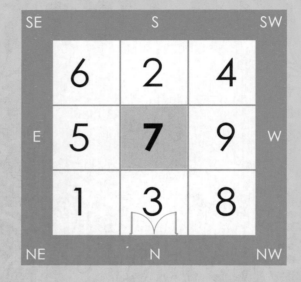

Overview

The #3 Jade Star is the annual star of conflict, and this year, the North sector is plagued by arguments, misunderstanding, and in severe cases – lawsuits and legal complications. So if you are using a North door, double-check your contracts and fine prints. Family members tend to me more impatient this year using this door, and communication tends to falter especially in months with negative stars.

In the presence of positive external features like a natural lake to the North, this indicates travel and reaping gains from to travel. Those in the sports arena will also do well with the aggressive nature of this Star #3. Those in the speaking profession will find the courage and clarity they need when using the positive aspects of Star #3.

If the physical forms of your North sector are less than ideal – for example, an incomplete Bright Hall which does not facilitate Qi-coagulation – then internally, divert the Qi flow from the North sector to the Northwest sector (location of the annual Wealth Star). This helps negate some of the negative effects from the #3 Star.

As far as human actions go: keep a relaxed attitude! Remember that there is no point arguing when neither party is actually listening. Use the Star #3 if you need to break away bad habits and start new ventures in life.

Main Door in Northwest Sector

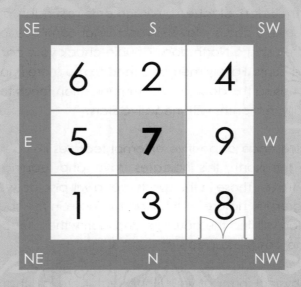

Overview

The wealth star for the year resides in the Northwest sector for 2011. Houses and offices using a Northwest door will benefit from the auspicious effects of the #8 White Star – financial stability, opportunity for gains, and career enhancement. If you do not have a door in the Northwest sector, you can activate this sector with an internal water feature. Water is a Yang component that can lend a 'buzz' to the Qi in the sector. Alternately, what you can do for your office is to relocate your water-cooler to this sector – that way, the constant human activity will stimulate the Star energies there. Work performance also increase as a side effect of this prosperous energy. The Star #8 in the Northwest is also perfect for establishing businesses and consolidations.

At the home front, having the Northwest as a living area or TV area will also activate the positive effects of this sector.

Having a mountain externally to the Northwest strengthens the positive effects of the wealth star. Established companies and business models will reap results under the influence of this Feng Shui configuration. Gua #2 individuals will see fastest results.

Main Door in West Sector

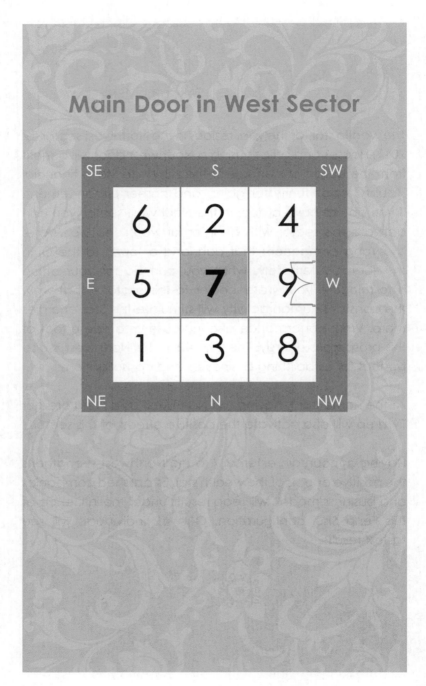

Overview

This year the West sector contains the #9 Purple Star of Happiness. If your main door is in the West sector, expect more good news coming your way this year. For those looking for promotion at work, try using a West sector entrance or even a West sector study room.

Businesses that well benefit especially from this Star #9 are the bridal industry, beauty, motivation, public relations, and spirituality. Offices should capitalize on this sector by having brainstorming meetings here. Managers already using this sector will receive the positive effects of Star #9 as well.

The positive effects are multiplied if externally there is a hill or higher ground. If the external forms are too Yang – a busy road or junction – then the positive effects are minimized instead.

Additionally, this star can also be considered a secondary Peach Blossom star, especially for couples looking to enhance existing relationships. For couples looking to start a family and conceive a child, this sector room would be ideal especially for those who belong to Gua #4 and Gua #1.

Main Door in Southwest Sector

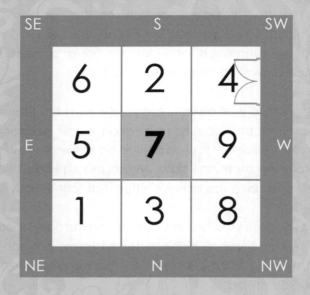

	SE	S	SW
	6	2	4
E	5	**7**	9	W
	1	3	8
	NE	N	NW

Overview

Replacing the dreaded #5 Yellow Star from last year is the #4 Green Star in the Southwest sector. The #4 Star is the bringer of romance, new relationships, and positive communication. As such, this star is also useful for businesses dealing with education, personal development, creativity, and beauty. If you are not already using a Southwest sector door – see if there is an entrance available here to tap into this flowery energy.

The Star #4 in the Southwest sector is especially beneficial for Gua #1 and #9 persons. Additionally, a water feature in this sector can help boost the positive effects. On the home front, however, caution should be taken – over-activity of this Peach Blossom star may not be appropriate for married couples and existing relationships. Those seeking new relationships can use the Southwest room as a bedroom or study.

All in all, keep this sector clear and open, unhindered by large structures like cabinets. Allowing the Qi to flow and meander in this sector facilitates fruitful communication throughout the year.

Main Door in South Sector

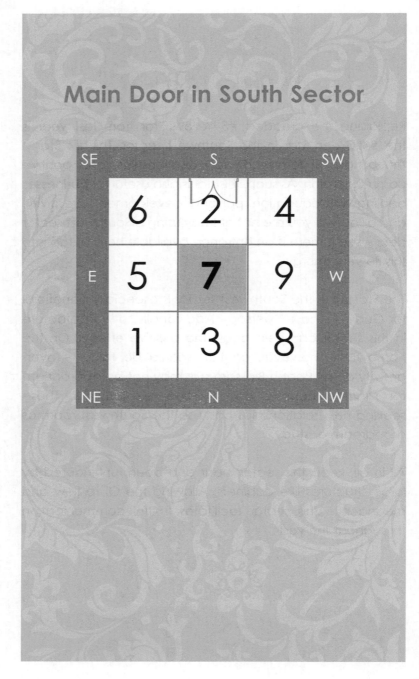

SE	S	SW
6	2	4
5 (E)	**7**	9 (W)
1	3	8
NE	N	NW

Overview

The illness star for the year flies into the South sector this year – if your door is in this sector, be prepared to battle weak health. Boost your immune system with vitamins and watch your diet. In more severe cases – either when afflicted by negative forms, or when coupled with a negative Monthly Flying Star – take care against stomach problems, skin disorders, migraine, and depression.

Persons who are more sensitive to the ill effects of this #2 Black Star are Gua individuals #1, #3, and #6. As with the negative Star 5 Yellow, elderly folk and pregnant mothers should avoid using a South sector room to avoid potential illnesses and problems.

For those of you using a South sector door, and with no option to use another entrance – redirect the internal Qi flow to the Southeast sector using a partition or screen. By physically 'waling through' the Southeast sector, some of the ill-effects of the South sector can be diminished. Another viable option is to activate the positive energy of the Southeast (#6 White Star) to minimize the negative #2 Black – a Water feature in the Southeast should help stimulate the positive Qi.

The only exception to the negative effects of the #2 Star is when there is a Huge Door mountain externally to the South. This denotes wealth and status through properties.

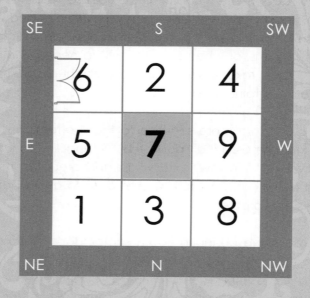

Main Door in Southeast Sector

SE	S	SW
6	2	4
5 (E)	**7**	9 (W)
1	3	8
NE	N	NW

Overview

The Star #6 White in the Southeast is the Star of power and authority, normally favored by managers and CEO's. Using this door enhances ones respectability and encourages wise wielding of power and execution. Using a Southeast room for work also facilitates this effect. A water feature can also be used to activate the energies of this sector.

In 2011, this sector is most effective for Gua #4 persons. Through proper execution, one is able to reap financial gains as well.

For Gua #3 persons, however, should take care against neck and finger injuries, in the presence of external Sha Qi in the Southeast.

A natural water feature externally indicates wealth from distant places or as a result of travelling. However, a straight-moving river cutting across the Southeast indicates accidents and injury from falling.

Main Door in East Sector

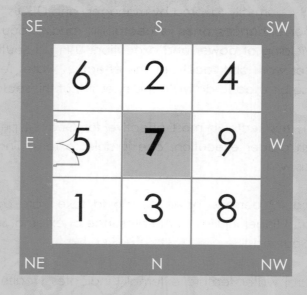

Overview

The East sector with the #5 Yellow Star would be the most negative sector for the year. Its volatile energies bring about misfortune and accidents. If you have your main door in the East, consider using another entrance for the year.

No renovation should be performed in this sector, even nailing and drilling (commonly done to hang a picture). There should not be water features in this sector as well, as this will activate the negative #5 Yellow. Also important to note that pregnant mothers and elderly folk should pay extra attention and caution when using this door – occupants tend to be more accident prone. Avoid using an East sector room altogether.

If the external forms are positive, like a Bright Hall which allows Qi to gather gently or wide open spaces like playgrounds – benefits can still be reaped. However, health-wise is still a risk due to the aggressive nature of the #5 Yellow.

The #5 Yellow at the main door is also sometimes a reminder to go for a medical check-up, especially if you have not been doing so. Gua #3 individuals using this door should pay attention to the liver.

If the external physical forms are afflicted by Sha Qi, it indicates possible accidents, bankruptcy, and major illnesses like cancer.

Main Door in Northeast

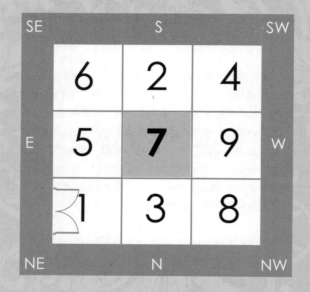

SE	S	SW
6	2	4
5	**7**	9
1	3	8
NE	N	NW

Overview

The Northeast sector houses the Star #1 White, also known as the Nobleman Star of the year. If your main door is in the Northeast – this is the year you will get favors you need, as well as to keep your eyes opened for potentially helpful people coming into your life. This is also especially useful for those in sales that thrive on meeting new customers!

Alternately, the Star #1 promotes creativity, brainstorming, and useful ideas – so those in the thinking and intellectual businesses will also benefit from using a Northeast sector door. Water-related industries like shipping, tourism, sanitation, and intellectual properties should also tap into the positive effects of this star – stimulate the Qi here with more human activity.

This star would be in its most positive and beneficial state when it is supported by mountains, hills, or higher ground externally. This indicates not only help from others, but help from powerful people.

12 Month
Room - by - Room
Analysis for the
8 Types of Houses

INDEX

Using the 12 Month Outlook based on Bedroom Location Section

To use this section, you must know the location of your property's Main Door, and the location of your bedroom. Note that your bedroom may be located on the Ground Floor or 1st or 2nd floor.

1. Identify the location of your Main Door.

In the example below, the Main Door is located in the West. So turn to page 145, for the section on the 12 month outlook for all 8 bedrooms for a West Main Door House.

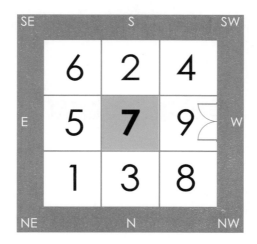

2. Identify the location of your bedroom.

In the example below, the Bedroom is located in the South. So turn to page 154, and you will find the 12 month outlook for your bedroom, located in a West Main Door house. (Note: Instead of the bedroom, you can also use the same analysis for your office or study room located in that sector.)

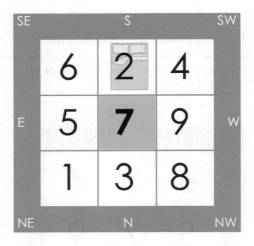

North Sector
Main Door

North Sector Main Door

This section contains the monthly outlook for all 12 months of the year, for different bedrooms in a property with a North sector Main Door.

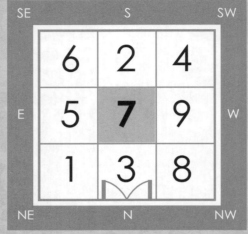

Ground Floor

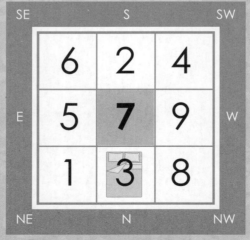

First Floor

農曆正月 (February 4th – March 5th) 庚寅

Those who have undergone recent medical procedures should avoid using the North bedroom this month, as there is a chance of complications setting in and causing some serious trouble. Make sure that good auditing procedures are in place, as employees may be involved in theft and fraud at this unsettled point in time. But this will be a good month to form alliances with partners or associates in far-flung corners of the world – or the ones simply residing abroad!

農曆二月 (March 6th – April 4th) 辛卯

Talk to others, and not about others. Communicate clearly with other parties, to minimize the possibility of running into problems and complications in your relationships that might continue to dog you into the future. You might also want to refrain from dealing in equities, shares or any form of financial trading this month; lest you find yourself troubled by financial and/or legal problems as a consequence of your transactions.

農曆三月 (April 5th – May 5th) 壬辰

If your marriage is important to you, then regardless of the problems that crop up this month, you will find the time and put in the requisite effort to address any dispute you may have ongoing with him or her. As far as business is concerned, check and double-check any decisions you make pertaining to your ventures, to mitigate the risk of suffering from financial losses, later on.

農曆四月 (May 6th – June 5th) 癸巳

Just when you least expect it, and think that nothing else could possibly stand between you and sweet success, a spanner is thrown into the works. In other words; it will be to your best advantage to not conclude major deals at this time. Nevertheless, professionals or part-timers in the counselling field will find their services benefiting those who seek their advice – so do continue using the North bedroom, to continue being of service to others!

North Sector Main Door

農曆五月 (June 6th – July 6th) 甲午

You'll find that opportunities to travel in a professional capacity actually boost your reputation and stature this month, enabling you to cement your good name regardless of the industry or field you're in. Where your bodily safety is concerned, be careful of potential accidental injuries to your back and spine; and take extra care when performing when any physically-demanding activities or sports.

農曆六月 (July 7th – August 7th) 乙未

Think before you say or do anything, especially if you find your relationship with your other half more strained than usual this month. It's perfectly normal for every relationship to go through the occasional rough patch, but that's no excuse to behave in an irrational manner. More room to breathe – quite literally, in most cases – is what is needed among couples using this room this month, and you'll find your relationship improving by leaps and bounds the more you give other space and increase tolerance.

農曆七月 (August 8th – September 7th) 丙申

Your friendship may be tested when you find yourself facing a lawsuit against your own friend. Hence, do watch out for any possible signs of a power struggle or dispute with your friends. Similarly, those using a North bedroom might end up feeling depressed or emotionally distraught this, more than likely as the result of an act of betrayal by those you thought you could trust, more so your family members and friends.

農曆八月 (September 8th – October 7th) 丁酉

Bear in mind that it will be a rather trying and testy month for those using the North. For one thing, be prepared for questions regarding your fidelity to your relationship from your partner as feelings of suspicion mount. Jealousy is a symptom that, if not treated in its early stages, could manifest into a strained relationship and loss of trust. Elderly males using this bedroom will also be more susceptible to lung problems.

農曆九月 (October 8th – November 7th) 戊戌

If you're the type who simply loves to gamble and take risks on your money, then be forewarned that this is not a good month to indulge in your interest for excitement. Any speculative or high-risk investments will most likely result in losses, and in some extreme cases, can also bode potential legal wrangles and lawsuits.

農曆十月 (November 8th – December 6th) 己亥

It never hurts to listen to good, sound financial advice – more so if you know you can use it to your advantage at any given point in time. So if money-making's on your list of priorities, you now know what to do! The North is also a good sector to use in terms of academic endeavours and studies. Businesspeople, however, should be wary of fraud or embezzlement – scrutinize all business transactions and legal documents very carefully, and be sure to double-check anything that arouses your suspicions.

農曆十一月 (December 7th – January 5th 2012) 庚子

Those working with heavy machinery should be careful of injuries whilst working shifts this month. This is not the time to lose focus and concentration and be careless with your safety, or accidents could happen. Rivals at the workplace will be going all out to prevent you from gaining the promotion you deserve and using a bedroom in this sector will only make things worse this month.

農曆十二月 (January 6th – February 3rd 2012) 辛丑

A surprise confrontation by employees might come to you as complete surprise this month. In order to prevent a rebellion that spreads far and wide, you will need to work and think hard about how to reach out to them and address their grouses. Speculative investments show a loss this month and any dealings will be fraught with financial losses or possibly even lawsuits. This is not a month to spend gambling, as your recklessness will lead to severe losses.

| Main Door | North | Bedroom Sector | Northwest |

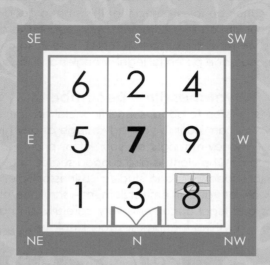

農曆正月 (February 4th – March 5th) 庚寅

Use the Northwest more frequently this month to enjoy good health and harmonious relationships. This is especially true for those of you in marriages and in relationships. You'll find that it's a good month to have discussions on sensitive or potentially-explosive topics as both partners will be willing to compromise and be patient.

農曆二月 (March 6th – April 4th) 辛卯

This month, you'll need to watch out for malicious, insidious types who may be trying to plot ways to derail you and to trip you up. Watch what you do and say. Your personal relationships will be off to a 'bad' start at the beginning of the month, but things will eventually smooth themselves out as the month draws to a close. It will benefit you to keep a cool head and to focus on trying to eliminate arguments and dissatisfactions.

農曆三月 (April 5th – May 5th) 壬辰

This month, be sure to check to see if there are any negative structures or features outside the Northwest sector, as these indicate the possibility of a lung infection afflicting those using a bedroom in this sector for the duration of the month. If possible, elderly folks already afflicted with pneumonia before, or suffering from weak lungs, will do well to be temporarily moved into another room.

農曆四月 (May 6th – June 5th) 癸巳

This is the time for budding entrepreneurs to prove your worth, and to show the world just exactly what you're made of. It's more than likely that you'd be off to a good start, so if not now, then when else? There is likely to be a more favourable time with a confluence of encouraging factors to help you along in your pursuits. And if you're a salaried employee, that promotion or raise you've been eyeing all this while might just be yours – sooner than you realise, even!

Main Door	North	Bedroom Sector	Northwest

農曆五月 (June 6th – July 6th) 甲午

You may find your boss pressing for deadlines that simply can't be met. Chances are, he or she is concerned about declining profit margins, and is projecting stress and anxiety onto you. Bear in mind not to take stress too lightly, however, as being constantly overwrought could affect your health, especially if you allow ill-will and anxiety to get to you. So guard against any ailment affecting your muscles, joints or even nerves!

農曆六月 (July 7th – August 7th) 乙未

It's a fairly profitable month for those involved in the forestry, dairy or agriculture business. That aside, this is definitely not the time of the year to engage in strategic negotiations, as you will only find yourself plagued by losses in the long-term. But there will be good profits to be made from property deals, but one may have to travel in order to conclude these deals.

農曆七月 (August 8th – September 7th) 丙申

Your wealth luck starts to take a dip this month, and it could well be that your career or business is encountering some serious problems. Plan carefully, and consider every alternative that would allow you to leverage on your position and capitulate on any of the gains you've made over the course of the year. It'll be important to focus on planning and taking measured, deliberate steps.

農曆八月 (September 8th – October 7th) 丁酉

You might want to consider relocating yourself to another bedroom, as illness and poor health in the form of gastrointestinal problems threaten to bedevil those using the Northwest room this month. For elderly people and pregnant women, in particular, it might not be the risk that is best to take. In your professional life, look out for rivals, co-workers or even subordinates who are bent on sabotaging whatever efforts you put in at work.

農曆九月 (October 8th – November 7th) 戊戌

The energies of the month augur well for personal and professional relationships. Hence, this is a good time to foster even closer ties with your business partners and loved ones. In fact, you'll find your network of contacts playing a pivotal role in enhancing your professional reputation and status; thereby contributing to your popularity within a surprisingly short period of time.

農曆十月 (November 8th – December 6th) 己亥

Rebellious children will get into fights at school, and end up getting hurt by sharp metal objects and metal implements. Parents will do well to monitor their activities a bit closely, and to respond with love and compassion even when they seem particularly stubborn or sullen. It's a phase that needs to be worked out. Business deals should be postponed, as there will be sudden changes in negotiations that could result in possible losses.

農曆十一月 (December 7th – January 5th 2012) 庚子

This is a month to dispose of property, as windfall gains can be expected. You can expect to make quite a bit of profit! Property dealers and real estate agents will make financial gains this month, especially if there is natural water outside this sector. Therefore, aim to be a bit more ambitious in your goals and to cultivate network connections you're your instincts tell you will lead to bigger deals.

農曆十二月 (January 6th – February 3rd 2012) 辛丑

Take advantage of support from superiors this month by launching your new ideas and projects. You'll find that your higher-ups will be willing to help you or offer some valuable advice, even if they seemed to be somewhat cold or not forthcoming in the past. Couples should focus on careers rather than relationships, as marital disputes may become serious and require some intervention to be resolved.

Main Door	North	Bedroom Sector	West

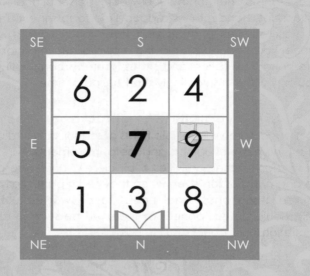

	SE	S	SW	
	6	2	4	
E	5	**7**	9	W
	1	3	8	
	NE	N	NW	

農曆正月 (February 4th – March 5th) 庚寅

If there are no natural water formations outside the West this month, then chances are, your relationships will prosper and remain harmonious! The likelihood of naturally-occurring water outside this area has the potential to bring about acrimonious personal relations and strained ties. Those intending to embark on a major research project, where substantial research and development expenditure is required, will find this a suitable month to look for sponsors.

農曆二月 (March 6th – April 4th) 辛卯

The profits are just waiting to be reaped, more so if you're involved in the fashion, beauty or cosmetics industry, so this is the month you'll have to give it your all and work doubly hard. If you play your cards right, you'll see your rewards and profits doubled or tripled in relation to the amount of effort you put in. In addition, this is also a good time of the year to go on a spiritual retreat, or take a respite from your hectic schedule, to clear your mind and metaphorically re-charge your batteries.

農曆三月 (April 5th – May 5th) 壬辰

Couples looking to conceive should harness the positive energies of the West bedroom this month, as the energy bodes well for conducive family and personal relationships. This is also a good time to cash-in on any real estate or property investments you've made earlier, as the profits will keep you laughing all the way to the bank! Ensure that you do not fall prey to extravagant spending at the same time, however.

農曆四月 (May 6th – June 5th) 癸巳

Businesses smart enough to tap into the power of the media and press publicity will experience a boom this month. There will be good opportunities to benefit from some good and positive attention and use it as leverage to build a bigger client and profit base. Couples using the West bedroom this month will, however, find their relationship at an all-time low. Be sure to communicate, and above all, be patient with one another. There will be a temptation to be short and curt, but this should be resisted for the benefit of the relationship.

農曆五月 (June 6th – July 6th) 甲午

If you typically use or are using the West room this month, you will increase your chances of getting that promotion, salary raise or recognition from your superiors, provided you've been performing at work all along, of course! If you know that you've been putting in good effort and letting your talents shine at the workplace, there is no reason for your performance to go unrewarded this month.

農曆六月 (July 7th – August 7th) 乙未

Keep a tight rein on your temper, more so if you happen to be using the West sector room this month when you're dealing with others. Otherwise, your relationships will only suffer due to your unintentionally harsh or cutting words due to your sense of aggravation and anxiety brought about by heightened anger. The presence of negative structures or features outside this sector will only worsen the situation, by bringing about health problems like food poisoning and/or liver-related problems.

農曆七月 (August 8th – September 7th) 丙申

If the academic or education field is your niche industry, you'll be pleased to know that this will be a favourable month for you, even though your rivals or competitors threaten to throw a damper on your efforts. Despite other people's insidious attempts, luck is on your side thanks to your solid reputation built upon your talent and hard work. And if you're a student due to sit for an important exam soon, use the West to study or as a bedroom, while preparing for your exams.

農曆八月 (September 8th – October 7th) 丁酉

Seek the advice of your seniors or an experienced professional before you actually engage in any investment deals this month. You lose nothing, and gain everything by doing so. This is not the month to take random risks based on feelings or even momentary greed. If you simply take the time to evaluate your decision and run it by a professional expert, your returns are likely to be more favourable.

農曆九月 (October 8th – November 7th) 戊戌

If metaphysical or esoteric studies are your area of interest, then you might want to tap into the energies of the West sector room this month. This will gradually allow you to develop your skills, enabling you to better understand and absorb principles and theories that might be completely new to you. You'll also derive a sense of fulfilment from being able to engage completely with your interests. What's more, long-term investments in real estate or properties will yield handsome financial gains, if undertaken this month.

農曆十月 (November 8th – December 6th) 己亥

It's a good month for personal relationships for those of you using the West room this month. However, it will be best to ensure that there are no naturally-occurring water formations outside the room. Those intending to embark on a major research project, where substantial research and development expenditure is required, will find this a suitable month to look for sponsors.

農曆十一月 (December 7th – January 5th 2012) 庚子

Those of you who work or are involved in the fashion, beauty or cosmetics industry will find this a good month in terms of success and profits. In addition, this is also a good time of the year to go on a spiritual retreat, or take a respite from your hectic schedule, to clear your mind. This will go a long way in helping you to recoup your lost energy from the previous months of the hectic year.

農曆十二月 (January 6th – February 3rd 2012) 辛丑

Those of you who are married or in relationships will enjoy a good month if using this room. Also, if you're keen to have children, this room bodes well for your efforts! This is also a good time to cash-in on any real estate or property investments you've made earlier, as your profits are likely to be quite substantial. Be sure to get the advice of an agent or consultant if you're wondering about the potential returns.

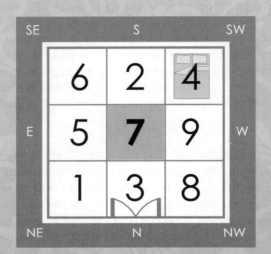

SE	S	SW
6	2	4
5	**7**	9
1	3	8
NE	N	NW

E (left side) · W (right side)

農曆正月 (February 4th – March 5th) 庚寅

Women using the Southwest room this month should go for a mammogram, or consult their physician, to check for breast cancer. Even if there are no risk factors in place, it will be best to simply get yourself evaluated to ensure that all is as it should be. This is certainly not the month to gamble or engage in any speculative, high-risk investments; unless you wish to end up poorer at the end of the day.

農曆二月 (March 6th – April 4th) 辛卯

This is indeed a good month to embark on a vacation, or leisure travel. And you might just be lucky enough to encounter a romantic fling! Be open to possibilities and don't cut yourself from anything just because it doesn't fit into your well-organised plans. At the same time, however, it will be important to adopt a low-key attitude and avoid expecting it to develop into anything lasting or long-term. Not everything needs to end in forever in order for it to be good for you.

農曆三月 (April 5th – May 5th) 壬辰

Keep a sharp eye on your kids, as they could well be influenced by peer-pressure to get themselves involved in rebellious or damaging activities. This is especially true if they become sullen and reticent. Find ways to spend more time with and draw them out in order to get them talking and communicating with you. Marital relations will also be strained and tense, so exercise tolerance and patience in dealing with your spouse.

農曆四月 (May 6th – June 5th) 癸巳

Women could well prove to be trouble-makers this month, especially if your workplace is one dominated by women. You really want to stay clear of any such disputes or quarrels involving these people, and instead, concentrate on your work. Keep your head low and avoid getting wrangled in any long-festering office politics.

Main Door	North	Bedroom Sector	Southwest

農曆五月 (June 6th – July 6th) 甲午

Students and candidates due to sit for examinations soon should use the Southwest, if you wish to optimize your results. Similarly, those involved in the literary or arts field might want to start looking for a company willing to publish their works, as the energies of the Southwest augur well for such an undertaking. Couples will also find their relationships blossoming into something stronger and more harmonious by using the Southwest sector for the duration of the month.

農曆六月 (July 7th – August 7th) 乙未

You might want to consider moving your kids to another bedroom this month, more so if you notice them behaving in a more rebellious and disobedient manner. If they continue to use this room this month, bear in mind that you'll have to be firmer than usual, and be prepared for some heady battle of the wills! Those of you who are single will this to be a most unsuitable month to engage in romantic flings, so don't be too easily swept off your feet by someone you've just met at your local pub, bar or disco!

農曆七月 (August 8th – September 7th) 丙申

In business, tensions will run high as a result of hidden agendas, so you will need to be cautious when committing to important deals. This will be especially true if the CEO is female. Play your cards right, and the best way to do this will be to be careful in your planning and to take measured, deliberate steps. Don't rush into something headlong, or out of spontaneous instinct.

農曆八月 (September 8th – October 7th) 丁酉

Handle all sharp instruments with care, to prevent yourself from suffering from a nick or cut – because the risk is higher if you're using the Southwest room this month. And scrutinize all legal documents very carefully before you commit yourself to them, to pre-empt any potential complications later on. Be sure to read the fine print thoroughly. Be careful of your interactions with others, as you might well find yourself being a party to a bitter or even violent dispute.

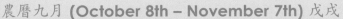

農曆九月 (October 8th – November 7th) 戊戌

Success favours the most persevering, so deal with difficult clients or parties in a patient and rational manner, and you'll reap the rewards of your equities or share deals. Those who are required to travel for business purposes will also find the energies of the month conducive enough to enhance their reputation and stature. So pack your bags, and get ready to embark on your next voyage! Expectant mothers should try to avoid long-distance travel this month, as this could result in accidents or pregnancy complications.

農曆十月 (November 8th – December 6th) 己亥

Those in the real estate business need to adapt their methods when speculating in property, as a change is needed for them to be able to capitalise on their investments. Sticking to the same old strategies and plans will only create negative and adverse scenarios, so attempt to brainstorm on how to improve and shake things up to your benefit.

農曆十一月 (December 7th – January 5th 2012) 庚子

Be careful of problems amongst the women, as this could lead to aggression or negative public attention. This may be especially true in the workplace, where long-brewing problems or disagreements could blow up in a detrimental manner if not diffused early on. Serious disagreements are possible between couples using this bedroom this month. Much like the previous month, a concerted effort will be needed to keep the relationship on a positive footing, as otherwise the relationship will have to endure some trouble.

農曆十二月 (January 6th – February 3rd 2012) 辛丑

Share and equity dealings will be profitable this month but concluding them will require some amounts of patience and effort. Avoid making any swift, emotional decisions that will only work against your overall plan. You need to be steady in mind and in action, and much profit could be reaped as a result. Your stature, reputation and name will improve if you travel to conduct business this month.

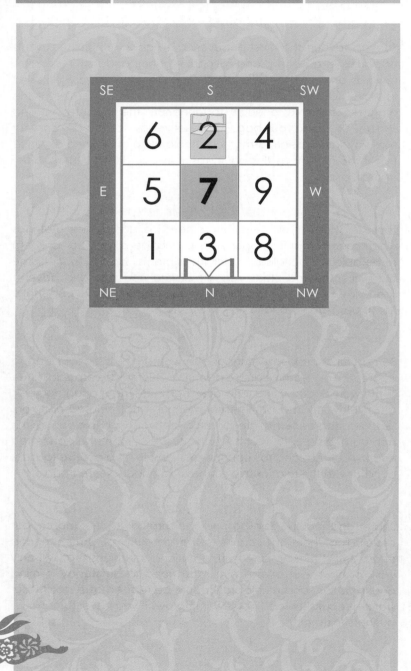

農曆正月 (February 4th – March 5th) 庚寅

On the professional and personal aspects of life, arguments, disputes and backbiting are the order of the day, so be sure to keep a cool head, as you seek to remedy matters. Don't play into office politics because once you enter the game, it's harder to extricate yourself from it. Be sure to be observant of what's going on, but try not to get involved in matters. You might also want to check to see that all fines, summonses and taxes have been settled, to avoid running afoul of the law.

農曆二月 (March 6th – April 4th) 辛卯

If you're in a relationship and find it to be encountering some problems, maybe it's time to give your partner some `personal space', so as to save your relationship. The best thing to do this month will be to retreat and let this cool down or blow over on its own accord. However, windfall gains favouring the elder female members of the family are very possible this month. Those of you who have previous investments might want to consider selling or cashing in as the profits could be very high.

農曆三月 (April 5th – May 5th) 壬辰

Be careful in handling your business dealings, as you certainly wouldn't want to be duped by anyone who's just bent on making a quick buck out of you, would you? Unfortunately, that would exactly be the case – or the risk, rather – this month, especially if you don't play your cards close to your chest. Refrain from trusting people too easily, particularly those whom you have just recently met or are new to you and your business concerns.

農曆四月 (May 6th – June 5th) 癸巳

Employees should ensure that they resist the temptation to be drawn into arguments, gossip and disputes in the work environment this month, as these could develop into large-scale problems. This is a good sector for those who wish to become involved in religious pursuits.

Main Door	North	Bedroom Sector	South

農曆五月 (June 6th – July 6th) 甲午

Stand up for your rights, and don't allow yourself to be made a scapegoat by a cowardly superior who isn't brave enough to admit his or her mistakes! This is not the time to sit by and allow someone else get away with something simply because they are higher-up than you on the hierarchy. It will behove you well to make a stand this month.

農曆六月 (July 7th – August 7th) 乙未

Confusion and lack of clarity comes into the decision-making process if you are using the bedroom this month so it is preferable not to make any important decisions at this point in time, particularly if those decisions will have a long-term impact in your professional or personal life. Couples need to watch for discord in marriage, arguments and family disharmony, and strive to deal with any quarrels with a sense of proportion and patience.

農曆七月 (August 8th – September 7th) 丙申

Use the South room for spiritual and religious pursuits if you wish to delve deeper into your area of interest. Keep a sharp look out, however, for the presence of any negative structures or features outside this sector, as they could cause health problems such as bone-aches and joint-pains. And in general, while there will be money to be made from real estate deals this month, your health may suffer. This means that you could end up feeling stressed at the end of the day.

農曆八月 (September 8th – October 7th) 丁酉

Misunderstandings and clouded thoughts threaten to mar the harmony you enjoy in any relationship, be it professional or personal. So maintain a low profile, and give other people the required breathing space to enable them to sort things out by themselves. On a similar note, disputes and negligence could well be the factors causing you to lose money, more so if you happen to be dabbling in the property or real estate business. This is a month of unforeseen problems; have your contingency plans in place.

農曆九月 (October 8th – November 7th) 戊戌

Those with literary talents will find the recognition and rewards they seek forthcoming will be forthcoming this month, bringing with it the possibility of good news and successful developments. Married women using the South bedroom, and living under the same roof as their in-laws might want to keep any contact with them to a minimal this month, as your relationship will tend to be frosty and tense.

農曆十月 (November 8th – December 6th) 己亥

Employees will find that they seem to work harder this month but income and deal closure do not seem to be concluded. If you feel that you are plugging away at the same old opportunity without any signs of interest or profit forthcoming, it might be time to give it a rest and focus your energies elsewhere. Those involved in spiritual pursuits or in gaining spiritual knowledge should use this bedroom this month.

農曆十一月 (December 7th – January 5th 2012) 庚子

Relationships need to be very low-key this month, as it will be a time of confused thinking and misunderstandings. Tensions should not be further aggravated. Give yourself time and space for emotional recovery, and if your partner or spouse wants to draw you into an argument, simply withdraw from it and suggest that the matter be resolved at a later time.

農曆十二月 (January 6th – February 3rd 2012) 辛丑

Those in real estate have the possibility of speculating in property related investments this month. If you've scoped out the market and know exactly how to proceed, this will be an ideal time to do so, as the profits could be high. Don't hold back if you're feeling fairly certain. This will also be a month that is conducive to self-cultivation, and if the opportunity arises, you should take a course in self-development or in any other course or program that interests you and will help improve your skills.

| Main Door | North | Bedroom Sector | Southeast |

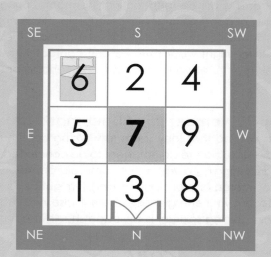

SE	S	SW
6	2	4
5	**7**	9
1	3	8

E — W
NE — N — NW

農曆正月 (February 4th – March 5th) 庚寅

Keep a low profile this month, as jealousy and rivalry will cause you trouble, and possibly lead to legal complications for those who are not wise enough lie maintain a low profile. Don't seek unnecessary attention unless you're quite prepared to deal with the consequences, which can be rather unnerving. Academics and legal professionals will find their skills much sought-after, and will find many opportunities opening up to further leverage on their knowledge and talents.

農曆二月 (March 6th – April 4th) 辛卯

Those who have worked hard will enjoy the rewards of their efforts, soon enough. This is a month that bodes well for rewards that come after some prolonged effort or labour. Similarly, employees in the printing, logistics and courier industries can look forward to a promotion and salary increment this month. There is a general upward trend in those particular industries for this month.

農曆三月 (April 5th – May 5th) 壬辰

Watch out for rebellious or disgruntled staff, as their discontent could cause them to betray you at any given time. Instead of allowing a mutiny to form, handle the problem with care and genuine interest in seeing how you can alleviate their concerns and promote a stronger sense of stability and loyalty. This is not a very suitable time to conclude any business deals, as they could well result in reverse takeovers, leaving you in the losing end in the process.

農曆四月 (May 6th – June 5th) 癸巳

Competitive athletes and sports professionals will find the energies of the Southeast to be favourable in allowing them to excel in competitions and tournaments this month. This is also a good room to be used by children or candidates who are going to write important examinations. Consultants, strategists and planners will also find their skills to be in great demand, although they may need to travel to have their advice implemented by clients.

| Main Door | North | Bedroom Sector | Southeast |

農曆五月 (June 6th – July 6th) 甲午

If either father or son happens to be using the Southeast bedroom, then look out for any signs of tension between them. Potential conflicts should be avoided as much as possible. Perhaps some physical distance between them might be beneficial. Good profits can be realised this month, but a more hands-on approach is required to maximise rewards. Those in travel will find this a challenging month, as competition leads to price wars where nobody will emerge the victor.

農曆六月 (July 7th – August 7th) 乙未

Couples looking to conceive should tap into the beneficial energies of the Southeast bedroom this month. Manufacturers and those involved in the production and manufacturing industry will also find this to be a favourable month, where disruptions are minimal, and output maximal. Elderly ladies should, however, be mindful of any potential health problems affecting their kidneys, or even cancer.

農曆七月 (August 8th – September 7th) 丙申

If you intend to impress your superiors and/or other important parties, seek the advice of your elders and mentors, before you plan how to go about being impressive. Relationships will also be favourable for you this month, so go ahead and seal that partnership with your business affiliate. Ensure that the terms and conditions of your agreement have been carefully ironed-out, of course.

農曆八月 (September 8th – October 7th) 丁酉

Stay away from speculative investments this month, but if you are in the engineering business this is the month to expand and seek new clients. There could be unexpected rewards in store. Elderly members of the family should pay serious attention to sudden health issues and not delay in getting medical help, as otherwise medical complications could arise.

農曆九月 (October 8th – November 7th) 戊戌

An ideal time of the year to immerse yourself in property or gilt investments, provided you're willing to take on a certain amount of risk. Some of you should be careful, however, of malicious parties out to sabotage your efforts. Where possible or necessary, seek the advice of your elders or mentors, as their suggestions will allow you to attain financial success at the end of the day.

農曆十月 (November 8th – December 6th) 己亥

A rocky relationship or business partnership on the verge of breakup can be amicably resolved if you are using the Southeast bedroom. Coaches and mentors are present so take their advice and act on these suggestions to achieve success. If your job involves strategic thinking or analysis, you will find that you have the chance to advance your career and gain a name for yourself within the company or the industry you're in.

農曆十一月 (December 7th – January 5th 2012) 庚子

Employers should be careful with labour relations or arbitration, as workers will challenge authority and be difficult to manage. Those in positions of power should be aware of challenges to their authority. There is also the possibility of sons challenging their fathers. In general, relationships with substantial power differentials will undergo some trials and tribulations this month, so it will be important to manage these in good faith and with an eye for an amicable resolution.

農曆十二月 (January 6th – February 3rd 2012) 辛丑

Investment and merchant bankers who engage in stock and corporate deals will put business on the books, and as a result increase the figures on the bottom line. Elderly members of the family should avoid using this bedroom this month, as there is a strong possibility that they may suffer from heart ailments. This is a good month for property or gilt investments so stick your neck out as you will make good financial gains.

農曆正月 (February 4th – March 5th) 庚寅

Continuous isolation and loneliness are never good for anyone, so seek the company of friends and family, especially if you need a listening ear or shoulder to cry on. This becomes especially heightened this month, as feelings of isolation tend to overcome you. Unfortunately, candidates due to write their examinations soon will find themselves easily distracted, so focus on what's important.

農曆二月 (March 6th – April 4th) 辛卯

If you're using an East bedroom this month, you need to remain vigilant, as your relationships, wealth and even safety may be threatened this month. Drive safely, ensure that the necessary insurance policies are in place, invest prudently, and above all, practice tact and patience with those around you. In fact, this is a month whereby all important decisions and investments should be postponed.

農曆三月 (April 5th – May 5th) 壬辰

Females who use the East bedroom may want to undergo a thorough check-up and mammogram this month to ensure that there are no untoward problems or risks. For everyone in general, the temptation to engage in speculative or high-risk investments, including gambling, should be resisted, as you only stand to lose more than gain.

農曆四月 (May 6th – June 5th) 癸巳

Arguments, quarrels and misunderstandings threaten domestic harmony, more so if the parties to a relationship are not willing to compromise. Therefore, make an effort to quell your temper and your frustration by trying to reach for a solution that doesn't involve ill-will or anger. Likewise, the energies in the Easy bedroom this month can also precipitate or increase the risk of heart problems or limb injuries.

| Main Door | North | Bedroom Sector | East |

農曆五月 **(June 6th – July 6th)** 甲午

Tread very carefully this month, as risky business dealings and/or property transactions will only serve to deplete your bank accounts. Generally speaking, it would be better not to use the East bedroom this month, unless you wish to risk acquiring gastrointestinal problems. Unsurprisingly, the presence of any negative structures outside the East sector will only increase the possibility and frequency of accidents, illnesses and disastrous outcomes for those using this bedroom.

農曆六月 **(July 7th – August 7th)** 乙未

Couples using the East bedroom should be careful not to allow disagreements to be blown out of proportion, as both partners are unable to think clearly and will end up saying things they do not mean. Success and promotion may come in the publishing field through hard work but there is always someone in the background who will try to undermine you from an intellectual point of view.

農曆七月 **(August 8th – September 7th)** 丙申

Niggling health issues are the main problem for those using the East bedroom this month especially in the form of eye and heart trouble. Fire hazards are also a potential hazard this month and electrical wiring should be checked where it is old and in need of replacement. Those in the political arena will find that friends and acquaintances will be around to help them with their political aspirations.

農曆八月 **(September 8th – October 7th)** 丁酉

Those in the insurance industry will have to put in hours of hard work and overtime to stave off financial losses this month. All forms of building expansion should be kept for a later time, and it would be better for you to focus on consolidation and motivation for the time ahead. Conservative, long-term property deals will bring positive financial rewards for you.

農曆九月 (October 8th – November 7th) 戊戌

Watch where and what you eat this month, and where possible, eat more frequently at home. After all, home-made food always tends to be more hygienic and healthy, especially since this month carries the risk of an upset stomach and stomach flu. Those dabbling in the communications industry should refrain from making an important financial investment or undertaking any business expansion plans this month as the chances of failure are high.

農曆十月 (November 8th – December 6th) 己亥

Stress and depression may end up causing some form of mental instability or neurosis this month among those who are prone to these issues, especially if negative Sha is located in the sector of the East bedroom. This may be especially true among elderly people using this room. Older males may find that the promotion to a position of authority ends up in a disastrous situation.

農曆十一月 (December 7th – January 5th 2012) 庚子

Avoid doing anything ambitious this month, and keep a low profile on the work-front as things will not go smoothly. It is not the time to make major career changes or decisions, as these will not have the consequences that you intend. All minor illnesses should be taken seriously as there is a tendency for health issues to take a turn for the worse at this point.

農曆十二月 (January 6th – February 3rd 2012) 辛丑

Be careful when travelling, as this could result in accidents that might require hospitalisation. If you have made profits from real estate, then it would be advisable to cash in these gains this month. Travel and courier businesses will feel a slow down this month and notice a sharp decline in clients and turnover.

| Main Door | North | Bedroom Sector | Northeast |

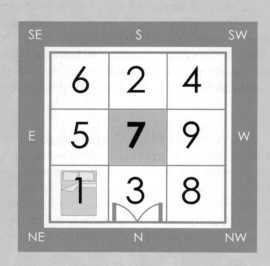

農曆正月 (February 4th – March 5th) 庚寅

It will be better to consolidate your position this month, as projects tend to stagnate and progress grinds to a halt. It will be rather foolhardy to try to push for development when you will do better to conserve your energy and plan for a later stage. Where romance is concerned, the green-eyed monster makes its unwelcome appearance this month.

農曆二月 (March 6th – April 4th) 辛卯

Speculative investments in asset acquisitions will return favourable profits this month, especially if these involved travel abroad. Therefore, grab the opportunity that allows you to travel as financial rewards are likely. Academics and people facing important examinations will do well this month in the Northeast bedroom, as it bodes well for scholarly pursuits.

農曆三月 (April 5th – May 5th) 壬辰

There will be those who spread rumours about you and your business this month, resulting in a loss of wealth and even the possibility of legal issues. Business relationships may be a little strained so avoid partnerships or new alliances this month, as the outcome will not be favourable. You will need to be more circumspect of the new connections you make, as otherwise only losses are likely.

農曆四月 (May 6th – June 5th) 癸巳

If you invest in property this month, you are likely to enjoy profitable deals. Therefore, be sure to follow up on other previous inquiries, or speak to a real-estate agent to see how you can maximise potential financial returns with astute decisions. Pregnant women who use the Northeast bedroom may encounter complications in their pregnancy.

農曆五月 (June 6th – July 6th) 甲午

This is a good month for those in the creative industries, as there is a chance to make a name for yourself and step into the limelight. This is not the month to be modest and retiring, as it won't bring you any benefits. There is a time to step back from the limelight, and there are times when it's necessary to step forward in order to get your just dues.

農曆六月 (July 7th – August 7th) 乙未

Avoid working with people you do not know very well, as they may let you down when you need to rely on them the most. This is a month to ask for the promotion you require as superiors will recognise your talents this month and be willing to show their appreciation! If you are involved in competitive sports, you will do well in international competitions this month.

農曆七月 (August 8th – September 7th) 丙申

Those in travel and logistics will find the opportunity to conclude new deals and build up alliances abroad. Those in the real estate business and those who conclude property deals will find business highly profitable and lucrative at this point in time. Keep your eye out for a good bargain in the property field, as many good offers abound. Business deals should be concluded this month, as the conditions will be in your favour.

農曆八月 (September 8th – October 7th) 丁酉

It will be a competitive month at work, with office politics at its full, no-holds-barred height. Focusing on romance this month is not a good idea, as it might end with your reputation in tatters and your spirits dejected. It will be better for you to focus on another aspect of your life instead. Those in the financial world will find new clients and customers, especially if they travel to solicit business prospects.

農曆九月 (October 8th – November 7th) 戊戌

This is a good room to use in preparations for important examinations this month. The energies in the Northeast bedroom this month will prove to be conducive for learning and academic activities, as it heightens focus and concentration and helps you tackle problems with a clear mind. Politicians wishing to rise up the ranks will find this a good month in terms of receiving support from people already in power or esteem within the government, or within their respective parties.

農曆十月 (November 8th – December 6th) 己亥

It will seem as though progress comes to a stop this month, so it will be fruitless to continue to push forward ambitiously. The smarter alternative will be to sit back and recoup your losses, and plan for a new strategy in the months ahead. Ask for help from mentors or trusted friends on what type of steps you should plan to take. You'll find romantic relationships plagued by jealousy this month, so you will need to be careful with your interactions with others if it bothers your partner.

農曆十一月 (December 7th – January 5th 2012) 庚子

Speculative investments in asset acquisitions will return favourable profits this month, especially if these involved travel abroad. Try to look for smart ways to invest in these types of investments, and get the advice from experts if you're unsure how to proceed. Academics and people facing important examinations will do well this month in the Northeast bedroom, as it bodes well for scholarly pursuits.

農曆十二月 (January 6th – February 3rd 2012) 辛丑

There is the risk of loss of wealth, and subsequent legal repercussions, due to some malicious gossip or rumour being spread about you or your business. It will be important to ascertain if this is someone within the company or an external force (a competitor, perhaps), but the main focus should be on fixing your reputation and strengthening your client and partnership or alliance base.

East Sector
Main Door

Main Door	East	Bedroom Sector	East

This section contains the monthly outlook for all 12 months of the year, for different bedrooms in a property with an East Main Door.

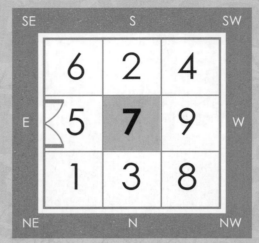

Ground Floor

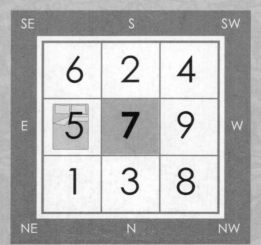

First Floor

農曆正月 (February 4th – March 5th) 庚寅

Look out for any negative structures or features towards the East sector, as these are the harbingers of emotional or mental problems, such as stress and depression. It seems that one's thoughts will be most susceptible to being under attack from stress and anxiety this month, but other types of health issues may also arise in the form of headaches or migraines. Prioritize your health and you should do just fine. Don't push yourself too hard where work or emotional problems are concerned.

農曆二月 (March 6th – April 4th) 辛卯

Those in the entertainment industry and market may also encounter some personal setbacks this month. The trick lies in remaining focused on your business goals, while not neglecting your own personal affairs at the same time. Those considering a joint-venture or partnership with another party might want to delay making such a move for the meantime, and wait for a more suitable time to put their plans into action. Avoid rushing into something even if you feel it is imperative to do so.

農曆三月 (April 5th – May 5th) 壬辰

If you simply have to travel on a frequent basis this month, then it would be wise to ensure that all the relevant insurance policies are in place. Above all, travel safely and be particularly attentive to your personal safety as well as to the general safekeeping of your valuables and important documents. Don't trust your belongings with someone new, even if they seem personable and friendly.

農曆四月 (May 6th – June 5th) 癸巳

Be mindful of any mental disturbance plaguing those who happen to be using an East bedroom this month, as any such condition left untreated could lead to severe complications in due time. There should be no stigma attached when it comes to seeking early psychiatric help or counselling for anyone who needs it. You may also find that head injuries and bone problems are prevalent, so exercise caution and avoid any risky physical activities.

農曆五月 (June 6th – July 6th) 甲午

Even if you happen to be single, and searching for the love of your life, avoid plunging into any new relationships this month, as they will only bring your heartache. Even if you succumb to the temptations of charm and good looks, ensure that you simply keep it low-key without investing too many hopes into it for the future. Females who have been suffering from stomach upsets or abdominal pains lately should consult their doctor at once. It will not be to your benefit to prolong your condition to a later time.

農曆六月 (July 7th – August 7th) 乙未

Do not be overzealous or overambitious as you go about your property transactions! Be wise and stick to a moderate plan of action. You should seek immediate medical treatment, especially if your stomach has been troubling you lately. Couples who find their relationship to be going through a rough patch this month should give each other some space to calm down and think things over. It will not be to your benefit to press the issue to breaking point.

農曆七月 (August 8th – September 7th) 丙申

This month, you may need to prepare yourself for some relationship issues. Relationships could be turbulent and acrimonious for those using the East bedroom, and there could be involvement of a third party. However, all is not doom and gloom; there are plenty of opportunities for improvement if both sides maintain openness and honesty. Avoid being tactless or overly blunt in your speech.

農曆八月 (September 8th – October 7th) 丁酉

For women using the East room this month, stomach and respiratory problems will plague you. Those of you who are involved in sports or play sports competitively should be careful of accidents this month which could result in bone and tendon injuries. These results could have serious implications in the future if left untreated or unmanaged, so don't ignore the warning signs.

農曆九月 (October 8th – November 7th) 戊戌

Lawyers, advocates and solicitors, and legal professionals will find it a rather difficult month to put their points across, and argue their cases successfully. As such, it might be wiser to put any legal issues that require litigation on hold for the meantime, or settle these as quickly as possible, as your chances of a victory in court are slim – to say the least. On the domestic front, be patient in addressing any disagreements and misunderstandings with family members and loved ones.

農曆十月 (November 8th – December 6th) 己亥

This is a month that can be overwhelming for some, as stress and work pressure will cause relationships to be tense and difficult. Schedule some time for heart-to-heart communication with your loved ones so that they understand your situation. Betrayal by employees making a play for power will bring you stress, so you will need to maintain courage under fire. Stay out of nasty office politics as much as possible in order to remain unaffected.

農曆十一月 (December 7th – January 5th 2012) 庚子

This month, do not get involved in high risk property deals as the outcomes could be unfortunate. You will need to continue to be conservative and extremely cautious in your financial endeavours, but this can only work to your benefit. Professional and personal relationships take their toll on you this month so avoid antagonism, especially if things are already rocky between you and others. Where possible, simply walk away from a tense situation – it could be wisest thing you do this month.

農曆十二月 (January 6th – February 3rd 2012) 辛丑

Competition and rivalry from competitors will affect those using the East room this month. This will become an emotional issue resulting that could result in manipulation and confrontation, so it will be best to take the proper precautions to prevent the situation from escalating. Where possible, try to leave your emotions out of the picture or it could hamper you and cause you to react or respond in ways that will lead to further arguments and complications.

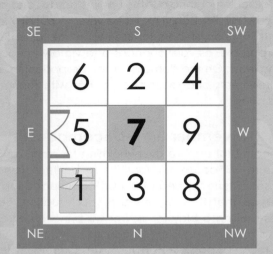

農曆正月 (February 4th – March 5th) 庚寅

This is an especially difficult month for those in the property business, as clarity of thought becomes a problem. You will find it difficult to make decisions, so if it possible to delay important decision-making, then you should. If major decisions need to be made, it will be best to consult someone else who can view the picture clearly without any potential confusion. Older men using this room should be careful of head injuries this month.

農曆二月 (March 6th – April 4th) 辛卯

Children facing examinations this month should be careful especially if there are negative structures outside the Northeast. It will be important to monitor them closely during their studies to ensure that their concentration and focus is not disturbed. Where possible, move them into another room temporarily in order to help them achieve the mental peace needed to aid in their studies and learning.

農曆三月 (April 5th – May 5th) 壬辰

Legal problems are possible this month as betrayals occur and people turn against you, spreading rumours about your business. You may need to get into damage-control mode to stem the rumours. This may cause you a certain amount of stress, so be prepared and don't castigate yourself if you need more space and solitary time. Ensure you get adequate amounts of rest. The gossip and rumours will affect you business relationships this month, so be prepared for some tense relations.

農曆四月 (May 6th – June 5th) 癸巳

Older men should take good care of their health this month and see a doctor even for seemingly minor problems. Any health troubles are best discovered early, as otherwise they could become quite serious or complicated the longer they are left untreated. There are good deals to be made in the real estate business but you will need to be very astute to choose the correct ones. Employ discretion and be thorough in checking out credentials.

| Main Door | East | Bedroom Sector | Northeast |

農曆五月 (June 6th – July 6th) 甲午

This is not the best month to make financial decisions as you will be easily deceived. Prolong any major decisions involving big sums of money to a future month. Romance doesn't fare too well this month, either, as relationships come under strain as one or both of the parties may be tempted into illicit affairs, and in some cases, it could lead to marital break-ups and separation.

農曆六月 (July 7th – August 7th) 乙未

Those in the entertainment business who want to expand should check all contracts carefully to make sure that everything is in order before signing. There is a likelihood that mistakes or oversights could turn out to be costly. Relationships are likely to be short-term this month so do not put too much time into them. This is not to say that you must avoid or ignore all socialising and pleasant flirtation, but it does mean that you should keep things in perspective to avoid getting hurt or disillusioned.

農曆七月 (August 8th – September 7th) 丙申

Those in the real estate business or who have property deals this month will find business highly profitable, but you'll also need to grab onto good opportunities as they come up. Don't think too hard on a decision and play it safe, because the month is good for some calculated risks that could yield big dividends or benefits. Where marriage is concerned, spouses may feel a bit neglected this month as one partner is busy making money and seems to have no time for the other.

農曆八月 (September 8th – October 7th) 丁酉

Jealousy resulting in marital discord could cause problems in relationships this month. Pent up resentments could come to the fore as a result of the green-eyed monster, so don't do anything that jeopardize your relationship, and be sure to be ready to talk openly should your partner or spouse wish to bring up some matters that are at the root of their insecurity. Don't judge or ridicule them for their responses.

農曆九月 (October 8th – November 7th) 戊戌

Personal reputations could be called into question this month, so you must pay attention to the things you say and do. Words and actions may have some stern consequences this month. Don't be ready to make offensive statements or jokes unless you're prepared to defend your point-of-view to people who are keen to make you do so. Understand that all that you say will be under observation.

農曆十月 (November 8th – December 6th) 己亥

Elderly males using the Northeast bedroom should be careful of potential head injuries or head-related symptoms and illnesses. This is an especially difficult month for those in the property business, because you will find it hard to zero in on the root of the problem and achieve some mental clarity. You will find it difficult to make decisions. Where possible, defer your decisions to another time when you're feeling stronger mentally.

農曆十一月 (December 7th – January 5th 2012) 庚子

Offshore deals and negotiations should be avoided this month, as finalising them now could only lead to a potential loss. It might be best to wait for a more favourable time in the future. Children facing examinations this month should be careful especially if there are negative structures outside the Northeast sector or room. It might be best to move them into another room for the duration of any important examinations.

農曆十二月 (January 6th – February 3rd 2012) 辛丑

Those of you who are married or in relationships will find that this month brings about the likelihood of extra arguments and fights if you're using the Northeast bedroom. You will have to be more circumspect with your words and actions. Try to avoid offending your partner simply because you feel angry and or unhappy. Legal problems are possible this month as betrayals occur and people turn against you, spreading rumours.

Main Door	East	Bedroom Sector	North

農曆正月 (February 4th – March 5th) 庚寅

Be mindful of your state of mind, as mental and emotional stress could lead to mild depression and lethargy. If you need to, spend more time with friends who make you see the bright side of things to avoid focusing too much on the negative this month. Also, scrutinize all business deals and contracts carefully and critically, to minimize the risk of being cheated or short-changed, this month. Pay attention to the fine print.

農曆二月 (March 6th – April 4th) 辛卯

Avoid being dragged or enmeshed into any family dispute or arguments, as you certainly wouldn't want to witness your family being divided as the result of a lawsuit or continuous bickering amongst other family members! You will, instead, do well to mind your own personal safety this month, as the possibility of being robbed or mugged looms over your head ominously, especially if you happen to notice any negative forms outside the North sector.

農曆三月 (April 5th – May 5th) 壬辰

Those of you involved in the real estate or property development business should market your products more aggressively this month, especially if you wish to generate more revenue in time to come. Have one eye toward the future as you make your plans for the present. Similarly, specialists in the services industry will find this month to be a fairly favourable one for business, as long as you ensure that all taxes due are paid. Otherwise, the long arm of the law may soon catch up with you.

農曆四月 (May 6th – June 5th) 癸巳

You may need to be prepared for a relationship, personal or professional, that has been stormy all throughout, to reach its end, sometime this month. But perhaps it's better to sever such ties now, instead of letting them fester and allowing yourself to be bogged down by them. Ensure that you remain clear-eyed and practical, and don't allow emotions to get the better of you, leading you to make some poor decisions.

| Main Door | East | Bedroom Sector | North |

農曆五月 (June 6th – July 6th) 甲午

Just when you least expect it, you find your competitors and rivals launching a surprise attack on you and your business interests. Their aim is simple: A hostile takeover of your enterprise, so it's up to you to thwart their attempts. Unfortunately, this is not a very good time to look around for more deals, as even those that are already in the midst of being negotiated may take time to finalize. This will be a challenging month resulting in financial losses but important lessons can be learnt.

農曆六月 (July 7th – August 7th) 乙未

This is a good month for concluding property deals but be very specific on the details as legal issues will raise their head if you are not careful. If there was a time to be nitpicky and a perfectionist, this is it! However, your relationships on a downturn this month, so no important decisions should be made. It will be best to let things slide for the time being. Marital relations have a strong chance of becoming tense and stressed this month, and there is a need for these discords to be addressed promptly.

農曆七月 (August 8th – September 7th) 丙申

Beware of fraud or theft if you're using the North bedroom, and ensure that all the proper controls to keep track of your finances are in place. It's always safer to err on the side of caution. Don't be so quick to trust people, especially the newcomers to your life. And if you've been feeling rather poorly of late, then in all probability, the North is not the most ideal sector for you to use, as the energies of the month could well aggravate your situation or any internal injuries from which you're already suffering.

農曆八月 (September 8th – October 7th) 丁酉

Good news will come to those who use the North room this month, so long as you are involved in travel in some form. Clarity of thought will favour those who need to make important decisions this month, so attempt to think things through and decide now instead of postponing decision-making to another time. Do not be deceived by conmen who offer unusually good investment deals as this will only result in loss of money and legal troubles.

農曆九月 (October 8th – November 7th) 戊戌

Postpone any important decision-making pertaining to your business deals, to avoid risking slander and other types of disputes unnecessarily. What's more, you need to monitor your employees closely this month, as by letting your guard down, even formerly loyal staff may attempt to deceive or steal from you this month. So, have all the necessary precautionary measures in place, and duly enforced.

農曆十月 (November 8th – December 6th) 己亥

There is a likelihood of a loss of wealth as a result of fraud or theft. Be careful of all your personal belongings and your material assets. Do not leave valuable jewellery lying about the house in easy-to-reach areas, and do also pay close attention to your personal documents – especially those relating to your financial accounts and statements. Confidential business documents should also be kept in a safe place and guarded closely.

農曆十一月 (December 7th – January 5th 2012) 庚子

Male teenagers using the North bedroom this month may be more rebellious than normal and should consider using a different room for the month. Using another room might temper their spirits a little and soften their harder edges. Also, if you're the parent of the rebellious child, avoid engaging in pointless battle of wills. Being understanding and giving them room to earn their independence will work much better in the long run for both parties.

農曆十二月 (January 6th – February 3rd 2012) 辛丑

There is a possibility of car accidents resulting in leg injuries this month for those who use the North bedroom. Be careful when you're driving, and remember that nothing is so important that you need to speed to the point where it's a danger to your personal safety! This is an ideal month for contractors to submit that tender for the job of a lifetime.

East Sector Main Door

East Sector Main Door

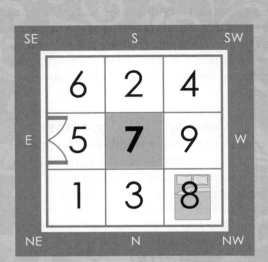

農曆正月 (February 4th – March 5th) 庚寅

Your relationships will be harmonious and smooth-sailing this month, especially for couples using the Northwest bedroom. Indeed, this is a good time of the year to embark upon a new venture or endeavour, with positive results awaiting the bold, diligent and persevering. You're likely to find obstructions melting away in the face of any issues, and it is the ideal time to embark on ambitious projects you've long put on hold.

農曆二月 (March 6th – April 4th) 辛卯

After what appears to be a slightly rocky start to the month, your relationship with your spouse will flourish and remain harmonious. Be sure to keep the lines of communication open, and things will proceed smoothly. Problems only arise when you start to hide the important things from each other. You need to be mindful though of jealous co-workers, who are only plotting your downfall. Be wary of offers for help or assistance that could only be a ploy to get you to reveal important information that will be used against you.

農曆三月 (April 5th – May 5th) 壬辰

Windfall gains may be realized this month, so check your list of portfolios, and mobilize any that appears to be promising, in tandem with the latest market trends. All in all, this is an ideal time to cultivate new business relationships or partnerships. So, utilize your network of contacts to bring in even more new clients, and there's no need to be modest in your aims.

農曆四月 (May 6th – June 5th) 癸巳

This will be a favourable month to embark on any ambitious projects that you have been planning on. You'll enjoy the support of your superiors, and this is certainly something to be taken advantage of. Consult them for valuable advice and insider tricks that could help you gain advances you may have only dreamed of. Traders involved in the futures, stock and equities markets will also find this month to be a fairly profitable one, as will investors involved in the property and real estate business.

農曆五月 (June 6th – July 6th) 甲午

This is not the most suitable of times to make any important decisions regarding your relationships. Give the other party some space of his/her own, and wait for a more appropriate time to act. And it would equally be wise to deposit your money in the bank, instead of using it to engage in speculative property investments. This month is not favourable for risk-taking, especially in finances.

農曆六月 (July 7th – August 7th) 乙未

Working in the management, marketing or consultancy line, and looking to widen your customer base? Then this will be the best time to utilise your network of contacts, and be proactive in seeking new openings to expand your business to previously unexplored markets. There will be profits to be made from all deals concluded abroad, although you should scrutinize every legal document carefully before signing it.

農曆七月 (August 8th – September 7th) 丙申

Progress on projects is good resulting in the employees being recognized for their success and being rewarded accordingly. This creates a general sense of wellbeing in the workplace and you'll find yourself increasing your productivity and achieving targets a at a better pace than you thought possible. Couples using this room will find this a harmonious month for relationships.

農曆八月 (September 8th – October 7th) 丁酉

You'll enjoy harmony and bliss in your relationships, so make the most of this favourable period to strengthen the bonds between you and your loved ones, and business affiliates. Nevertheless, keep a sharp eye open for rivals, subordinates or co-workers who are only out to sabotage your efforts. You may sometimes be too kind and trusting, but there are times when steeling your heart and presenting an intimidating front can be of use in warding off the insincere hangers-on!

農曆九月 (October 8th – November 7th) 戊戌

Do not overwork and overexert yourself, as you will only be prone to bladder or kidney problems at the end of the day. And know that no matter how successful you may be, there will always be jealous parties out there plotting your downfall. Hence, it's important that you learn how to manage your stress levels wisely. The energies of the month augur well for short-term gains from speculative investments.

農曆十月 (November 8th – December 6th) 己亥

There are big changes coming out of the blue that will help revive stagnant careers and business this month. You can expect to see your ventures getting a jumpstart in newer, fresher ways, but you must be ready to accept change when you see it and be ready to think and operate in slightly differently. Adults using this sector should focus on academic activities and educational improvement, as the outcome is good these endeavours. You will a stronger interest in self-cultivation as a result.

農曆十一月 (December 7th – January 5th 2012) 庚子

Your relationships are positive and harmonious this month for partnerships of both a professional and personal nature. You will see many obstructions melting away in your dealings with others. This will be the ideal month for you to capitalise on those relationships that could lead to greater professional opportunities in the future. Those who have invested in property and real estate will see bumper financial profits this month, which you get you excited!

農曆十二月 (January 6th – February 3rd 2012) 辛丑

This is a good month for those in the food and beverage industry, as there is an obvious increase in profits. Use the good energies of this month to promote the name of your restaurant or business as the response will be favourable. Good status and reputation will lead to an increase in contacts and connections in your field, and your popularity will grow exponentially. This is a good month for relationships, which should generally be happy and harmonious.

Main Door	East	Bedroom Sector	West

農曆正月 (February 4th – March 5th) 庚寅

You will make great strides in both your professional and personal relationships, so now's the time to foster even closer ties with your business partners, and loved ones. Where it's possible to boost relationships with colleagues and superiors, you should take the opportunity to cultivate it.

農曆二月 (March 6th – April 4th) 辛卯

The energies of the West room augur well for pursuits of the spiritual or religious kind, so use this sector if you wish to meditate or develop your mind-power. It will help you focus your mind and your energies, and will spill over into all other aspects of your life, as well. Likewise, politicians or budding ones should harness the positive energies of the month, to take on their opponents at the grassroots level.

農曆三月 (April 5th – May 5th) 壬辰

Couples using the West bedroom will enjoy harmony in their relationship throughout the month. Use this month to have meaningful heart-to-heart conversations about issues or potential issues that you need to discuss. The energy will be smooth, and arguments will be pushed aside for a solution or a compromise that benefits both of you. Indeed, this is also a good time to propose marriage to your loved one!

農曆四月 (May 6th – June 5th) 癸巳

Business owners should be mindful of competitors or rivals launching a bid for a hostile takeover of their business this month. Remain vigilant for any underhand or aggressive tactics to bring about their downfall. Check to see if there are any negative structures or features outside the West as well, and if you notice any, bear in mind the risk of a potential fire hazard.

East Sector Main Door

農曆五月 (June 6th – July 6th) 甲午

It's best to be disciplined and careful, should you wish to continue engaging in metal, futures, equities or stock trading. Don't rush into anything recklessly or with haste simply because you want to make a quick kill. This will not be the month to indulge in such risk-taking. This is also not a good time to challenge or question the authority of your superiors, as your attempts will only end in defeat and embarrassment for you.

農曆六月 (July 7th – August 7th) 乙未

This month, it will be imperative for you to maintain a healthy lifestyle, and seek the advice of your physician at the first sign of trouble; to prevent the onslaught of illnesses such as eye or heart disease, or even leukaemia. Where possible, refrain from making any important decisions this month, as your thoughts would most probably be affected. And unless you wish to land in hot soup, watch your temper, and think before you act.

農曆七月 (August 8th – September 7th) 丙申

Students, scholars and candidates due to sit for examinations soon might find the going tough this month. Where possible, use another bedroom for your studies or revision, and to sleep in. This will help you clear your mind and help you with your focus. Female employees may find it difficult to get the support of their superiors, so watch how you go about your responsibilities, and seek the necessary approval in black-and-white before you undertake any important decision.

農曆八月 (September 8th – October 7th) 丁酉

Recognition, promotion and rewards are the order of the day for the diligent and persevering! You'll find this a good month in terms of recognition and praise, especially if you've been keeping your head down all these months and engaging productively in your work. Those in the counselling, advisory and psychology fields will also find their advice and skills much sought-after.

農曆九月 (October 8th – November 7th) 戊戌

Use the West bedroom this month, to enjoy good romance luck. You will be able to meet new people who will prove to be interesting romantic potential, or else those of you already in relationships will enjoy a relatively smooth and trouble-free month. However, in general, you will need to be more patient and tactful in handling tacky situations, as you would only be doing yourself disfavour by acting hastily or in a foolish manner.

農曆十月 (November 8th – December 6th) 己亥

It's a very good month for both you professional and personal relationships, so now's the time to foster even closer ties with your business partners, and loved ones. Cultivate more business partnerships and get to know more people in general as it will greatly benefit you. It's also a good month to tap into the energies of the West bedroom for education, learning, and scholarly activities – students in particular are likely to benefit.

農曆十一月 (December 7th – January 5th 2012) 庚子

Those of you in the political field should harness the positive energies of the month and attempt to garner support at the grassroots. Players in the cosmetics and fashion industries should also take the opportunity to promote their products to as many markets as possible. There's money to be made this month, but only for those who are willing to work hard, and take calculated risks.

農曆十二月 (January 6th – February 3rd 2012) 辛丑

The West bedroom will bode well for couples using this room, as the energies are conducive to romantic luck. Indeed, this is also a good time to propose marriage to your loved one if it's something you've been considering for a long time. Married people who are looking to start a family should utilise the West bedroom. People involved in real estate or property industries will find returns profitable this month.

Main Door	East	Bedroom Sector	Southwest

SE	S	SW
6	2	4 
5	**7**	9
1	3	8

| NE | N | NW |

E — W

農曆正月 (February 4th – March 5th) 庚寅

People using the Southwest room or sector should watch out for potential health issues involving the liver, while females have to do a thorough check-up to rule out any risk of cancer. Business owners and entrepreneurs should also ensure that all their deals are above-board, or you risk facing the full brunt of the law. Playing with fire in the legal sense this month could certainly backfire in a bad way, so it will be best to err on the side of caution.

農曆二月 (March 6th – April 4th) 辛卯

Expectant mothers should avoid using the Southwest bedroom this month, to prevent any pregnancy complications or a miscarriage. Where possible, move into another room for the time-being just to keep any potential risks at bay. However, those using the Southwest to study or revise for their impending examinations can definitely be optimistic in the hope of positive outcomes in their papers.

農曆三月 (April 5th – May 5th) 壬辰

You may expect some unfriendly competition, or even intense rivalry in whatever you do, if you happen to be using the Southwest bedroom. Indeed, the negative energies present within the Southwest will bring about emotional and psychological problems for those who unwittingly tap into them, so it will be best to be on guard against potentially explosive arguments. This will be equally true to both relationships at work and in your personal life.

農曆四月 (May 6th – June 5th) 癸巳

If you're married, it would be wiser to minimise contact with your in-laws this month, to save yourself and your partner a great deal of unnecessary stress. Marital relationships will be strained this month and it would be better to give each other space. Try not to get in each other's way and it could a long way towards easing the tension.

| Main Door | East | Bedroom Sector | Southwest |

農曆五月 (June 6th – July 6th) 甲午

If you have interest in writing, and making a name for yourself from it, then perhaps the time has come for you to look for a publisher who's willing to put forth your works for sale. This is a beneficial month for just such endeavours. And those whose line of work involves extensive research and development will be pleased to know that any changes within your organisation will invariably bring about positive outcomes and financial benefits.

農曆六月 (July 7th – August 7th) 乙未

This promises to be a favourable month for those daring enough to invest in high-risk, speculative deals, as all negotiations will have the likelihood of going well. And as for more good news; this is also an ideal time of the year to play the field, and see whether your efforts will land you a romantic prospect or otherwise! Those travelling this month should expect some sudden changes or last minute problems which necessitate the buying of travel insurance.

農曆七月 (August 8th – September 7th) 丙申

It does pay to treat your staff or employees fairly, and reward them as they deserve. And if you've been doing so all this while, then you'll be pleased to know that the loyalty of your workers will make them go the extra mile, in bringing you the results you desire. You might want to, however, scrutinize all legal documents before signing them, to avoid the possibility of any legal entanglements later on.

農曆八月 (September 8th – October 7th) 丁酉

Scrutinise all legal documents very carefully this month, and read the fine print before you apply your signature to the dotted line. Most importantly, you need to be certain of your obligations as far as any legally binding contract is concerned. It would also be wise to stay away from quarrels and disputes, as things may take a turn for the worse. This is a good month to engage in business expansion or build alliances with partners abroad.

農曆九月 (October 8th – November 7th) 戊戌

This is favourable month to foster even closer ties with your business affiliates, co-workers and loved ones, if you wish your professional and personal relationships to remain harmonious, and long-termed. Those who find it necessary to travel in the name of business will find their stature and reputation greatly enhanced. Women in the entertainment industry will find this a month of reward, recognition and promotion.

農曆十月 (November 8th – December 6th) 己亥

This is a good month to enter into property deals, so you need to be ready to make the right move when the opportunity strikes. Strokes and migraines may be a problem for older women who use this bedroom; it will be wise to pay close attention to any of the warning signs. As early as possible, if something seems amiss, it will become necessary to seek professional medical advice. Don't put it off or ignore the symptoms.

農曆十一月 (December 7th – January 5th 2012) 庚子

Keep away from disputes and quarrels this month as they may take on a violent nature. It is better to be proactive rather than to end up in disharmony. This is especially true if you find your temper fraying quite frequently and easily. Then, instead of saying what's on your mind, it might be best to heed the sage advice of not saying anything at all if one can't be compelled to say anything nice!

農曆十二月 (January 6th – February 3rd 2012) 辛丑

Relationships take on a new level of commitment as harmonious energies prevail in this sector. This will be a good month for couples to have important talks they've been putting off for some time, or to make important decisions together. Family discussions on important and big changes or decisions will go well this month, too, as will the brainstorming sessions at work.

| Main Door | East | Bedroom Sector | South |

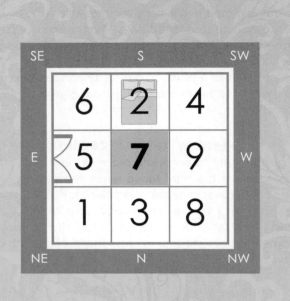

農曆正月 (February 4th – March 5th) 庚寅

Where possible, couples should refrain from using a South bedroom, as the energies present in that sector will not augur well for their relationship. Likewise, it would also be advisable to refrain from making any significant investments, or embarking on any new projects this month. You will only stand to lose from poor decision-making which will be exacerbated from cloudy thoughts and weak reasoning this month.

農曆二月 (March 6th – April 4th) 辛卯

Medical professionals and practitioners will benefit from the energies of the South this month. You'll have a boost to your reputation and increasing number of patients who will prefer your services. However, expectant mothers are advised to refrain from using a South bedroom, and seek the advice of a doctor, to prevent the occurrence of a miscarriage or any other form of pregnancy complications.

農曆三月 (April 5th – May 5th) 壬辰

Arguments resulting in disharmony threaten the tranquillity of home-life this month, so where possible, avoid using the South bedroom. You should also be especially careful in evaluating all deals that involve monetary transactions, as otherwise you could well end up being duped by unscrupulous parties. Pay close attention to all that takes place verbal negotiations and meticulously read through the fine print in contracts and documents.

農曆四月 (May 6th – June 5th) 癸巳

Take good care of your eyes, any ailments or problems affecting them will only cause your health, and peace of mind, to suffer this month. On the work front, you may find your employees more hard-headed than usual, thereby compromising their ability to think and plan logically. This situation could lead to some bad decision-making, which in turn, will result in your company suffering from financial losses.

Main Door	East	Bedroom Sector	South

農曆五月 (June 6th – July 6th) 甲午

The energies of the South could well produce spiritual or religiously-inclined persons, more so if they happen to already harbour interest in such matters. However, seek immediate medical treatment if you feel unwell, to prevent nagging or recurring ailments. This is not the month to take risks with your health.

農曆六月 (July 7th – August 7th) 乙未

Avoid signing documents and contracts this month as they may not be what they seem. Read the fine lines, and pay special attention to what's being said in between the lines as well! Students should avoid using this sector for a study if they are facing important examinations this month. Arguments and family disharmony is a problem for those using the South room, so choose your words carefully.

農曆七月 (August 8th – September 7th) 丙申

This month, care should be taken with new property deals as these could result in financial losses. It will be better to be safe than sorry, so spend that extra bit of time verifying credentials. Negative socialising will be a problem this month so be aware of the difficulties as a result of too much gambling. In effect, avoid temptations that require use of substances, or some form of risk-taking with money.

農曆八月 (September 8th – October 7th) 丁酉

If you need to change your home, this is a good time to sell as you will make favourable profits. The market is good for property at this point. Those in real estate will make money on property deals this month but just make sure that all the legal issues are well taken care of. Confusion will cloud thought processes this month. Read documents carefully or consult a lawyer so that possible losses can be avoided.

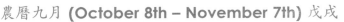

農曆九月 (October 8th – November 7th) 戊戌

Use your experience, knowledge and expertise in the real estate field, to make as much money as possible from your investments in properties, this month. On the domestic front, however, there could be strife and disharmony between the in-laws. So, be extra patient with them, and deal with any problem as it arises. And mind your spleen and other internal organs, unless you wish to acquire an illness affecting them, which could lead to more serious health problems in the long-run.

農曆十月 (November 8th – December 6th) 己亥

Mental and emotional stress may cause depression and even hallucinations for those using the South bedroom. It will be important for you to talk to people close to you or seek help if you find yourself becoming increasingly confused and disoriented, and unable to deal with regular, day-to-day problems that you had no problem with before. This sector is best suited for those in religious pursuits or for gaining spiritual knowledge.

農曆十一月 (December 7th – January 5th 2012) 庚子

Those in merchant banking, shares, stocks and equities will find this a very difficult month as deals go belly up in many cases and profits start to dwindle. You'll have to think swiftly on your feet in order to avert potential disasters or catastrophes. Don't be too reticent – seek advice from others and discuss strategies with others in your field to see how you can play the game a little different.

農曆十二月 (January 6th – February 3rd 2012) 辛丑

Arguments between mother-in-law and daughter-in-law will become more prevalent for those using this room and may even result in gossips and slander. Any tension should be diffused from the get-go, because if left to simmer can result in long-term emotional tumult and upheavals. Stress at work may cause gastrointestinal problems and ulcers. While work stress cannot be avoided, how you manage it will make a world of difference.

| Main Door | East | Bedroom Sector | Southeast |

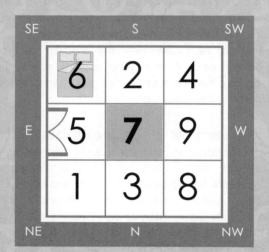

農曆正月 (February 4th – March 5th) 庚寅

Keep a sharp eye out for rivals and competitors who are out to undermine you, whether you're the boss, or even just a salaried employee trying to make a decent living. It would be wiser to concentrate on what you're doing, and maintain a low profile. That way, you will be able to minimize the possibility of running into any trouble. Avoid being sucked into office politics or high dramas.

農曆二月 (March 6th – April 4th) 辛卯

Those using the Southeast room need to be mindful of health problems, which may assume the form of headaches or kidney problems. If need be, seek immediate medical advice and treatment. Those of you already suffering from complications related to these areas might do well to temporarily use another room.

農曆三月 (April 5th – May 5th) 壬辰

There's no shame or dishonour is asking for help, especially in times of need. You may need a helping hand, especially if your business endeavours appear to be more challenging than usual. So, consult an expert or someone wiser to turn your fortunes about for the better. The advice that they give you could prove to be eye-opening and useful in more ways than one.

農曆四月 (May 6th – June 5th) 癸巳

This promises to be a favourable month for those working in the consultancy or any other field that requires strategic thinking. Your reputation will be greatly enhanced through any good work that you produce. Likewise, there will be substantial financial gains to be made from speculative investments and stocks, although it's only wise not to flaunt your wealth!

| Main Door | East | Bedroom Sector | Southeast |

農曆五月 (June 6th – July 6th) 甲午

This is the time to maintain a low profile, and concentrate on your core business, instead of attempting to expand it. Any important decision-making can wait for the right time, of course. Furthermore, all forms of investments, particularly high-risk ones, should be avoided this month, to minimize the risk of any consequential legal problems. The good news is; employees and workers in the engineering field will enjoy the support of their superiors.

農曆六月 (July 7th – August 7th) 乙未

This is a month of potential scams and betrayal by disloyal employees which could be expensive, cause setbacks, and may result in legal issues. Family relations are strained and tense but it is better just to keep the peace as this is not a good time to thrash it out. It will be best to wait for a better time in order to have heart-to-heart conversations. Do not conclude business deals this month as these could lead to reverse takeovers.

農曆七月 (August 8th – September 7th) 丙申

Those in speculative investments or stocks and equities will make good profits this month if they use this room, so be prepared for the good outcome headed your way! This is a good month to travel for both business and leisure especially if you are doing a fact finding mission or are involved in research and development ventures. Couples using this room will enjoy harmonious relationships this month.

農曆八月 (September 8th – October 7th) 丁酉

Employers and bosses might find their staff behaving in a rebellious manner this month, where your authority and decision will be duly challenged. Be patient, and seek to understand your employees' points of view, instead of just pulling rank on them. Minor health issues could be a problem this month. Do not consider these unimportant as it could lead to more serious conditions requiring greater medical treatment and care further down the road, so get them sorted out early.

農曆九月 (October 8th – November 7th) 戊戌

This will be a month for celebrations, as a result of auspicious news received. To begin with, your relationship with your partner will be harmonious. Hence, you should take advantage of this, to foster even closer ties with your loved one. And as far as wealth luck is concerned, there will be notable financial gains from any investments in real estate or property, regardless of whether these investments were undertaken on a commercial or personal basis.

農曆十月 (November 8th – December 6th) 己亥

Those in the logistics, courier and tourism businesses should benefit from increased profits this month. If your job involves strategic thinking or analysis you will find that you have the chance to advance your career and gain a name for yourself this month – so don't be hesitant in putting your best foot forward and making strategic attempts to improve your reputation.

農曆十一月 (December 7th – January 5th 2012) 庚子

Those in positions of power should be aware of challenges to their authority. It could even manifest in sons challenging their fathers' authority, and this could result in tense relations. At the workplace, you might have to deal with rebellious subordinates or even colleagues who are bent to undermine your authority. Long-term investments will return a profit this month for those using the Southeast room, but try not to make any short-term investments.

農曆十二月 (January 6th – February 3rd 2012) 辛丑

This month, investment and merchant bankers who engage in stock and corporate deals will make good financial profits. They will be able to see the dollar signs quicker than expected! There will also be good news awaiting couples who are using this bedroom, and this could improve ties and forge closeness between the partners.

Northeast Sector Main Door

| Main Door | Northeast | Bedroom Sector | Northeast |

This section contains the monthly outlook for all 12 months of the year, for different bedrooms in a property with a Northeast Main Door.

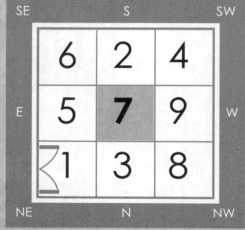

SE	S	SW
6	2	4
E 5	**7**	9 W
NE 1	3	8 NW

Ground Floor

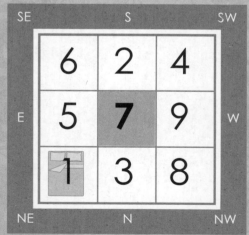

SE	S	SW
6	2	4
E 5	**7**	9 W
NE 1	3	8 NW

First Floor

農曆正月 (February 4th – March 5th) 庚寅

Speculative investments, especially equity investments and gambling, should be avoided this month as there is a risk of significant financial losses. Leave all speculative and risk-taking financial plays to another time, where the outcomes are likely to cause less damage. Those in frail health should avoid this room this month as there is a chance of breast or liver cancer. Couples using this bedroom must communicate more with each other, as suspicion may rear its head.

農曆二月 (March 6th – April 4th) 辛卯

This is a favourable room for children facing important examinations this month. It will work well during the preparations for the exams as it will help with clarity of mind and focus. Even if children don't use this room as a bedroom, they can conduct their studies and revision here. Any deals involving asset acquisitions concluded this month should do very well, especially if these are overseas investments or if you're dealing with contacts abroad.

農曆三月 (April 5th – May 5th) 壬辰

Those of you in the furniture industry will find this a bumper month, as significant profits and returns are likely. However, be on the alert for anyone who might potentially be a backstabber, as betrayals will cause a loss of wealth and result in legal problems this month. Don't trust people too easily, especially if they seem overly eager to help you or assist you. Partnerships and new alliances should be avoided this month, as they will result in a financial loss for you that will be hard to overturn.

農曆四月 (May 6th – June 5th) 癸巳

Elderly women who are ill or frail should not occupy this room this month, as the chances for ill health are likely. Avoid picking fights over small things this month, or it could result in serious arguments for couples who are using the room in the Northeast. The energies of this sector are favourable for those in the real estate business, as deals are likely to be quite profitable this month. Ensure that you make the most of any potential leads that come up. Sacrificing them for fear of being too forward or eager may result in some losses for you.

| Main Door | Northeast | Bedroom Sector | Northeast |

農曆五月 (June 6th – July 6th) 甲午

If you're using the Northeast room this month, be prepared to receive lots of media attention, publicity and recognition. You may have to get used to being in the spotlight! But make sure you make the attention and the elevated reputation work in your favour, as it will help you tremendously in cementing your career. This is a month to make changes for the better and begin anew on certain matters, as there will be substantial rewards awaiting you.

農曆六月 (July 7th – August 7th) 乙未

Students who are facing important examinations this month should use this room for their preparations, as academic results should receive a boost. Your passion and excitement abound this month and it should be channelled into opportunities for career advancement, especially if you are in the entertainment industry. Don't put a lid on your enthusiasm or you might limit the opportunities available to you. Your talents and abilities are finally recognised by your superiors who will give you the promotion and financial reward you have been waiting for. In essence, this month is all-systems go!

農曆七月 (August 8th – September 7th) 丙申

Those in the oil and gas industries will have a bumper month if they take advantage of the opportunities that arise this month. You should be alert and quick enough to capitalise on the chances that might crop up. If you're a salaried employee working on special projects, you will have a chance to shine, as the projects in question take off spectacularly. Expect to revel in a lot of praise and recognition!

農曆八月 (September 8th – October 7th) 丁酉

Interpersonal relationships amongst family members should improve this month, and you should be able to enjoy closer ties. You should also make sure that your health and travel insurance is up to date if you're intending to go on a trip. There is a chance of mishaps during travel resulting in possible injuries to the limbs. Be circumspect about the people with whom you share your work, and exercise some form of caution.

農曆九月 (October 8th – November 7th) 戊戌

People involved in competitive sport should find advancement this month in terms of your career progress and development. If you're in politics, this is a good time for politicians to push your new policies, as you will find good support this month from your constituents. In general, this is also a good month for networking and making new contacts, so put your best foot forward and aim to impress.

農曆十月 (November 8th – December 6th) 己亥

This is not a good month for speculative investments, especially equity investments and gambling. There is a likelihood of losses otherwise, and some may have more serious consequences than expected. It will be best to play it safe this month. Couples who use the Northeast room may have to battle issues concerning jealousy and suspicion. In terms of health, breast or liver cancer risks could be heightened in this particular area.

農曆十一月 (December 7th – January 5th 2012) 庚子

Make a go at asset acquisitions this month, as the returns should be very good. This is especially true for trading or investments that take place abroad. Make an effort to travel in order to see to it that all is proceeding as well as it should. Parents will find that children who use the Northeast room will experience good results in examinations and their studies in general. Relationships on the whole progress very well, be it personal or professional.

農曆十二月 (January 6th – February 3rd 2012) 辛丑

This month, it will be important for you to be on the alert for anyone who might potentially be a backstabber, as betrayals will cause a loss of wealth and result in legal problemsIf you have a chance to set it right, be sure to eliminate your ties to such people because you don't need these problems in your life at this point in time. Partnerships and new alliances should be avoided this month, as they will result in a financial loss for you that will be hard to overturn. It will be best for you to strike out on your own, for the most part.

Northeast Sector Main Door

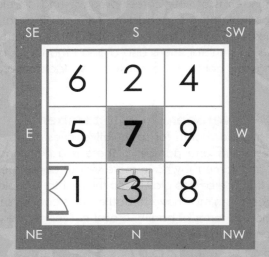

農曆正月 (February 4th – March 5th) 庚寅

Theft and fraud is a problem this month, especially by close friends and family members. If would be advisable to put extra financial controls in place. Don't allow emotions to get in the way of true and authentic evaluation. Be sure to assess matters in a practical and straightforward manner. Windfall gains can be attained from deals made with overseas partners and contacts abroad. Those who are already in poor health should be careful of internal injuries this month, so if something seems amiss then it's best to get a doctor's opinion.

農曆二月 (March 6th – April 4th) 辛卯

There is a possibility of a new position with more power and authority for those who are due career advancements. But with authority comes more responsibilities, so be prepared for the onslaught. Male teenagers using this bedroom this month may be more rebellious than normal and should consider using a different room for the month to temper their spirits. Power disputes between friends may turn sour and end up in the law courts this month, so try to diffuse any strong tension as early as possible to prevent this outcome.

農曆三月 (April 5th – May 5th) 壬辰

Speculative investments will show a loss this month and any dealings will be fraught with financial losses or even lawsuits. Health problems will surface in the form of ulcers, gallstones and liver problems this month, and those who live in rural areas may have a problem with unexpected snakebites. This is not a month to spend your hard-earned money on gambling, as losses will more than likely be severe and leave you in dire straits. Therefore, ensure that you strive to put away your money instead of taking a risk or a gamble on it.

農曆四月 (May 6th – June 5th) 癸巳

Emotional and psychological problems may hamper the occupants of the North bedroom this month. Those in research and development will have opportunities to gain prominence in their profession this month, especially so if you are involved in dealings with overseas companies. Those of you who are part of a couple should make an effort in your relationship this month, as there could be competitors on the horizon if you neglect your duties and responsibilities.

Main Door	Northeast	Bedroom Sector	North

農曆五月 (June 6th – July 6th) 甲午

Car accidents are likely if you use this bedroom so you will need to take special care when travelling on the road this month. Be sure not to get behind the wheel when you're ill or exhausted, especially when you need to make long-haul trips. Some common-sense and reason applied to your commute will help divert potential risks. Those wishing to further their political career and who need to rely on oratory skills will likely do well this month.

農曆六月 (July 7th – August 7th) 乙未

Property deals that come out of the blue this month should do well, but be very specific on the details, as legal issues may arise if you are not careful. Get the matter assessed by a lawyer or someone familiar with the legalities if you're unsure of it yourself. Relationships are on a downturn; so no important decisions should be made this month as the outcome will be less than pleasing. There may be problems with the authorities in the form of outstanding taxes and fines this month, so if there are any outstanding payments it will be best to clear them early before legal action is taken.

農曆七月 (August 8th – September 7th) 丙申

Those who artistically inclined, especially sculptors and carvers, will find a sudden increase in new clients looking for help and support. This will be a favourable month for those in the construction industry, especially if you are required to travel to conclude your deals. Those in unsettled relationships, both personal and private, may find yourself at the end of the road this month – it will require you to make a decision that will bring a definite outcome. Don't waffle over a hard decision, as executing it and dealing with it will become that much harder. Where possible, be firm and swift in your choice.

農曆八月 (September 8th – October 7th) 丁酉

Competitors will attack you from out of the blue this month, which could even end in hostile takeovers. Deals will be hard to come by and those that are available need to be concluded carefully, even if it means stalling for time if necessary. Occupants of this bedroom will make good gains this month. Fortunately, you will have the wisdom to protect it, but you will need to be extremely cleaver to outsmart the conmen who will plague you this month.

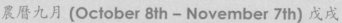

農曆九月 (October 8th – November 7th) 戊戌

You will do well financially this month but be careful of those who are jealous of your success. Resentment and ill thoughts may be brewing while you are blissfully unaware, so it will be best to stay away from those who seem too overly concerned with your affairs. This is a good month to make money from property and real estate using your past experiences and superior knowledge to best advantage. Those involved in fashion and clothing retail will make excellent gains this month.

農曆十月 (November 8th – December 6th) 己亥

People who are having health problems should be on extra guard this month, especially if using the North bedroom. There is the risk of injuries, and if one does take place then don't ignore the symptoms or resulting consequences. You'll find it easy to make a good financial profit from deals made with overseas partners or contacts abroad. But bear in mind that you should put extra financial controls in place this month. This should be adhered to because theft and fraud are likely to take place, especially among people you thought you could trust.

農曆十一月 (December 7th – January 5th 2012) 庚子

Be careful of any disputes and arguments that you get into with friends this month. As much as possible, temper your words with kindness and avoid provoking someone or pushing them into a corner. Otherwise, a legal trouble just might come out of it! Be aware of the tension from early on, and seek to diffuse it. You're likely to see some career progress this month, as well, and it comes with an elevation in power and status, as well as authority. But be prepared also for the increased work and responsibilities.

農曆十二月 (January 6th – February 3rd 2012) 辛丑

This month, keep a tight rein on your spending, and don't be tempted to fall into activities like gambling or speculative risk-trading and investments. Losses are likely to befall you, and the consequences can be quite harsh. Most financial investments this month will be tinged with the likelihood of loss and potential lawsuits. Those of you using the North room may also have to deal with a few physical symptoms that affect your health, including ulcers and gallstones, or potential liver diseases or trouble.

| Main Door | Northeast | Bedroom Sector | Northwest |

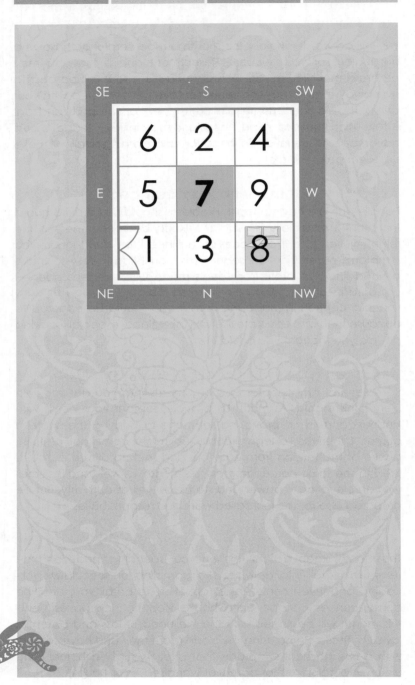

農曆正月 (February 4th – March 5th) 庚寅

This is a difficult month generally but by making key changes this can be turned around into a positive situation. Don't let your troubles overwhelm you to the point where you're unable to think clearly. If it helps you to discuss your problems with someone else, then that is what you must do. It would be best to keep young children out of this room this month, as they may be prone to injury by sharp metal objects. At best, keep sharp implements out of their reach.

農曆二月 (March 6th – April 4th) 辛卯

Speculative investments in real estate will provide handsome profits this month, but make sure that the details have been taken care of by lawyers. Relationships will tend to be smooth sailing with little or no stress and tension. Problems in communication will tend to melt away and you'll enjoy closer ties. Those who are in high authority or of high social status will find that things are in their favour this month so take advantage of any opportunity that comes your way. It will give you an opportunity to exercise your rule and display your leadership skills.

農曆三月 (April 5th – May 5th) 壬辰

Those in the construction and engineering business will find that business picks up this month, and there will be a chance for you to make good investments abroad. Even if it involves travel and some time away from your current business, you need to grab the bull by the horns and travel if that is what will bring you likely returns. Investments bloom for those who took investment positions in the preceding months, especially for fund and investment managers. Marital relationships proved to be harmonious and rewarding this month for those in the Northwest bedroom.

農曆四月 (May 6th – June 5th) 癸巳

Good news and celebrations await those using the Northwest room this month, especially if you want to start a family. Recognition comes to those of you who have excelled in your specific field or for something in which you've been specifically involved and have helped drive to its conclusion. This will bring about some moments of genuine pleasure as others come to recognise your true talents and achievements. This is a good month for those in the travel or construction industry, as profits will show a pleasant improvement.

Northeast Sector Main Door

農曆五月 (June 6th – July 6th) 甲午

Deals will be financially worthwhile this month, but it may take some concerted effort to conclude these deals. If you need to put in the extra hours to help matters along further, then you should be willing to make the appropriate sacrifice as the rewards will be immense. Employees wanting to make a breakthrough need to first find out what are the obstructions to progress. It could be something so subtle that it misses your immediate attention. If you are looking for a new partner, there will be no shortage of dates this month.

農曆六月 (July 7th – August 7th) 乙未

If you are in the share and equity markets, this month should show a good profit if you cash in your shares. It is important that you bank the money rather than let it slip through your fingers. Children sitting for important examinations this month will find positive support from the good energies in the Southwest bedroom. This will be a happy and harmonious month for couples using this bedroom. Windfall gains are possible this month, so look to realise these profits in your portfolio. This is a good month for networking and developing new client and business relationships. You will need to engage your diplomatic skills and put your best foot forward, but the results will be good and better than you expected.

農曆七月 (August 8th – September 7th) 丙申

Deals that require you travel to conclude it will be especially profitable, so persist in finalising the deal abroad if you can. Those in the banking industry can look forward to a promotion or advancement in career this month. Those in futures, share and equity trading will do well this month, as will those who invest in property and real estate. Family businesses are also likely to prosper. In addition, any form of travel abroad will bring good quality, new business, resulting in increased profits for your business.

農曆八月 (September 8th – October 7th) 丁酉

Wealth Luck is generally favourable for those using the Northwest sector this month. Couples using this bedroom will find that this is a good room to be in this month, as the quality of the relationships can be expected to increase, and you can derive fulfillment from your ties. Employees may find that they are more stressed this month as superiors step up the pressure for them to perform. Expectations are rather high and this may increase your stress levels, so you will need to learn how to manage anxiety and turn it into useful energy.

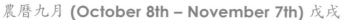

農曆九月 (October 8th – November 7th) 戊戌

This is a good month to unbundle your property portfolios if you have them, as there are generous profits to be made. Those taking important examinations this month will do well to use the Northwest bedroom or study, as the academic results are likely to be good. It is a generally good sector for you to help you focus your energy and develop your levels of concentration, as well. Overseas opportunities will become more lucrative for those using this bedroom or sector this month as profits and new clients abound for those involve.

農曆十月 (November 8th – December 6th) 己亥

Although this month might prove to be taxing in many respects, it will be important for you to keep your spirits up in order to turn negative events in positive outcomes. Try hard to see the silver lining in every cloud – and without a doubt, there always is one, even if it's not apparent at first! Young children using the Northwest room might be prone to injuries by small and sharp metal objects. Where possible, monitor them closely and keep such implements away from them.

農曆十一月 (December 7th – January 5th 2012) 庚子

This month, your relationships will proceed smoothly with nary a hitch or a problem. With the minimal stress comes increased and more effective communication, and while this will make life a breeze on the homefront, it will also help you engage more effectively with your colleagues, superiors, and subordinates at the workplace. If you are in a leadership role or have some form of power or authority, you can expect to enjoy a very good month indeed. Dabbling in speculative real-estate investments will provide good profits this month.

農曆十二月 (January 6th – February 3rd 2012) 辛丑

Those of you who are married and using the Northwest room will find that marital relationships prove to proceed without a hitch, and minus any form of tension. Arguments will lessen, and you can make use of the time to have some major or serious discussions about issues and concerns you've put aside. Alternatively, consider taking a holiday together, especially if both of you have been very stressed out by work of late.

Main Door	Northeast	Bedroom Sector	West

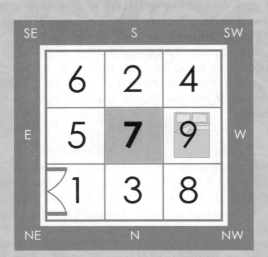

農曆正月 (February 4th – March 5th) 庚寅

Things at work start to get a little demanding, and you might have to juggle multiple projects to please your superiors. If it becomes overwhelming, you need to speak up and ask for help. There is no shame in doing that, because you only succeed in providing half-hearted work if you don't have the time or the energy to give it your best! Be sure to outline exactly what it is you find troublesome in your daily tasks.

農曆二月 (March 6th – April 4th) 辛卯

Those of you using this room will find it a very good month for romance. If you're already in committed relationships, you'll find that your relationship can progress comfortably to the next level with very little effort on your part. If you're single and looking, this is the month to step up the pace (or make a move if someone has already caught your eye!). Those of you working in the engineering or travel industry should go forth and ask for a promotion this month as results are likely to be good.

農曆三月 (April 5th – May 5th) 壬辰

This will prove to be a very good month, professionally, for people using this room. There are strong chances for a promotion for salaried employees, while those among you who are self-employed or own businesses will be able to enjoy an enhanced reputation. Fame and increased business are likely to be the results of that. Personal relationships will also do well this month, so make an effort to forge closer ties with your loved ones.

農曆四月 (May 6th – June 5th) 癸巳

Make this your month of self-improvement, as any attempts at self-cultivation will be fruitful and leave you feeling satisfied. Consider embarking on a new program for living, or take up meditation and other soul-replenishing activities. Clarity of thought is at its unvarnished prime this month, so it will be a good time to make an important decision you've been holding off. Health will generally be good, but ensure that there are no negative features located outside this sector.

| Main Door | Northeast | Bedroom Sector | West |

農曆五月 (June 6th – July 6th) 甲午

People using this bedroom will be able to celebrate with some good news this month. Married couples may be able to welcome a new crying, squirming bundle of joy into their arms! The rest of you in committed relationships should be able to go forth and pop the question – and receive the desired answer. In terms of finances, it's all looking quite rosy as well – as property investments are likely to bring in positive results.

農曆六月 (July 7th – August 7th) 乙未

Bad temper proves to be a problem this month, as your mood will be lot sourer than usual due to the effects of sleeping in this room. This might lead you to be very anti-social, and you'll find it difficult to get along with others and simply enjoy a good time. Don't worry too much or push things along, because it will blow over soon. Partners in relationships should avoid being too clingy this month, as both of you need more space.

農曆七月 (August 8th – September 7th) 丙申

Trouble comes this month in the form of openly defiant and rebellious subordinates and employees. Try to find out the reasons behind this, as they are most likely disgruntled over some issue that proves to be quite significant. This is not the time for heavy-handed authority, as they are more likely to respond positively when you show some compassion. This way, the problem can be easily solved and everyone is able to move on.

農曆八月 (September 8th – October 7th) 丁酉

Health concerns come to the fore this month, leading up to some troubling matters if you're not careful. In particular, food poisoning is very likely, especially if there are negative structures located outside this sector. If you are not careful, it's likely to lead to stomach and digestive problems that cause you much discomfort, even if it's not serious. Stick to low-profile, conservative investments this month, as financial loss rather than gain is likely to be the norm.

農曆九月 (October 8th – November 7th) 戊戌

You'll face quite a bit of difficulty at work this month, as very little support is received for your ideas and projects. Without the encouragement and help from others, the obstacles in place are likely to be harder to overcome. If possible, avoid starting any major or important projects this month. It will be better to just lay low and do your planning at this stage, conserving your energy and productivity for a more fruitful time in the future.

農曆十月 (November 8th – December 6th) 己亥

Those of you who are salaried employees will find that your employers' expectations start to increase tenfold this month! Dealing with their demands will be somewhat difficult, yet all you can do is to try to fulfill them to the best of your ability. If however, you find that the workload is too much to cope with, endeavour to discuss this with your superiors and try to find a middle ground that works for everyone.

農曆十一月 (December 7th – January 5th 2012) 庚子

People working in engineering, or in the travel industry, will find this a good month where promotions and profits are concerned. Be bold enough to ask for a promotion if that is what you want. People using the West bedroom will find it an ideal month for romance, so singles might want to take advantage of the situation and ask out the person they've had an eye on for some time.

農曆十二月 (January 6th – February 3rd 2012) 辛丑

Personal relationships continue to do well this month, so use this time to become closer with the people in your life. Put work aside and try to put your family, friends, and loved ones at the top of your priority list. Salaried employees may have a good chance at promotion. Those of you who are self-employed or run your own businesses are likely to see an increase in your public profile and reputation. As a result, new business opportunities may start coming in.

| Main Door | Northeast | Bedroom Sector | Southwest |

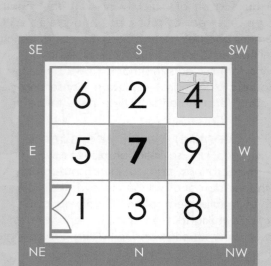

農曆正月 (February 4th – March 5th) 庚寅

This month can bring about an increase in status and authority for those using the Southwest room. Promotion, recognition and advancement will finally come to those who use this room this month, especially if they are involved in the property and real estate fields. This is the month to go for it! Health issues may arise in the form of back and spine injuries this month. This is the month to get involved in joint ventures. If this is in your line, then it is suitable to get involved in gilt bonds or shares.

農曆二月 (March 6th – April 4th) 辛卯

Those in the furniture business will do well this month but just be extra vigilant when signing documents, as this could have legal implications. Pay attention to the fine print and get the legal help or consultation of a lawyer if something proves to be particularly dense or confusing. This month, be careful of what you say as your words might come back to haunt you or you may easily be misunderstood. It will bode well for you to watch your speech and to think carefully before you express yourself.

農曆三月 (April 5th – May 5th) 壬辰

Personal and professional relationships will see an improvement this month so if you wish to build on these relationships, then this is the month to do so! Work on improving communication ties and the benefits will become apparent. Speculative investments in equity, shares and futures should be kept to a minimum, as losses are possible this month, especially if you are careless and decide to act on impulse instead of forethought and planning. Your stature, reputation and name will improve if you travel to conduct business this month, so strive to make as many business opportunities abroad!

農曆四月 (May 6th – June 5th) 癸巳

Those involved in speculative investments, specifically involving property or real estate, should withdraw from their deals or divest from them before losses are experienced. Gambling should be avoided this month as it may end in financial losses, and these losses might prove hard to sustain. This is a month to play it safe and to stick to the rules. There are problems on the health-front for women, and you would do well to have a mammogram this month as a precaution. This is especially true if you already sense or feel that something is amiss. Don't put it off to another time.

農曆五月 (June 6th – July 6th) 甲午

Asthma and bronchitis are the health problems that plague those using this bedroom this month, so it would be best if you have these symptoms to take any precautionary methods as necessary. See your doctor if symptoms seem more pronounced than usual to rule out any unnecessary complications. Avoid gambling this month as you stand to endure heavy losses. Much as the previous month – playing by the rules will yield better results.

農曆六月 (July 7th – August 7th) 乙未

Children using this sector could be encouraged by peer pressure to get involved in rebellious activities. If you're a parent, it pays to be more aware of your children's friends and their leisure habits. Those of you who are artistically creative should market your products abroad, as the demand for quality work is high, and people are more willing to pay for good creative work. Those travelling this month should expect some sudden changes or last-minute problems that may necessitate the buying of travel insurance

農曆七月 (August 8th – September 7th) 丙申

Female employees will have an excellent month. You will bring in increased turnover especially if you are in the real estate industry. This is a good month to invest in self-cultivation, either by attending new courses or learning a new trade. There are problems with the in-laws this month and it is better to avoid contact with them or be more patient in your outlook. If meditation and reading are your interests, this will be a good room to use this month.

農曆八月 (September 8th – October 7th) 丁酉

Authors and journalists should look for new publishers this month if you want to release new publications. Media attention and publicity will bring fame to those who use this bedroom, especially if they are in the arts and culture industry. You can expect to prepare for your moment in the spotlight. Academic luck is strong in this sector, and you should use this room to your advantage if you're facing important examinations this month. This is a good month to build alliance partners abroad, or embark on business expansion.

農曆九月 (October 8th – November 7th) 戊戌

It will be favourable to conclude deals this month in order to benefit from the lucrative investment opportunities available. This is the month for you to go forth and seal the deal! Relationships are generally on the upswing this month and those using this bedroom should take full advantage of them. Ensure that you spend more time you're your spouse or partner and with your loved ones; this will help to cultivate more closeness that will benefit you greatly. This is not a good time to travel, as your rivals will make inroads into your client base whilst you are away.

農曆十月 (November 8th – December 6th) 己亥

Joint ventures will benefit you greatly this month, especially if you're already using the Southwest room. If possible, try to dabble or try your hand in gilt bonds and shares to see how you will do. The likelihood is that you'll be able to rake up the profits! In general, those using this room will enjoy a good month especially if involved in the real estate and property industry. There is a good chance that you'll see a marked increase in stature as a promotion or likely recognition comes your way. In general, profits come from the property market.

農曆十一月 (December 7th – January 5th 2012) 庚子

Those of you who work in construction or have to spend a fair bit of time on worksites need to be extra cautious this month, as there is the potential risk of injury from sharp objects and machinery. However, be careful about potential fraud and cheating by scrutinising all documents, contracts, and forms that need to be signed. Pay attention to what you say this month, especially if you use the Southwest room, as otherwise you may end up hurting, offending, or angering someone with your speech.

農曆十二月 (January 6th – February 3rd 2012) 辛丑

This month, speculative investments in equity, shares and futures should be kept to a minimum, as losses are possible this month. Don't rush into anything without thought. Your stature, reputation and name will improve if you travel to conduct business this month, so strive to make as many business opportunities abroad! Make the time to meet with new people and their associates.

Main Door	Northeast	Bedroom Sector	South

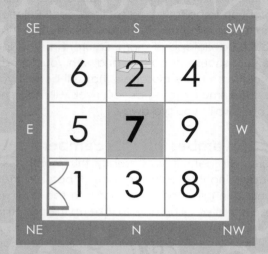

農曆正月 (February 4th – March 5th) 庚寅

If there is a need to sign legal documents, be particularly careful this month. You will need to exercise extreme caution in all your legal dealings because the possibility of fraud and cheating is rampant. Be sure to keep your eyes and ears peeled. Financial loss as a result of negligence or disputes is possible, especially for those of you directly involved in the world of finance. There is a risk of financial loss, so you must take the necessary steps to mitigate them. Abdominal illness is a problem this month, and it will typically affect older women in the home or using the South bedroom.

農曆二月 (March 6th – April 4th) 辛卯

Arguments between mother-in-law and daughter-in-law will become more prevalent for those using this room, so some patience will go a long way this month. If you're either one of the above, it will be best to exercise tact and diplomacy in your dealings with the other! Women in the literary field will have a time to shine this month, as they will receive awards and achievements. This is a time for self-cultivation and if the opportunity arises, you should take a self-development course. It is a good month to work on improving yourself.

農曆三月 (April 5th – May 5th) 壬辰

Make sure that all taxes and fines are up-to-date this month, or you may find yourself in trouble with the law otherwise! Couples should make sure that they spend as little time together as possible, as they will end up with tense and stressful situations if they share this room this month. You actually need the space and time to allow yourself both the room to deal with whatever stresses and problems on your own terms. This is a good sector for those who wish to become involved in religious or spiritual endeavours. It will also help in meditation activities, as the energies here are conducive for peaceful thought and reflection.

農曆四月 (May 6th – June 5th) 癸巳

If you're in the medical field, you will find that your skills are in great demand this month, and can expect to enjoy an increase in profits. There will be an accompanying boost to both your reputation and stature as well, and you will be able to enjoy some welcome accolades. Those of you wishing to invest in property will find that this a good month to get involved in the venture, as the returns will be quick and profitable. Women who are pregnant should avoid this sector this month, as the chance of miscarriage is possible.

| Main Door | Northeast | Bedroom Sector | South |

農曆五月 (June 6th – July 6th) 甲午

While your financial luck is still somewhat good, you will need to exercise some caution and not get too carried away. Don't be tempted to make lavish purchases or display extravagant forms of generosity. Maintain good ties with your friends and family and don't let any arguments escalate out of control. Don't be too gullible this month as people may tend to take advantage of you, and the more you are willing to hedge around and give them room, the bolder they will become.

農曆六月 (July 7th – August 7th) 乙未

It is important not to make any important business decisions this month, as confusion will play into the decision-making process. This could cloud the entire process, resulting in some bad choices being made. Arguments and family disharmony will be a problem for you this year, so you need to be mindful of the way you interact with your family members. There is a possibility of miscarriage this month for pregnant women who use this sector, so move to another room if possible. At the very least, take all proper precautions to prevent any complications and see your doctor at the first sign of trouble.

農曆七月 (August 8th – September 7th) 丙申

Paranoia and superstition may set in this month, resulting in emotional setbacks for those you who succumb to the worries. The key thing is to maintain some form of emotional strength despite the negative feelings. Share your problems with others and talk to people in order to help yourself get a better grasp on the situation. Gastric and intestinal problems will plague those using this bedroom this month.

農曆八月 (September 8th – October 7th) 丁酉

There is a possibility for you to make money this month from side investments that will return good profits. If you make smart decisions, you can expect to enjoy a well-padded wallet! If you're a doctor, you will find that you have increased business. This is not because more people are ill, but because there is a demand for your skills in many sectors. Couples in this house may find that they are unable to have children, and using this bedroom this month will complicate things further. If possible, you should try shifting to another room.

農曆九月 (October 8th – November 7th) 戊戌

As an employee, you will find that you are working harder this month, but income and deal closure do not seem to be concluded. In other words, the benefits of your hard work are not clearly visible. Don't let this get you down, however, by focusing too much on the end results. Use your level of personal satisfaction as your benchmark. Those involved in religious pursuits or those gaining spiritual knowledge should use this bedroom this month, as it is conducive for those types of activities.

農曆十月 (November 8th – December 6th) 己亥

Health issues come into the fore this month, and typically for elderly women using the South room, this will come in the form of abdominal illness. Don't put off a medical consultation for too long. It will be best to consult your doctor at the first signs of discomfort. Be careful when signing legal documents this month, because all legal dealings are fraught with potential risks at this point in time. This is especially true for those of you working or involved in finance and trading.

農曆十一月 (December 7th – January 5th 2012) 庚子

Typically, this is a month for potential success for those in the literary field and publishing, especially women. There will be awards and achievements, and an increase in your reputation and stature. It's a good time to simply let the good times roll and allow yourself to feel good for being in the centre of the attention! However, mothers-in-law and daughters-in-law may find themselves at odd this month, so be careful in your interactions with each other. It's also a good month to work on self-improvement.

農曆十二月 (January 6th – February 3rd 2012) 辛丑

Couples should make sure that they spend as little time together as possible, as they will end up with tense and stressful situations if they share this room this month. You actually need the space and time to allow yourself both the room to deal with whatever stresses and problems on your own terms. However, the South room is good for those who wish to become involved in religious or spiritual endeavours. It will also help in meditation activities, as the energies here are conducive for peaceful thought and reflection. Ensure that all taxes and fines are up-to-date this month, or you may find yourself in trouble with the law and having to dig yourself out of a messy spot.

| Main Door | **Northeast** | Bedroom Sector | Southeast |

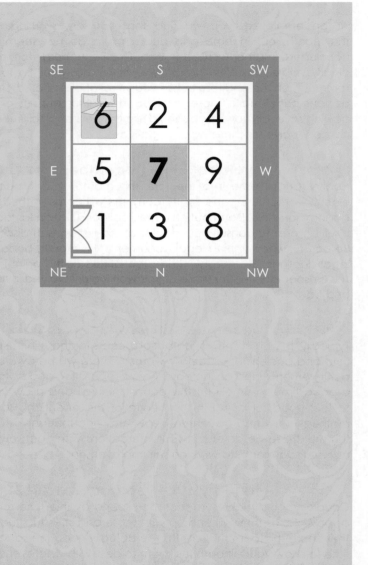

農曆正月 (February 4th – March 5th) 庚寅

Entrepreneurs and those wishing to start new ventures should use the good energies of the Southeast bedroom to go out and make a start. It will provide auspicious vibes for new beginnings. A rocky relationship or business partnership that is on the verge of a break up will be exacerbated if this room is used this month. If you're facing any troubles in your romantic or professional relationships, you may want to take extra care in your dealings with the other party.

農曆二月 (March 6th – April 4th) 辛卯

Avoid putting children in this bedroom this month, as they will be rebellious and difficult to control. Parents will do well to find a way to manage the rebelliousness, or it might be a difficult future ahead! There may be internal bickering this month so you will need to keep a low profile at work, and make sure that you keep out of the office politics. Older men should take care of their health, especially with regards to high blood pressure or lung disease.

農曆三月 (April 5th – May 5th) 壬辰

A change in career, a pay raise, or some form of career advancement is likely this month, and this could result in financial rewards that will have you smiling all the way to the bank! Investment and merchant bankers who engage in stock and corporate deals will make good financial profits this month. You will find that there are coaches and mentors around to offer good advice, so take heed of their suggestions. You are able to achieve financial success if you consider their suggestions wisely.

農曆四月 (May 6th – June 5th) 癸巳

Jealousy and rivalry amongst males could result in physical fights, which could end up in the law courts. Therefore, it might be good to put the bravado aside and consider the situation using reason instead of brawn, and ugly legal wrangles can be avoided. This is a month for short-term flings rather than long term relationships, and if you're comfortable with that then you should be able to enjoy it. If you're not, avoid putting too much expectation into any new relationships formed.

農曆五月 (June 6th – July 6th) 甲午

Employees may become rebellious this month, and superiors will find them difficult to handle. Good profits can be realised this month, but a more hands-on approach is required to maximise

| Main Door | Northeast | Bedroom Sector | Southeast |

profits – so you should not be hesitant to get your hands dirty! Getting involved in your business and enterprise can also help you to assess where financial leaks or losses occur. This bedroom will benefit you if you're into professional sports and are participating in any competitive events this month.

農曆六月 (July 7th – August 7th) 乙未

Family relations are strained and tense but it is better just to keep the peace, as this is not a good time to thrash it out with the family. Heart-to-heart conversations that may require quite a bit of emotional involvement are best left to another time. Legal challenges may arise from the sacking of staff and employees, as industrial labour relations are likely to play a big role this month. There are opportunities to make money from property investments this month, but you will need to have a good knowledge of the market to be successful in this venture. In other words, study the property market inside out before attempting anything in it!

農曆七月 (August 8th – September 7th) 丙申

Those in the academic and literary fields will benefit from new ideas and inspiration that are likely bring favourable financial gains this month. Children who are facing important examinations should make use of this room to make their preparations, as academic results are likely to be favourable. If you are in the psychological, counselling or mentor fields, you stand to gain respect and recognition this month as the demand for wisdom and intelligence increases among the public. This is a good month for those who wish to use travel as a means of producing more income.

農曆八月 (September 8th – October 7th) 丁酉

Travel-related problems could result in leg injuries this month, so be especially careful on any of your travel trips. Minor health issues could be a problem as well, but do not think that these are unimportant or it could end up as more serious conditions that will require more trouble and expenditure further down the road.. There is an increased risk of car accidents and injuries this month, so be careful when driving and out and about. Employees in the engineering field will benefit from the support of superiors, which could result in financial reward and recognition

農曆九月 (October 8th – November 7th) 戊戌

Those in the metaphysical or spiritual development fields should do well this month, so ensure you use this room if you want to have a clear mind and some peace and quiet to focus on your meditation and reflection. Salaried employees may find that you face obstructions in career prospects this month, but you need to be patient and wait it out, as this is only temporary. Women may experience gynaecological problems this month if they use the Southeast bedroom, so any complications or troubles should be medically checked-out early.

農曆十月 (November 8th – December 6th) 己亥

Those of you who are experiencing a rocky relationship or a floundering business partnership will most likely have to face the end of the tie or connection if you use the Southeast bedroom this month. However, don't think of it as a bad thing, because it paves the way for auspicious new beginnings. But be sure to take extra care of your manner of speech and behavior with your partner for those of you going through a rough patch with your other half. Those of you in the spa and tourism business will do well to do some travelling because it will help lead you to new business prospects and contacts.

農曆十一月 (December 7th – January 5th 2012) 庚子

Elderly males who use the Southeast room need to take special care of their health this month, and monitor their blood pressure as hypertension or high blood pressure is likely. Also, there is the increased risk of lung disease or illnesses. Children who use this bedroom are likely to be somewhat tempestuous and strong-willed, so parents will do well to be expect moments of rebellion and high drama! Be sure to deal with it calmly, as that will help to defuse the tension. At work, it will be best to lay and refrain from getting involved in office politics.

農曆十二月 (January 6th – February 3rd 2012) 辛丑

Investment and merchant bankers who engage in stock and corporate deals will make good financial profits this month. You will find that there are coaches and mentors around to offer good advice, so take heed of their suggestions. There is a likelihood of you making it big financially if you pay attention to their expertise. There is likely to be a change in your career this month, or at the very least a pay raise or some form of career advancement is likely this month. Therefore, be sure to put your best foot forward at the workplace and show others why you've earned the accolades!

| Main Door | Northeast | Bedroom Sector | East |

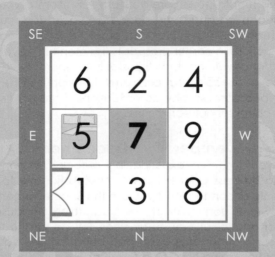

農曆正月 (February 4th – March 5th) 庚寅

Mentors and superiors are not around to help you this month, and as a result you may find business contracts drying up. You will need to learn some of the skills quickly in order that you are able to manage matters yourself should the need arise. Couples using the East bedroom will feel anxious, stressed and mentally pressured, resulting in lots of disputes and fights. Niggling health is the main problem facing those in the East sector this month, especially in the form of kidney and ear problems.

農曆二月 (March 6th – April 4th) 辛卯

Conservative property related deals will bring good financial gains this month, while those in business will lack the leverage to benefit from positive investment outcomes. Business owners should avoid any expansion this month and rather, should focus on consolidating their options. Pay extra attention to customers and clients, as disloyalty amongst employees is rife, and they may be sabotaging your enterprise or company by leaking unwanted information towards your customer base.

農曆三月 (April 5th – May 5th) 壬辰

Competition and rivalry, especially from competitors, will affect those who use the East bedroom this month. This will become a very emotional issue resulting in psychological warfare. You will need to be on guard, but don't overreact and resort to petty responses. Lawyers will find it difficult to put their case across this month, and may need to use every ounce of strength to fight. Accidents could be caused by mishaps with other people, resulting in muscle and tendon injuries.

農曆四月 (May 6th – June 5th) 癸巳

Professional sportspeople will find competitions an uphill battle this month, and should instead use the time for some physical improvement that can bring future benefits. Stress and depression may end in mental instability or neurosis this month, especially if there is negative Sha outside the East sector. Health issues may also arise in the form of migraines or headaches, so try to relax more and not let worries and anxieties get to you.

農曆五月 (June 6th – July 6th) 甲午

It will be best to avoid from the fashion and apparel industries, as the outcomes for those industries are likely to be quite disastrous this month. For business owners this month, everything that can go wrong, will, and even those things that usually run smoothly will cause trouble and obstruction. Pregnant women should be careful when using this bedroom this month, as there is a risk of complications and troubles.

農曆六月 (July 7th – August 7th) 乙未

Speculative investments and gambling should be resisted this month, as it is likely to bring financial losses. Problems arising this month will be difficult to solve as the cause is not easily evident, and your rivals will take quick advantage of this factor. Stay away from casual relationships this month, as it is likely to result in sexually-transmitted diseases and will be more trouble than it's worth.

農曆七月 (August 8th – September 7th) 丙申

You should avoid lending money to anyone this month, but especially to family members, as it may end up in discord. This is a good month for lawyers and those in the dispute resolution business, as this is a month of petty disputes and conflicts resulting in harmful end results and lingering problems. Males who use this bedroom this month may find themselves entangled in lawsuits arising out of car accidents.

農曆八月 (September 8th – October 7th) 丁酉

Mothers and older women who use the East sector this month will find an increased risk of kidney problems and related ailments. Negative structures outside the East sector will enhance the bad effects of the energies of this sector, which will give rise to unforeseen problems in the form of illness and accidents. Ensure that there are no negative structures outside the East sector. Do not try to make property acquisitions this month, as this will likely end in failure.

農曆九月 (October 8th – November 7th) 戊戌

Business partners should be aware of possible fallout from tension and stress as this will eventually result in a loss of wealth. Try to salvage what you can of your professional connections instead of simply writing it off. Health is severely affected this month, resulting in bladder and kidney problems. Those involved in lawsuits should try to settle out of court or it will end up costing a lot more for all involved.

農曆十月 (November 8th – December 6th) 己亥

You may find your business networks somewhat dwindling this month, due to a lessening of mentors and superiors. It will be best for you to adapt to learning some of the necessary skills yourself so that you can cope with it should the need arise. Those of you in romantic relationships or marriages might feel pressured and stressed due to constant arguments. Take extra care of your health this month, as well, and watch out for any ear problems or kidney diseases.

農曆十一月 (December 7th – January 5th 2012) 庚子

If you own or run a business, this will not be the month to focus on expansion and growth. Use this time to consolidate your current interests and to brainstorm for future strategies. While you're at it, pay special attention to your customers and clients as well. Ensure that no disgruntled employees are being treacherous behind your back. Financial wealth is likely to come from modest and conservative property deals.

農曆十二月 (January 6th – February 3rd 2012) 辛丑

Accidents could be caused by mishaps with other people this month, so be careful. Muscle and tendon injuries are likely. Competition and rivalry, especially from competitors, will affect those who use the East bedroom this month. You will need to be on guard, but don't overreact and resort to petty responses. Strategise wisely. Lawyers will find it difficult to put their case across this month, so you will have to rely on strong willpower to carry on.

West Sector
Main Door

Main Door	West	Bedroom Sector	West

This section contains the monthly outlook for all 12 months of the year, for different bedrooms in a property with a West Main Door.

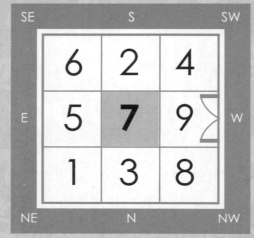

Ground Floor

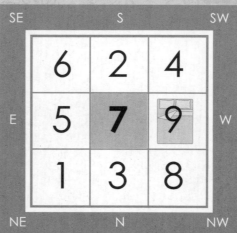

First Floor

農曆正月 (February 4th – March 5th) 庚寅

Academics and scholars will do well to tap into the energies of the West sector this month. Do so and you'll find plenty of opportunities to be recognized and rewarded, in terms of better perks and a possible promotion at work. What's more, those using the West will also find their relationships to be harmonious and thriving this month, so use this period in time to further consolidate your ties with others.

農曆二月 (March 6th – April 4th) 辛卯

You'll be pleased to find your thoughts coherent and clear, with your decision-making capabilities impeccable this month. So use this period of time well to generate more gains from your investment portfolios and make long- term decisions. No matter if it involves your professional or personal life, ensure that you do all major thinking and planning for the year now, when your thinking is unclouded.

農曆三月 (April 5th – May 5th) 壬辰

If you're looking for a good time to divest of some of the properties under your investment portfolio and cash-in on your investments, now's the time to do so. Likewise, good news and celebrations await politicians and civil servants, as they find their status and position elevated, due to their tireless efforts. Ensure that you do your best to prop up your professional reputation with sustained work.

農曆四月 (May 6th – June 5th) 癸巳

Beware of frayed tempers and other problems arising from miscommunication, as this could lead to a rocky month for those using the West room. Curb your tendency towards a sharp tongue. But otherwise, models, actors and actresses and those involved in the dramatic arts will benefit from good publicity provided by the mass media this month and it would be a perfect time to use it to your advantage.

West Sector Main Door

農曆五月 (June 6th – July 6th) 甲午

This promises to be a profitable month for speculative investments in metal trading, futures, equities and stocks. But you'll need to keep abreast of current market trends in order to capitalize on any favourable situations that may arise. Expect changes at the workplace as well, which could come in the form of staff transfers. Females in the household are particularly susceptible to eye and heart-related ailments this month.

農曆六月 (July 7th – August 7th) 乙未

You may find yourself feeling stressed and under pressure this month, so it would be a good idea to postpone any important decision-making, as your mental faculties aren't functioning at their best. Be vigilant and mindful of any fraudulent activities that could cause you legal problems as well. This is a time to be extremely caution in handling monetary and financial issues, as disputes over money are very likely during this month.

農曆七月 (August 8th – September 7th) 丙申

You stand to reap substantial profits this month by expanding your business as well as your network of contacts, so go ahead and get in touch with all of your old friends and associates. The fact that the mass media aids in your business expansion process with positive coverage serves to further enhance your reputation and status. On the home front, be mindful of tension in your relationships, especially where ladies of the household are concerned.

農曆八月 (September 8th – October 7th) 丁酉

Legal issues will rear its ugly head this month, so seek the advice of your mentors and experienced seniors in attempting to work out an amicable solution to your woes. Look out as well for any minor ailments, and have them treated at once to avoid it festering into something more serious. You'll be pleased to know that the ability to make money from your investments and the wisdom to invest your gains wisely will benefit you.

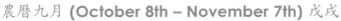
農曆九月 (October 8th – November 7th) 戊戌

Health problems may assume the form of heart and eye ailments this month, so those who have existing cardiac problems and those with existing eye issues should be doubly cautious. Romance luck will smile upon you this month, so now's the time to take your relationships to the next level or to seek out a potential partner. Those working in the engineering and technical fields might want to seek an appointment with their superiors, and present your case for a promotion – it is bound to go well.

農曆十月 (November 8th – December 6th) 己亥

Those of you who use the West room will notice a significant improvement in your personal relationships this month, and perhaps even your general working relations with colleagues and clients will improve. This sector also bodes well for scholarly activities throughout the month, and so those of you in academia or studying for exams will do well.

農曆十一月 (December 7th – January 5th 2012) 庚子

Those of you involved in the fashion industry may need to travel to conclude major deals but this could also be an indication of better profits as a result. Make the effort needed even if it creates a more hectic schedule; the pay off will be worth it. And if you're into all matters spiritual or religious, then the energies of the West will aid you in your meditative and self-development endeavours.

農曆十二月 (January 6th – February 3rd 2012) 辛丑

This will generally be a favourable month for those in the diplomatic corps, as positive publicity will turn the tide of things in their favour. Those of you in the civil service or in the government will find that the month generally brings positive development, more so if you use the West room as a bedroom. It's a good month to forge diplomatic ties and build new social connections.

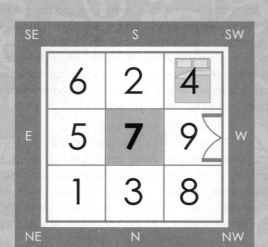

農曆正月 (February 4th – March 5th) 庚寅

Health issues in the form of skin problems or breast malignancies may plague the ladies of the household this month, so it's an ideal time to go for an immediate medical check-up, even if you may feel perfectly well. Avoid all gambling activities as well, unless you wish to end up incurring massive financial losses by succumbing to your urges. Financial risk-taking will not go down well this month.

農曆二月 (March 6th – April 4th) 辛卯

Artists and those of you who consider yourself artistically-inclined should publicise your skills at an exhibition if possible, or at least to draw attention to your creative output. The time is ripe to do so. Likewise, those specializing in the car or auto accessories business should market their products and services more aggressively this month as well. Couples however, will need to put in a little extra effort into their relationship to preserve the harmony at home.

農曆三月 (April 5th – May 5th) 壬辰

Any tension that exists between couples this month will more likely affect the women, compared to the men so exercise tact and tolerance in dealing with your partner. Pick your arguments wisely, and don't indulge in verbal swordplay simply to be the one to "win". In fact, unhealthy rivalry and deceit may well prove to be an issue for many individuals this month, across the board, especially those involved in the literary field.

農曆四月 (May 6th – June 5th) 癸巳

Journalists and astronomers will find this to be a good month for them, as they may attract funding or potential sponsors. You're also advised to change your property portfolio this month, as you'll stand to reap the rewards of doing so, especially if your investment managers are women. Nevertheless, be mindful of ailments affecting your internal organs (including your spleen) this month. Elderly ladies should consult the doctor, at any sign of pain or discomfort.

Main Door	West	Bedroom Sector	Southwest

農曆五月 (June 6th – July 6th) 甲午

Scholars and students sitting for important exams soon should use the Southwest room to study and sleep in, to benefit from the positive energies present in this sector throughout the month. In fact, your relationships will also blossom and thrive, more so if there's no body of water in the sector. Fame and recognition will also come rolling to those in the arts and culture industries due to the positive publicity and media attention received this month.

農曆六月 (July 7th – August 7th) 乙未

Establish a joint-venture to widen your niche market by identifying a suitable partner who will complement your capabilities. This is the month in which to do it. Likewise, those looking to finalize any business deals should do so this month, as the outcomes will be in your favour. Specialists in the metaphysical and services industries will also benefit from the energies of the Southwest, as long as they do not have to travel to generate their income, as any travelling will result in reduced revenues for them.

農曆七月 (August 8th – September 7th) 丙申

Elderly or ailing folk using the Southwest room face the risk of suffering from a stroke or arterial blockage due to poor blood circulation, so it's advisable to take them for a medical check-up as soon as possible. Married couples will also find themselves more at loggerheads with each other than usual, so it's important to exercise tolerance and patience in dealing with each other. Don't be too quick to retort with anger.

農曆八月 (September 8th – October 7th) 丁酉

Prioritise safety this month, especially if your job requires you to work with sharp instruments or knives on a regular or daily basis. And if you've already been feeling rather poorly of late, you need to guard against acquiring a lung ailment this month – see your doctor, at the first sign of a cough or wheezing. Note as well that disputes and arguments amongst women could lead to a more serious situation, or worse still, a lawsuit at the end of the day.

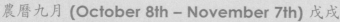

農曆九月 (October 8th – November 7th) 戊戌

If you are a politician or civil servant, be careful when it comes to matters involving real estate, as serious disputes could arise if you let your guard down. However, athletes and sportspersons travelling to participate in competitions will do better than those whose field of work does not involve travel. Indeed, this is a favourable time to travel to conclude deals, as they will bring you greater repute, status and fortune.

農曆十月 (November 8th – December 6th) 己亥

This month, those of you involved in speculative investments, especially property or real estate dealings, are advised to pull out early before the market takes a plunge and burns a hole in their finances. This is not the ideal month to take a risk or a gamble with finances, as the fall-out is likely to be quite significant. It would be best to lie low and do things the foolproof way for the time being.

農曆十一月 (December 7th – January 5th 2012) 庚子

Those of you in relationships or marriages will find it a bit hard-going this month, and so you will have to make more of an effort to ensure that you're off on an even keel. Spend more time with each other and don't bring home stress from work, or allow individual family obligations and problems to take over. Those of you who are artists will find this a bumper month for which to boost your portfolio and your name.

農曆十二月 (January 6th – February 3rd 2012) 辛丑

This is a month of tough choices and slim pickings, especially for those of you in the literary and publishing world. Nevertheless, do not be disheartened but instead, travel to conclude your deals, more so if your area of specialty lies in the artistic, marketing or consultancy business. This way, you'll broaden your base of contacts while taking in new sights and sounds that will rejuvenate you.

Main Door	West	Bedroom Sector	South

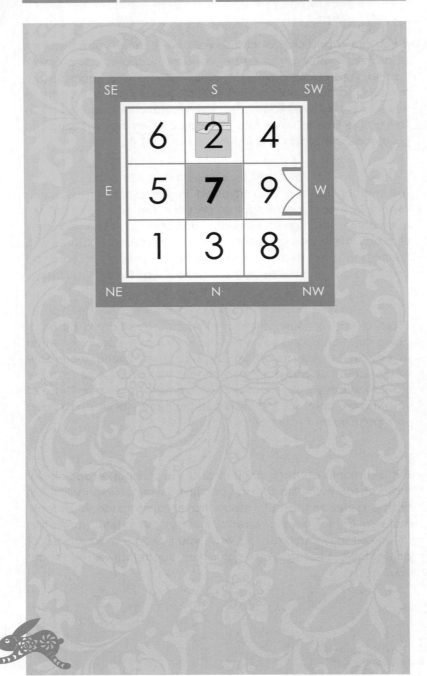

農曆正月 (February 4th – March 5th) 庚寅

Be sure to settle all outstanding fines, summonses and taxes, unless you wish to long arm of the law to catch up with you. Stay out of office politics as well, more so if you find arguments, gossips and backstabbing to be rampant at the workplace this month. Couples are also advised to give each other some breathing space this month, to minimize the possibility of getting into unnecessary arguments or quarrels that may affect their relationship.

農曆二月 (March 6th – April 4th) 辛卯

Frail health threatens to plague those using the South bedroom this month, especially those who have already been feeling sickly of late. Unsurprisingly, medical practitioners will find their advice and services highly sought-after, while medical researchers will be successful in making breakthroughs in their work. Those who deal in real estate or property stand to make handsome gains from their investments in land.

農曆三月 (April 5th – May 5th) 壬辰

Competitive or professional athletes will do well this month, especially if an event requires you to travel. However, car accidents are possible as well, so watch how you move around, especially when you are on the road. Expectant mothers should also go for a full medical check-up, as the risk of running into pregnancy complications is a strong likelihood for those using the South this month.

農曆四月 (May 6th – June 5th) 癸巳

This promises to be a rather trying month and possibly even a hazardous one. For starters, take good care of your eyes; otherwise you may risk running into some complications, more so if there are any negative features outside the South sector. And mind your stress levels as well, especially if you've been filled with anxiety lately over your property dealings. Indeed, it would be wise to leave all negotiations and decision-making to a more favourable time, as your thoughts will tend to be clouded this month.

Main Door	West	Bedroom Sector	South

農曆五月 (June 6th – July 6th) 甲午

There will be handsome financial profits to be enjoyed by those shrewd enough to invest in viable properties or real estate this month. In fact, there will be plenty of opportunities to improve your fortunes and financial standing. Nevertheless, the South isn't really an ideal room to be used by those who have been feeling rather poorly in terms of health.

農曆六月 (July 7th – August 7th) 乙未

The potential for windfall gains are high this month, so a small gamble or the occasional lottery ticket may bring you some financial gains. Just be careful not to get carried away and only spend what you can afford. On the work-front, arguments and jealousy abound, and it would be advisable for women to stay clear of such disputes, as these will most probably end up in disaster for all involved.

農曆七月 (August 8th – September 7th) 丙申

Legal practitioners and professionals will find their skills in great demand this month. And if you're a businessperson, make sure that any deal you sketch this month does not require too much capital, as the potential for financial losses are on the cards if the risks are high. Bosses are also advised to communicate more coherently and tactfully with their subordinates, to mitigate the risk of running into any legal complications.

農曆八月 (September 8th – October 7th) 丁酉

Pregnant ladies using the South room should be cautious this month, and all others should be looking out for potential appendicitis. Couples using this sector should also exercise tolerance and patience with one another to ensure any disagreements do not get out of hand. This is not a good time of the year to conclude any business deals or investments as well, as you may find yourself on the losing end.

農曆九月 (October 8th – November 7th) 戊戌

You may find the ladies in your household disinclined to treat each other in a civil or tactful manner, with arguments amongst them rife, so where possible, move them out of the South sector of the home. Nevertheless, the energies of the South augur well for self-cultivation and development pursuits, so use this sector if you seek self-growth. Academics, scholars and candidates sitting for exams this month will also do well if using this room.

農曆十月 (November 8th – December 6th) 己亥

This month, couples will undergo a trying time if using the South bedroom, and should therefore be prepared to be more patient and tolerant than usual. It will best to leave things be instead of forcing issues and arguments. It's also best to be on the right side of the law, and have all your outstanding fines and penalties settled before things get messy.

農曆十一月 (December 7th – January 5th 2012) 庚子

People involved in the real estate and property industry will enjoy a good month, as investments made are likely to pay off in a big way. In general, it's a thriving atmosphere. However, those of you who have been feeling poor of health lately should take precautions when using the South bedroom; the energies here could exacerbate illnesses and symptoms.

農曆十二月 (January 6th – February 3rd 2012) 辛丑

Pregnant women are liable to suffer from some complications this month if using this room, so they are advised to see their doctor for any issues that come up – even if it seems minor at first. Everyone else should be wary of potential car accidents and should be doubly-cautious while on the road.

Main Door	West	Bedroom Sector	Southeast

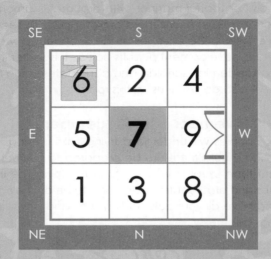

農曆正月 (February 4th – March 5th) 庚寅

This looks set to be a month of intense competition and rivalry, especially at the workplace. Learn how to maintain a low profile, although this doesn't mean that you should let your guard down. On the contrary, remain vigilant, but keep your cool as well, to prevent any issues from escalating into something more serious. Where possible, don't burn any bridges because you'll never know when you might need those connections.

農曆二月 (March 6th – April 4th) 辛卯

This is a favourable month insofar as both professional and personal relationships are concerned. Take this opportunity to foster even closer ties with your business partners, co-workers and loved ones. Nevertheless, be mindful of the possibility that your employees could adopt a more rebellious stance this month, with superiors equally difficult to please. Don't let this stand in your way of making a financial gain, although a more hands-on approach will suit you best!

農曆三月 (April 5th – May 5th) 壬辰

This is not an ideal month to look for love, so focus on your career instead. Be wary of competitors launching a hostile takeover bid for your business and make plans to ward them off, just in case. Similarly, employees need to be careful as to how they handle workplace disagreements and conflicts, if they wish to keep their job at their current company.

農曆四月 (May 6th – June 5th) 癸巳

Couples using the Southeast bedroom this month will find the energies of this sector beneficial to their relationship. Similarly, athletes and sportspersons should make an extra effort as this month will support their endeavours. Employees will also find their diligence and capabilities recognized by their superiors, who may also entrust you with more complex projects or assignments. Prove your worth, and that promotion may be just around the corner.

| Main Door | West | Bedroom Sector | Southeast |

農曆五月 (June 6th – July 6th) 甲午

Teenagers and youngsters using the Southeast bedroom will be predisposed towards behaving more rebelliously this month – so moving them out of this sector is a good idea. Elderly family members are also advised to take good care of their health, and seek immediate medical attention for any health issues arising; lest these manifest into something more serious if neglected.

農曆六月 (July 7th – August 7th) 乙未

The presence of negative forms outside the Southeast sector will render elderly family members even more susceptible to health problems, particularly kidney and stomach ailments. Nevertheless, couples using this bedroom will enjoy a harmonious time with each other, and their loved ones. Meanwhile, if you've any real estate investment portfolios under your name, now's a good time to divest of some of them and cash-in on your profits.

農曆七月 (August 8th – September 7th) 丙申

Use the Southeast sector room if you're due to sit for an important examination soon. Bankers will also find their efforts and capabilities duly recognized by their superiors, which could lead to a promotion. Similarly, entrepreneurs and budding business owners should utilize the energies of the Southeast, if they wish to make a good start of their ventures.

農曆八月 (September 8th – October 7th) 丁酉

Couples using this sector will tend to enjoy a harmonious relationship, as well as excel in their respective career fields. This is a time to engage in only conservative business deals, although preferably, one should refrain from making any significant moves, as far as commercial deals are concerned. It would be better to bide your time, in waiting for a better moment to make your move.

農曆九月 (October 8th – November 7th) 戊戌

You may find yourself affected mentally or emotionally, or even at best, feel lonely and isolated from the rest of the world. Seek the company of loved ones and friends, to bolster your spirits. Couples wishing to formalise their relationship by tying the knot should use this month to embark upon this latest phase in their lives. Likewise, employees who've worked hard the last six months of the year may find their reward coming to them this month.

農曆十月 (November 8th – December 6th) 己亥

This month, concentrate on your career and work, instead of trying to look for a long-term romantic relationship, as chances are, Cupid's arrow won't really hit the mark for you this month. There are benefits to this, in that you'll be able to throw yourself whole-heartedly into your career without a worry about how your personal life is going to play out.

農曆十一月 (December 7th – January 5th 2012) 庚子

Those of you who run a company or own a business will find that your employees prove to be a little difficult than usual. You may have some particularly rocky instances where outright rebellion leads to wasted time and productivity. This won't necessarily get in the way of financial profits if you play your cards right, but you need to be sure you're ready to get your hands dirty in terms of finding a solution.

農曆十二月 (January 6th – February 3rd 2012) 辛丑

Some conflicts and disagreements are likely at the workplace, lending an air of strained tension among colleagues. It will behoove you to learn how to juggle workplace tensions without letting it interfere with your performance. Otherwise, you'll have trouble holding on to your job in the long run. Romance does not fare well this month; career-focus will be the way to go.

Main Door	West	Bedroom Sector	East

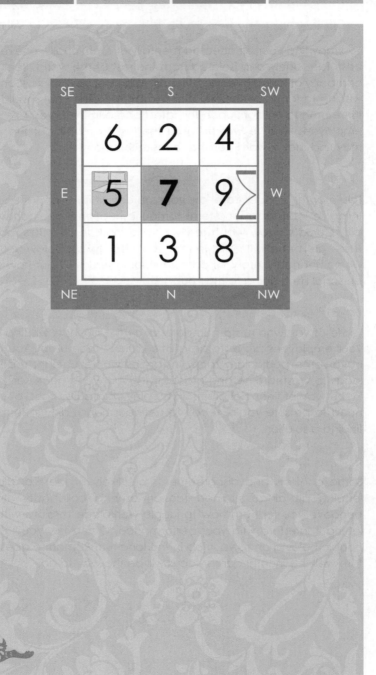

	SE	S	SW	
E	6	2	4	
	5	**7**	9	W
	1	3	8	
	NE	N	NW	

農曆正月 (February 4th – March 5th) 庚寅

Those using the East bedroom may feel lonely or even unwanted this month. Seek the company of friends and loved ones, as this is only a temporary situation, which should soon pass. Indeed, individuals who are prone to, or already suffering from depression, are advised not to use this bedroom for the duration of the month – as the energies present therein will only exacerbate your situation.

農曆二月 (March 6th – April 4th) 辛卯

Always seek a mutually amicable solution to even the trickiest situation, especially insofar as your relationships are concerned. There's no point in being antagonistic, only to win the battle... and lose the war. Unfortunately, professionals in the IT industry will find the outcome of their work to be disproportionate to the amount of effort they've put in. Stay clear of any joint-ventures this month, as they will most likely end up in disaster!

農曆三月 (April 5th – May 5th) 壬辰

Those of you using the East bedroom are particularly susceptible to liver problems this month – so see a doctor, if you feel unwell. And if you've profited from your investments, this is a good time to cash-in on your gain but bear in mind to avoid playing the share market lest you end up broke at the end of the day. Cash should be brought in, but preferably not gambled out this month.

農曆四月 (May 6th – June 5th) 癸巳

The risk of meeting with a car accident is very likely this month, so care should be taken whenever you're on the move. You may also find your children to be more rebellious and disobedient than usual this month if they use the East room(s); employ tact and patience in handling them. This promises to be a favourable month for lawyers and mediators.

Main Door	West	Bedroom Sector	East

農曆五月 (June 6th – July 6th) 甲午

Postpone all major decision-making for a better time, as these will only bring about negative outcomes if you rush into them. Look out as well for acts of betrayal from within your workplace, and be sure to remain alert of any such potential threats. Family-run businesses may also be plagued with disputes and arguments amongst family members, and things may get out of hand very quickly if left unchecked.

農曆六月 (July 7th – August 7th) 乙未

Kidney stones are amongst the variety of health issues that could plague those using the East bedroom this month. Stay away from unhealthy activities such as smoking and drinking, as these will have negative consequences on your health in the long run. That aside, CEOs and those in managerial positions will find their wisdom and intelligence bringing about positive outcomes for the company and as a result, you may have just earned yourself an elevation in status – and authority!

農曆七月 (August 8th – September 7th) 丙申

Stroke or internal bleeding poses a serious threat to those using the East bedroom this month – especially if they've already been feeling poorly of late. Couples using this bedroom will also find their relationship to be more strained and tense than usual, so give each other some breathing space and don't sweat the small stuff! Nevertheless, professionals in the IT industry will do well this month, thanks to your network of contacts and recommendations from satisfied, existing clients.

農曆八月 (September 8th – October 7th) 丁酉

Relationships won't exactly be your forte this month, and those using this room need to be a little more patient in dealing with their loved ones. Pregnant women using this room may have to take extra care. And while there will be money to be made from conservative property-related deals, those in business may find that they're lacking the leverage to benefit from their positive investment outcomes.

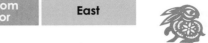

農曆九月 (October 8th – November 7th) 戊戌

This promises to be a challenging month for legal practitioners and lawyers, who'll be hard-pressed to put their cases across. Worse still, you may also be bedevilled by health issues, including mouth and speech-related problems! Arguments and tension will cause discord amongst couples, but only as much as you allow them to. Be sure to exercise patience and tolerance in dealing with your partner or spouse.

農曆十月 (November 8th – December 6th) 己亥

This month, those using the East room especially should avoid all forms of speculative investments, lest they cause you to lose more than you gain! Financial losses are a very real risk, coupled with some emotional imbalance and tensions that might lead you to feeling melancholy, with the risk of slight depression. Talk to a trusted friend or professional if you're feeling particularly down.

農曆十一月 (December 7th – January 5th 2012) 庚子

This month does not bode well for any joint-venture projects or businesses, as the outcome is likely to earn both or all parties a major loss. Those of you working in the computer industry will find that your rewards are not in keeping with the amount of blood, sweat, and tears you feel that you have been putting in. Relationships will require your consideration in seeking out solutions that benefit all involved.

農曆十二月 (January 6th – February 3rd 2012) 辛丑

Those of you who have made investments in the past will find that this proves to be a good month to liquidate or cash in on those, because the returns are likely to be very good. However, where this month is concerned, it will be best to avoid becoming involved in shares and trading because the risk of financial loss is very strong. Females using the East room may have to deal with some health complications.

Main Door	West	Bedroom Sector	Northeast

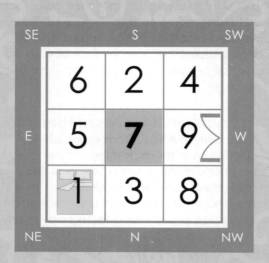

農曆正月 (February 4th – March 5th) 庚寅

Pregnant ladies are advised to avoid using this room for the month, or it could otherwise lead to unwanted complications. Stay on the safe side, and opt to rearrange your sleeping and living arrangements for a little while. If you're in the real estate and property industry, then you're likely to enjoy a month of progress and developments. Make the most of the opportunities to further enhance your career prospects.

農曆二月 (March 6th – April 4th) 辛卯

Those of you using this room will find the spotlight trained on you this month, bringing you lots of positive publicity and recognition. Make the most of it in order to gain more attention for yourself and your career, or even your business. However, where health is concerned, elderly individuals should be careful of potential kidney problems. Those of you involved in the travel, tourism, or even courier and logistics industries will be able to enjoy some positive benefits this month as a result of using this room.

農曆三月 (April 5th – May 5th) 壬辰

Don't be retiring this month, because this is a good month to show off your true talents and capabilities to your superiors! You'll be duly noticed and recognised, and may even be in line for a possible promotion or career advancement. If you're in the midst of business negotiations or closing a deal, you might find that things will go smoothly and in your favour.

農曆四月 (May 6th – June 5th) 癸巳

Those of you who are single, unattached, and on the prowl, this room bodes well for you on the relationship front this month. Turn on that charm and go all out in ensnaring a potential romantic mate. People in the construction industry and literary field will benefit from a surfeit of opportunities headed their way. In terms of investment opportunities, there is a chance for you to enjoy a good agreement and be able to seal the deal!

| Main Door | West | Bedroom Sector | Northeast |

農曆五月 (June 6th – July 6th) 甲午

This is the month to lay low and avoid poking your nose, even if it's just the tip of it, into other people's affairs. If you go ahead and do it anyway, you must be prepared for anger – which can lead to arguments and discord, and a general feeling of ill-will that will be directed at you. As long as you keep this in mind, this month in general sees an improvement in your ties with friends and family members.

農曆六月 (July 7th – August 7th) 乙未

Relationships that have endured some strained complications, or even estranged, will find itself being amicably straightened out this month. Things will seem to go back to normal and ties will once again be friendly. In that case, it will be a good room to use if you're ensnared in a divorce or corporate break-up, as the energies present here can lend an air of agreeableness and cordiality to the proceedings, instead of bringing up resentments and ill-feeling.

農曆七月 (August 8th – September 7th) 丙申

Couples using this room must make an effort to communicate more with each other, as otherwise suspicion and jealousy will make their unwelcome entrance! This could lead to general discord and friction, souring what could otherwise be a sweet connection. So do your best to prevent this from happening. Pregnant women should also avoid using this room for the month, because possible complications include miscarriage, and that's something to definitely avoid.

農曆八月 (September 8th – October 7th) 丁酉

If you have children who are sitting for examinations this month, this is the room you want to put them in! The energies here are very conducive to revision and studying, and you'll find that their heightened sense of concentration and focus will enable them to pass their exams and do quite well. In general, academics and scholars will benefit greatly from using this room too.

農曆九月 (October 8th – November 7th) 戊戌

Couples who use this room will generally find their relationships being plagued by quarrels and disagreements. Exercise fortitude, because giving in to your impulse to say cutting words could lead to greater trouble. Make an effort to try to understand what your partner is going through, and don't only focus on your personal point of view. Business opportunities will be good for those in the publishing and furniture industries.

農曆十月 (November 8th – December 6th) 己亥

This will be a good month to sell off property, as you'll find the profits to be quite numerous and of good value. Investing in property will also be a good idea this month, as the future outcome for investments made this month is likely to be favourable. Expectant women should avoid using this room, as the chances for complications and miscarriage are quite high.

農曆十一月 (December 7th – January 5th 2012) 庚子

Elderly people using the Northeast room this month will find some health troubles plaguing them, especially in the form of kidney problems. Be sure to check out any signs of trouble early on. The rest of you will find that attention comes your way this month, especially in the professional sense. Make sure you get your name out there and make the effort to forge new alliances and connections.

農曆十二月 (January 6th – February 3rd 2012) 辛丑

It's a good month for relationships, as couples using this room will find themselves enjoying greater communication and smoother connections. Those of you in the midst of business deals and negotiations should find that obstructions melt away and it becomes much easier for you to forge ahead. All in all, it should bode well for positive developments both on professional and personal fronts.

West Sector Main Door

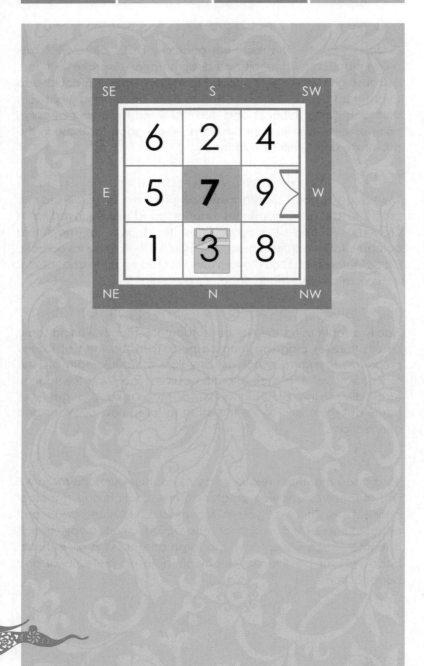

| Main Door | West | Bedroom Sector | North |

農曆正月 (February 4th – March 5th) 庚寅

Business owners need to be vigilant, and be mindful of what their rivals or competitors could possibly do to undermine their efforts. Indeed, any underhand tactics employed by your rivals – including fraud and embezzlement – could well cause you a pretty penny, if you let your guard down. Even romantic relationships could be fraught with mistrust this month.

農曆二月 (March 6th – April 4th) 辛卯

Watch out for any problematic situation at the workplace, which could develop into a more serious scenario if left unchecked. Take stock of your security procedures and measure as well, as the risk of a robbery is likely, this month. Those using the North bedroom are also advised to drive carefully, to minimize the risk of meeting with an accident while on the road this month.

農曆三月 (April 5th – May 5th) 壬辰

Be sure to respect your spouse or partner enough, to discuss all decisions with him or her… unless you wish to strain your relationship unnecessarily! In any case, speculative investments – especially in the futures market – will generate substantial profits for you, this month. And do scrutinise all business deals and contracts carefully, as the slightest oversight may prove to be costly to you later on.

農曆四月 (May 6th – June 5th) 癸巳

Take good care of your health, in particular your liver, this month. Nevertheless, those interested in embarking on their own business venture or changing careers should do so – as the energies of the North room augur well for such endeavours. Public relations specialists may, however, find this a challenging month, with unexpected problems cropping up from seemingly all directions! Be patient, and plan carefully.

農曆五月 (June 6th – July 6th) 甲午

Mind your own business this month instead of meddling in the affairs of others by offering unsolicited advice that will not be appreciated. Those using the North room this month will enjoy the ability to make profits, and the wisdom to safeguard it, as long as they use their wits to outmanoeuvre the fraudsters who may lie in wait to cheat them out of their wealth. Students using this sector to prepare for their examinations will also enjoy good academic luck.

農曆六月 (July 7th – August 7th) 乙未

Health problems in the form of gastrointestinal ailments and limb injuries could prove to be the bane of those using the North room this month. Likewise, enjoy your path to success this month by all mean, but only be sure to keep an eye open on any jealous rivals who are out to undermine you! And as for those who happen to dabble in the metals and equities markets, this is a good time to use your experience and expertise to your advantage.

農曆七月 (August 8th – September 7th) 丙申

Friends may also find themselves at loggerheads over a power-struggle this month, and this could lead to the end of their friendship... and a possible court case, should things get really out of hand. Unfortunately, you may also need to ensure that all security procedures are in place, as your employees or even family members may defraud or steal from you. It's a particularly turbulent month.

農曆八月 (September 8th – October 7th) 丁酉

Feeling stressed and lonely lately? Then moving out of the North bedroom for the time being may do you a world of good. In other aspects, subordinates will be inclined to challenge their superiors and sons their fathers for those using this as a bedroom. Elderly males are advised to go for a full medical check-up, to minimise the risk of suffering from an internal injury or bleeding.

農曆九月 (October 8th – November 7th) 戊戌

Unfortunately, those using the North bedroom won't exactly be privileged to enjoy robust health; especially males, who will be particularly susceptible to liver problems, ulcers and limb injuries. Couples need to communicate with each other more coherently and tactfully this month, as well, as you'll be inclined to listen to others, but ironically enough, not your partner. Avoid all forms of speculative investments and gambling, if you wish to safeguard your wealth.

農曆十月 (November 8th – December 6th) 己亥

This month, you'll need to pay more attention to your partner, as there may be other parties vying for his/her affections, if you fail to `take good care' of him/her! Don't be so oblivious to the warning signs, and taking your partner for granted because of work or other obligations. A relationship is like a garden – it needs to be watered and tended to daily.

農曆十一月 (December 7th – January 5th 2012) 庚子

Those of you using the North as a bedroom need to be extra careful when you get behind the wheel, as driving accidents are likely. Also, ensure that you refrain from driving while intoxicated or fatigued and sleepy. Avoid exacerbating the risk. Be on the alert for any potential problems at work, as it could become something much bigger if the warning signs are simply ignored.

農曆十二月 (January 6th – February 3rd 2012) 辛丑

Whatever business dealings you make this month, ensure that you give it your full attention. Being careless or negligent at this point in time will not benefit you at all, as there could be some costly mistakes. On the homefront, some attention needs to be paid to your marriage. Namely, ensure that all major decisions you make are vetted through with your spouse first.

| Main Door | West | Bedroom Sector | Northwest |

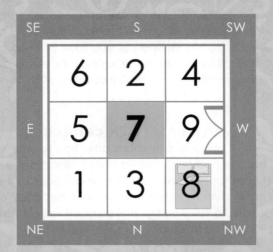

SE	S	SW
6	2	4
5 (E)	**7**	9 (W)
1	3	8
NE	N	NW

農曆正月 (February 4th – March 5th) 庚寅

This is a good month in which to focus on romantic endeavours and long-term relationships. Should you be thinking of proposing, this is also an ideal month. Good news and celebrations are also the order of the day for those using the Northwest, especially couples trying to conceive. And as for those who have worked hard throughout the last six months, your efforts will be deservingly recognized and even rewarded this month.

農曆二月 (March 6th – April 4th) 辛卯

You'll find plenty of opportunities to make money headed your way, but unfortunately, you won't really be able to capitalise on most of them. Nevertheless, this is a good time of the year to engage in speculative investments in the real estate and property sector, if you have a healthy appetite for calculated risks. Use this month to consolidate both your personal and professional relationships as well, even if the initial start may seem to be a little rocky.

農曆三月 (April 5th – May 5th) 壬辰

Children using the Northwest bedroom will enjoy good academic luck this month and potentially excel in their studies. Relationships are also on the upswing, but don't be too disheartened if they turn out to be short-lived, or fall short of your expectations. Negotiators and those who rely on their persuasive powers to make a living should utilise the energies of this sector. It will enhance their capability to gently sway others to their point of view when closing any important business deals.

農曆四月 (May 6th – June 5th) 癸巳

If you work in the banking or financial industry, and have been putting in more than your fair share of effort, then it may indeed be reasonable for you to look forward to that hard-earned promotion and salary increment this month. In fact, projects will progress smoothly, with employees being accorded due credit for their respective contributions. And don't hesitate to venture abroad to conclude that deal you've been negotiating over the previous months or years, the time is right and your persistence will finally pay off.

Main Door	West	Bedroom Sector	Northwest

農曆五月 (June 6th – July 6th) 甲午

Try to concentrate on your career this month instead of looking for love, as romance won't exactly be on the positive upswing. And you also need to be extra careful, especially if you've a penchant for extreme or dangerous sports, to minimize the risk of injuring yourself. There will be plenty of property deals for you to consider, but make sure you really know what you want – and what you're in for – before signing on that dotted line.

農曆六月 (July 7th – August 7th) 乙未

This is a favourable month to pursue any overseas business opportunities, as they will likely yield positive outcomes for you. Weavers, textile manufacturers and those involved in this industry will also enjoy a productive month, with increased profits being the final outcome of the day. Nevertheless, keep a sharp eye on your employees this month, as dishonest or disloyal staff may well prove to be your bane, if left unmonitored.

農曆七月 (August 8th – September 7th) 丙申

Despite what appears to be a challenging month, you'll be relieved and pleased to find that any changes occurring or made will bring about positive consequences. Still, refrain from making any important business decisions this month, as they will not likely work in your favour and may even cause you to suffer losses ultimately. However, this is a good sector for adults seeking to focus on academic endeavours, or engage in self-cultivation activities.

農曆八月 (September 8th – October 7th) 丁酉

Keep an eye out for the presence of any body of water in this sector, as it augurs well for property-related endeavours and investments. And if you already happen to be in a position of authority or high social status, then you should take advantage of any opportunities headed your way. Elderly ladies should, however, seek immediate medical treatment at the first sign of ill health or stomach ailments, to prevent them from developing into something serious.

農曆九月 (October 8th – November 7th) 戊戌

Marital relationships will prove to be harmonious and blissful for couples using the Northwest bedroom this month. And those who have prudently invested their money into viable portfolios stand to see their investments do well, especially fund managers. Likewise, the construction and engineering businesses will prosper this month, with opportunities to invest abroad being more to your advantage.

農曆十月 (November 8th – December 6th) 己亥

In the professional sense, if you've been putting in hard work throughout these months and endeavouring to make your work known to your superiors, you will find that due recognition and a likely promotion or increment comes your way this month. It's also an ideal month for matters of the heart, as couples who have long thought of marriage will formalise their arrangements this month.

農曆十一月 (December 7th – January 5th 2012) 庚子

This is a good month to further work on your professional and personal relationships. Bear in mind that while the beginnings of such ties may be turbulent, they will often work out well in the long run. So don't be afraid to push for some good opportunities, especially in terms of professional networking. Opportunities to make money are somewhat fleeting this month; nothing worthwhile particularly sticks.

農曆十二月 (January 6th – February 3rd 2012) 辛丑

People who need to count on the strength of their words to persuade and influence others will benefit tremendously from using the Northwest bedroom this month. You will find yourself blessed with a gift of the silver tongue! Young children or students using this room will also be fortunate enough to enjoy good academic luck that will provide for scholarly excellence. Romance, however, tends to be sweet but short-lived.

Southwest Sector Main Door

This section contains the monthly outlook for all 12 months of the year, for different bedrooms in a property with a Southwest Main Door.

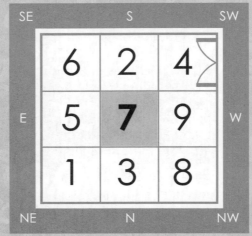

Ground Floor

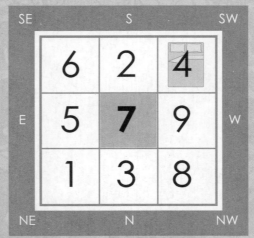

First Floor

農曆正月 (February 4th – March 5th) 庚寅

All forms of gambling and speculative activities should be avoided this month, unless you wish to sustain huge financial losses. Money matters are fraught with risk and better left to a better time in the future. Certainly, property deals are a big no-no. Ladies, consult your gynaecologist for a full check-up, as you could be afflicted by some complications that could lead to something serious in the future. Best to get it sorted out early.

農曆二月 (March 6th – April 4th) 辛卯

Couples, especially newlyweds, should tap into the energies of the Southwest room this month so that your relationship may bloom and thrive happily. Likewise, candidates due to sit for their exams soon are advised to use the Southwest to optimise your academic luck. However, if you need to embark on any form of travel this month, ensure that the necessary insurance policies are in place as carelessness is likely.

農曆三月 (April 5th – May 5th) 壬辰

Professionals using the Southwest bedroom may find business to be a bit slow this month, especially if they happen to deal in the real estate or property industry. However, those in the fashion, apparels and cosmetics industries will find this to be a fairly profitable month, with your business connections bringing in the money! You need to guard against injuring your spine, though, as it could result in more serious complications involving your limbs in the future.

農曆四月 (May 6th – June 5th) 癸巳

This month, wives living under the same roof as their in-laws will find it hard to see eye-to-eye with them. It would be best to minimise any form of contact to prevent any unpleasant scenarios from taking place. That aside, those in the media, travel, tourism and farming industries will find this to be a fairly favourable month, especially if they care to invest in viable properties.

農曆五月 (June 6th – July 6th) 甲午

Couples using this room this month will find this a month of happiness and growth in their partnership. If you're part of a serious couple you need to be sure to make use of this. It would be advisable for those who are pregnant to use another room this month, as it could result in complications otherwise. This is a month for travelling; if you have a long-awaited trip or holiday to go for, then this is the time to do so.

農曆六月 (July 7th – August 7th) 乙未

Those in the food and beverage industry should be careful of office politics this month, as there will be unfriendly rivalry that could possibly escalate out of control and lead to serious repercussions. Marital relations will be strained this month so tolerance and patience will need to be exercised by those involved. Domestic disputes and family matters are likely this month, and this is more likely to affect the females using this bedroom this month more than the males.

農曆七月 (August 8th – September 7th) 丙申

This is a good room for those who intend on doing some self-help course or self-cultivation, or those who wish to improve themselves by attending a workshop or seminar of some sort. Be careful of female subordinates or superiors causing trouble at work this month. Those who are travelling this month should invest in travel insurance to circumvent any possible problems or issues in this area.

農曆八月 (September 8th – October 7th) 丁酉

Academic luck is strong this month, and those facing important examinations should use this room to their advantage. If you are in the literary field you should look for publishers in order to put out new work this month. This is a good month to build alliance partners abroad or embark on business expansion, as the outcome is likely to be favourable.

農曆九月 (October 8th – November 7th) 戊戌

Although athletes and journalists will enjoy a fairly positive month in terms of output, it will be your reputation that will be enhanced, for the meantime. Similarly, those in the financial industry and literary field should be able to finalize deals abroad, which will serve to enhance their reputation and fame. Look out for kidney and lung ailments, though, more so if you notice any negative features outside the Southwest.

農曆十月 (November 8th – December 6th) 己亥

Those in forestry and dairy farming will find that business demands grow for their products this month. Entrepreneurs and businessmen will find that employees will go the extra mile to produce what is needed as a result of their loyalty to the company. Marital problems are likely to affect couples using this sector this month so spouses should try to travel more to give each other more space. This is likely to improve relations between the partners.

農曆十一月 (December 7th – January 5th 2012) 庚子

The will be some marital tension this month, with women being the most argumentative and bearing the brunt of the consequences. Female politicians who need to conclude contracts with their employers this month should make use of the legal profession to finalise these, as the contracts will be highly beneficial for them. You will need to check all electrical wiring in your home this month, as there is a chance of fire or a potential fire hazard.

農曆十二月 (January 6th – February 3rd 2012) 辛丑

Travelling will bring about an improvement in your stature, reputation or name in your industry or field this month. Equity or share deals will be profitable this month but concluding the deal will require some patience with difficult opposition or clients. This is a good month to consolidate personal and professional relationships, and you should consider formalising these ties where necessary.

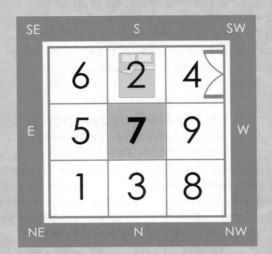

農曆正月 (February 4th – March 5th) 庚寅

Settle all outstanding traffic fines, summonses and taxes at once, unless you wish the long arm of the law to eventually catch up with you. And if you use the South bedroom, you may well find yourself arguing and quarrelling with your partner or spouse more frequently than usual this month. Indeed, the energies of this sector tend to bring about disagreements, misunderstandings and disputes.

農曆二月 (March 6th – April 4th) 辛卯

Those looking to invest in real estate, and make a quick buck by doing so, should invest now. Medical practitioners will also find plenty of opportunities to serve the sick and needy, as the demand for their skills starts to increase. Males who are in the midst of divorce proceedings will find matters tough-going as their partners gain more leverage over them for benefits and assets.

農曆三月 (April 5th – May 5th) 壬辰

Pregnant ladies using the South room will have to guard against complications and see their doctor at the first sign of trouble. Meanwhile, couples using the South bedroom might want to consider temporarily moving out of it, as the energies present in this sector will only cause unnecessary disharmony between both partners. Expect arguments to be rife this month.

農曆四月 (May 6th – June 5th) 癸巳

Those in relationships will spend the month quarrelling and arguing continually if they use this bedroom this month. Ensure all traffic fines and outstanding taxes are up to date, as you might be plagued by the revenue offices throughout the month otherwise. Those in the property development business should be really aggressive this month as there is a good chance of making surprise profits from real estate.

農曆五月 (June 6th – July 6th) 甲午

Women who are pregnant should avoid this bedroom this month, as the chance of miscarriage is possible especially if there is negative Sha outside the South bedroom. If there is water outside the South sector, property deals should take a backseat as these could result in heavy losses. There is a chance of windfall gains this month – and this is especially true for the older women of the family.

農曆六月 (July 7th – August 7th) 乙未

Students should avoid using this sector if they are writing examinations this month. Confusion will come into the decision making process if you are using this bedroom this month; therefore it is preferable not to make any important decisions. It won't bode well for all activities requiring deep thinking and critical analysis. Arguments and family disharmony might well become a problem this month, so greater tolerance and fortitude are needed.

農曆七月 (August 8th – September 7th) 丙申

There will be a tendency for women of the house to be stubborn and foolish this month. No important decisions should be made this month as well, as otherwise this could result in less than sensible decisions being made that may cause some regrets later. Do not take any new relationships seriously this month, as these may not be what they seem and may start to lose their initial lustre after some time.

農曆八月 (September 8th – October 7th) 丁酉

Those in real estate and property development will make beneficial investments in property this month. Those expecting to be promoted to positions of authority and high social status could find this a fulfilling month in terms of achieving their desired expectations and goals. Heart and eye problems will cause worry for people using this bedroom this month.

農曆九月 (October 8th – November 7th) 戊戌

Be careful of burns and scalding by hot water this month if you are using the South bedroom. In terms of romance, this bedroom will not be conducive to couples wishing to start a family, so avoid it if that's your purpose. Judges and doctors will find this a time when people come to them for help and advice, especially if times are particularly difficult.

農曆十月 (November 8th – December 6th) 己亥

Those in the legal field will find that their skills will be increasingly in demand this month by their clients and even potential new ones! In terms of finances, make sure that any deals done this month will not rely on any capital, as this may end in losses for you. Employees will find it difficult to make money this month no matter how hard they work.

農曆十一月 (December 7th – January 5th 2012) 庚子

It will be better to lay low this month and try not to get involved in the financial markets, as there is a good chance that you might sustain heavy losses if you do so. Illness and accidents will plague women who use this room this month, and this could result in serious illness and complications. Those in merchant banking, shares, stocks and equities will find this a very difficult month, as deals go belly-up in many cases and profits start to dwindle.

農曆十二月 (January 6th – February 3rd 2012) 辛丑

Gastrointestinal problems will plague women this month, and these complications should not be left unattended, as it is likely to result in more serious issues. Those in the media, marketing and consulting business will find that investment in property yields good returns this month. If you need to spend time with in-laws, it would be better to use alternate accommodations or take a holiday as there is likely to be continual conflict throughout the month.

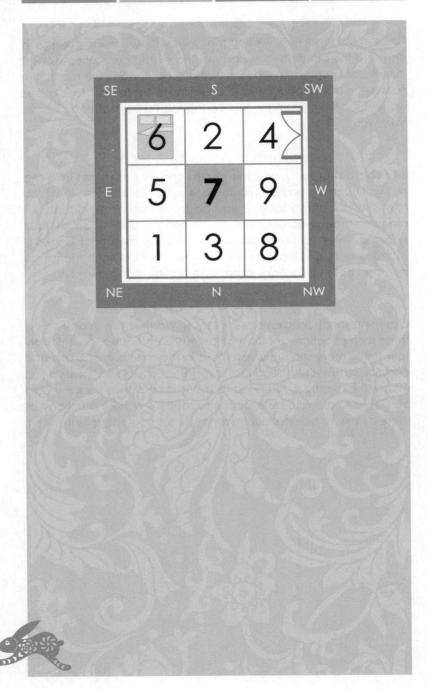

農曆正月 (February 4th – March 5th) 庚寅

Business partners may well find themselves disagreeing with each other, over who gets what and who controls what. In any case, it is very likely that the older or more experienced partner will prevail at the end of the day. Similarly, couples using the Southeast room will also squabble and bicker endlessly. See if you can take some time away from your home, and go on a vacation together to iron things out. Elderly folk, in particular, should also look out for ailments affecting their kidneys this month.

農曆二月 (March 6th – April 4th) 辛卯

Jealous rivals and enemies seek to undermine you this month, and you'll need your wits about you, to counter their cunning and devious schemes. Nevertheless, competitive athletes participating in tournaments should do well, so go for gold! Likewise, those seeking to carve a name and reputation in their chosen profession should work hard and smart, as this is a month for promotions and career advancements.

農曆三月 (April 5th – May 5th) 壬辰

This looks set to be a challenging month for those in the banking, equities and financial industries, so do not sign any major deals yet, as these will only bring you more headaches and stress! Indeed, certain employees may also be only too keen to betray their superiors. Elderly ladies should also refrain from using the Southeast bedroom, if possible, as the energies present there will make them more susceptible to lung infections.

農曆四月 (May 6th – June 5th) 癸巳

This is a good month to travel for those using this bedroom, especially for newly-weds who will find it a growth experience in many respects. Those in the academic and literary fields will benefit from loads of inspiration and new ideas that are likely to bring good financial gains this month. Speculative investments in equities and stocks will bring about good financial gains but care must be taken to conceal this windfall.

| Main Door | Southwest | Bedroom Sector | Southeast |

農曆五月 (June 6th – July 6th) 甲午

Wealth luck smiles upon those using the Southeast this month and the presence of any water forms in this sector will only enhance your wealth prospects even further. So, why not consider engaging in some form of speculative but viable investment? Couples using the Northwest will also find their relationship to be harmonious and smooth sailing. However, salaried workers and employees may find themselves feeling stressed or even exhausted due to the increased amount of pressure to perform imposed upon them by their superiors. Keep in mind to manage your work-life balance carefully.

農曆六月 (July 7th – August 7th) 乙未

Those in the real estate industry should take advantage of these good energies and invest in property deals, as these will return good profits this month. Those in the insurance industry should venture out and attempt to expand their business, as this is generally a beneficial month for them. Those using the Southeast bedroom will find bouts of depression creeping in, so if you are prone to emotional disturbances, then a change of room would be better for you this month.

農曆七月 (August 8th – September 7th) 丙申

Your health and relationship prospects will be good this month, and those involved in the logistics, courier and tourism industries will prosper accordingly as well. What's more, if your job entails strategic decision-making or sound analytical skills, then go ahead and show them what you're made of! That will allow you to carve a reputation for yourself, which in turn, should further brighten your career prospects.

農曆八月 (September 8th – October 7th) 丁酉

There may be internal bickering at work this month, so you will need to keep a low profile and make sure that you stay out of all office politics. This is the best time to be on the neutral and sit on the fence during all arguments! If there are any negative structures outside of the Southeast sector this month, then there is a high chance that the son may turn against the father. Family discords are possible. Older men should watch their health, especially with regards to blood and lung disease.

農曆九月 (October 8th – November 7th) 戊戌

Here's some good news for investment and merchant bankers concluding deals in the share and equity markets: there will be profits for you to enjoy, soon enough. Indeed, all your diligent efforts are finally being recognized by your superiors, so you may certainly look forward to that long-awaited promotion and salary increment! However, those using the Southeast bedroom may find themselves feeling somewhat lonely and emotional this month.

農曆十月 (November 8th – December 6th) 己亥

This should be a good month for those in the legal fields, as there will be a strong demand for your skills. However, you need to be careful of unwanted gossip. Relationships will be short-term, passionate flings rather than long-term partnerships. You might want to take a back seat this month and keep a low profile, as jealousy and rivalry will be intense, resulting in possible legal issues.

農曆十一月 (December 7th – January 5th 2012) 庚子

Faithful employees will find that long awaited rewards within the company come to fruition this month as a result of your efforts throughout this time. Lighten up on your staff this month if you wish to achieve your goals, as they will respond better if you if you take the pressure off them. This is a good month for those in professional sports, as you are likely to outshine your competitors in the sports arena.

農曆十二月 (January 6th – February 3rd 2012) 辛丑

Those using the Southeast bedroom this month will find that their efforts go unnoticed by their superiors this month. You may need to work harder than ordinary to get even the simplest form of acknowledgement. Invest in property transactions this month, as there is a chance of making good financial gains. Anxiety, stress and mental pressure will take its toll on those who use this bedroom this month.

| Main Door | Southwest | Bedroom Sector | East |

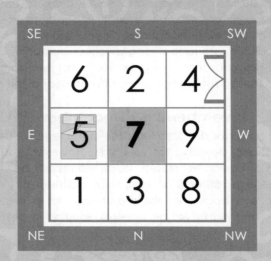

農曆正月 (February 4th – March 5th) 庚寅

There will be a tendency amongst your employees or subordinates to be disloyal this month. Look out accordingly for any potential signs of disgruntlement or trouble. Some of you may find yourselves feeling rather anxious and mentally stressed-out, and should seek medical treatment if necessary. This is not an ideal time to finalise any deals, so wait until a better opportunity presents itself, to make your move.

農曆二月 (March 6th – April 4th) 辛卯

Those of you using this room are particularly susceptible to heart ailments and complications; consult your physician at the first sign of trouble. Those specialising in the fashion and beauty industry are also advised to maintain a low profile, as this looks set to be a difficult month, at best. As such, no important decisions or investments ought to be made, as they will most likely result in loss of wealth.

農曆三月 (April 5th – May 5th) 壬辰

It's one thing to overindulge in alcohol, and another altogether to get involved in a casual relationship or one-night stand, as a result! Those occupying the East sector need to prioritise hygiene, unless you wish to be plagued by any form of skin disease, this month. And where possible, avoid travelling during this time of the year, as your travels may be fraught will difficulty and problems causing you stress and exasperation in the process.

農曆四月 (May 6th – June 5th) 癸巳

If investments need to be concluded this month, it is better to stay with the blue chips for the best chance of returns. This is not a good month to rely on employees, as they may create more trouble that they are worth – so you might want to avoid ventures and projects which require the support of your staff. Arguments and disputes will cause disruptions to couples and those in serious relationships.

Main Door	Southwest	Bedroom Sector	East

農曆五月 (June 6th – July 6th) 甲午

Avoid risky business dealings and property related transactions as financial losses are most profitable. As health is poor this month, it is better not to use the East bedroom if you suffer from gastrointestinal problems. Stay away from starting anything new this month as lots of obstructions may end up in failed ventures and some broken spirits. It is best to use this time to lie low and recuperate from the previous months.

農曆六月 (July 7th – August 7th) 乙未

This is a difficult month for business owners and managers, as sales targets will be difficult to meet, especially for those in the tourism, travel and media business. This will not be a peaceful month for couples so they should use another bedroom if things become strained, as staying on in this room could exacerbate troubles and cause more stress for both parties. Your health may be severely affected this month, resulting in bladder and kidney problems.

農曆七月 (August 8th – September 7th) 丙申

Fire hazards are a problem this month and electrical wiring should be checked where it is old and in need of replacement. Religious enthusiasm could end up in fanaticism for those using the East bedroom this month. Delay all investment deals and focus on employee motivation instead, as a distraction by monetary issues could result in financial ruin for you from which it'll be hard to extricate yourself.

農曆八月 (September 8th – October 7th) 丁酉

Do not get involved in high risk investment deals, as the outcomes could be disastrous especially where the property industry is concerned. Emotional and mental instability may be exacerbated by monetary and relationship problems this month. Business owners should avoid doing any expansions this month and should instead focus on consolidating their position.

農曆九月 (October 8th – November 7th) 戊戌

Couples should communicate openly and clearly to avoid misunderstandings this month. Throat and mouth cancer may be a problem for those using the East bedroom, so if early signs suggest something quite amiss, then you should get it checked with a doctor as soon as possible. Problems will be difficult to resolve this month as the cause is not readily identifiable.

農曆十月 (November 8th – December 6th) 己亥

CEOs should take stock of their companies this month and spend time motivating their staff rather than driving to improve strategic and financial directives. If you don't, you may find your staff's lack of motivation to be more of a problem in the coming months than anything else. Health-wise, kidneys and eye problems have a strong chance of occurring this month. Those who use the East bedroom will find that relationships will be at best frosty and distant! You might want to consider switching to another room.

農曆十一月 (December 7th – January 5th 2012) 庚子

Avoid risky business dealings as losses related to property transactions are likely. All minor illnesses should be taken seriously, as there is a tendency for health issues to take a turn for the worse this month. Pregnant women should be careful when using the East bedroom as there is a possibility of complications. Where possible, expectant ladies should use another room for this month.

農曆十二月 (January 6th – February 3rd 2012) 辛丑

Rivals are out to get you this month so prepare for an uphill battle, leaving you emotionally and psychologically drained for much of the month. Avoid drinking too much as this could result in complex casual relationships with unfortunate outcomes. Speculative investments and gambling should be resisted this month, as these will bring serious financial losses.

| Main Door | Southwest | Bedroom Sector | Northeast |

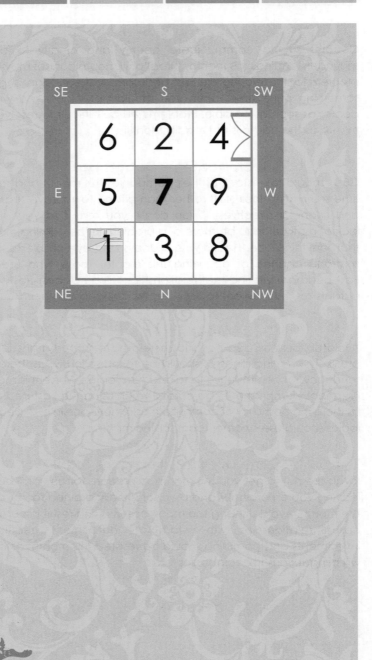

農曆正月 (February 4th – March 5th) 庚寅

Speculative investments – especially equity investments and gambling – should be avoided at all costs this month, as there is a risk of significant loss of wealth. Health-wise, you need to look out for lung and head injuries this month. Business owners will find it hard to make progress in anything this month so if you're one of them, lie low and consolidate your position at this point.

農曆二月 (March 6th – April 4th) 辛卯

Academic luck is strong in this sector this month, and students using this room as a study or bedroom will have success in their examinations this month. Provided there is no natural water in the Northeast sector, this will be a good room to use to further any serious relationships this month. You will need to conclude and close any overseas deals this month, especially if it involves asset acquisition and are concluded abroad.

農曆三月 (April 5th – May 5th) 壬辰

This is a boom month for those in the furniture business. Couples may find their relationships under strain this month, and both parties may need to exercise greater tolerance and patience during this time. Lawsuits and people talking behind your back could prove expensive this month, so you will need to watch your behaviour.

農曆四月 (May 6th – June 5th) 癸巳

It will be unwise to use this room if you are unwell or frail, as you may be more susceptible to illnesses. Pregnant ladies may wish to move out of this room this month, as there are chances of miscarriage. This is a month of marital tension, so couples using this room should be more tolerant of each other and learn to adjust their expectations of each other accordingly.

| Main Door | Southwest | Bedroom Sector | Northeast |

農曆五月 (June 6th – July 6th) 甲午

Use your inner talents, wisdom and knowledge to make inroads at work this month. You'll find that you will make good headway if you are proactive at doing this. This is also a good month to showcase your talents and work towards building your reputation. Relationships are good and all will go well with regards to work this month, with the strong likelihood of travel in the cards.

農曆六月 (July 7th – August 7th) 乙未

There will be career advancements for those in the transportation industry who will find that they receive the promotion they have been hoping for. Those in the entertainment industry should seek opportunities for career advancement this month as your passion and excitement will make you ready for something new. Those who work in the technical industry or in hands-on work will find this is a good month for them, as there are many benefits to be had.

農曆七月 (August 8th – September 7th) 丙申

Those who work with machinery or are involved in professional sports will excel this month, especially if you take advantage of the opportunities at your disposal. This is a good month for investment opportunities especially for those involved in the real estate industry. This is a good room to use if you are single and looking to form a relationship, as the prospects are good.

農曆八月 (September 8th – October 7th) 丁酉

This is a bad month for relationships, as these are likely to end badly and might even cause some damage to your reputation. Intensely jealous co-workers and peers will compete openly with you this month. It will be best for you to take no notice and refrain from getting involved, or it will work against you. There is an increased risk of car accidents this month especially if you have been drinking or driving when fatigued.

農曆九月 (October 8th – November 7th) 戊戌

Politicians and those in public service will have a good month, enjoying excellent public support which may even end in them rising up the ranks in government or their respective political parties. You will need to network more this month, as this is the time to make new contacts and connections. Foreign markets and alliances, or partnerships with business owners in other countries, will be profitable this month for those using the Northeast bedroom.

農曆十月 (November 8th – December 6th) 己亥

Those of you who own or run your own businesses will find it difficult to get going this month, so don't worry too much or push yourself too hard. It will be best to lie low and simply gather ammunition to launch an improvement in the future. Steer clear of speculative investments this month, especially those involving direct gambles or even equity investments. Loss of wealth is likely.

農曆十一月 (December 7th – January 5th 2012) 庚子

It's an ideal time to conclude deals that were done internationally, particularly if it involved asset acquisition. Don't continue to be further involved as this is the right time to bring it to an end. Students or people using the Northeast room will find themselves the recipients of good academic luck. It's also an ideal room for romantic relationships to do well.

農曆十二月 (January 6th – February 3rd 2012) 辛丑

This month proves a bit rocky where interpersonal relations are concerned, as people will talk behind your back – rendering betrayal an unfortunate inevitability. Also, be on guard of potential legal problems that arise as a result of that. Couples who use the Northeast room will have a bit of turbulence this month, but career-wise, those in the furniture industry will see a rise in profits and business.

Southwest Sector Main Door

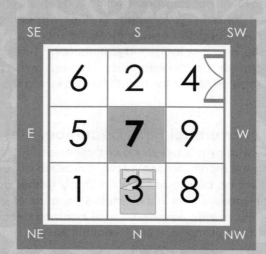

SE	S	SW
6	2	4
E 5	**7**	9 W
1	3	8
NE	N	NW

農曆正月 (February 4th – March 5th) 庚寅

Professionals in the engineering and technical fields will find their skills duly recognized by their superiors, resulting in a possible promotion and salary increment. However, as an employer, don't be surprised or disheartened to find your subordinates seemingly working against each other. Perhaps they just lack clear direction and a sense of purpose. Emotional problems may hound you this month, so don't delay in seeking professional help if you feel you are in need of it, or talk to a trusted friend.

農曆二月 (March 6th – April 4th) 辛卯

You might be somewhat on the wrong track this month, but you can fix matters if you're willing to be flexible and ready to make some changes. And while it's perfectly normal to feel anxious when you encounter a problem at work, don't worry too much as things will sort themselves out in time. This promises to be a productive month for those in the scientific, research and analytical fields, as they find their skills much sought-after by interested parties.

農曆三月 (April 5th – May 5th) 壬辰

Try to avoid high-risk investments this month as there could be hidden problems in the investments; problems that could be of a legal nature. It will be best to avoid such investments or otherwise you might find yourself smack dab in some legal troubles. Marital relationships could be improved by giving each other more space this month.

農曆四月 (May 6th – June 5th) 癸巳

Business owners should be careful of rivals posing as allies, as this will result in losses for their enterprise. Couples should make an effort in their relationships this month as there could be competitors on the horizon if they negate their duties. In other words, don't slack off paying attention to your partner, or you might find others are more than willing to step into your shoes. Newfound fame and enhanced reputation will bring an increase in wealth for those in the literary and creative arts field.

Southwest Sector Main Door

農曆五月 (June 6th – July 6th) 甲午

Those in the analytical or scientific fields will benefit from the good energies of this sector and find breakthroughs in their line of work. Those in the mining and construction businesses will find that they make inroads into their competitors' markets this month. This will be a challenging month for those who are reluctant to implement the changes that are required in their line of work.

農曆六月 (July 7th – August 7th) 乙未

Speculative investments, especially in the futures market, will return favourable profits. Couples using this bedroom need to be tolerant of each other as disputes and arguments will be prominent this month. You may suffer a loss of income through legal issues caused by financial problems this month, so you will need to be on guard and be careful or otherwise those losses will be difficult to recoup.

農曆七月 (August 8th – September 7th) 丙申

Although those in the legal field will do well financially this month, the money and rewards from your efforts can only be collected later. Security should be scrutinized thoroughly as the risk of robbery is increased this month. Those who want to change careers or who want to start new businesses should do so this month, as the opportunities for beginning new things or starting anew are quite good.

農曆八月 (September 8th – October 7th) 丁酉

Strategic decisions should be put into action this month as clarity of thought is at its peak and positive results will be forthcoming. Do not be deceived by conmen who offer unusually good investment deals, as this will not only result in loss of money but may end up in legal issues as well. This is a favourable room for children to use this month as far as educational activities go.

農曆九月 **(October 8th – November 7th)** 戊戌
If there are negative forms in the North, then those using this bedroom this month will find problems with the eyes. Be careful not to let any eye troubles develop. If you are in the restaurant business, this is an excellent month to expand the business. This is especially so if travel is required to close the deal or conclude an agreement. Those in their own businesses who need to work hard to float their companies will find this a good month to do so, as the month will be kind to you in terms of those endeavours!

農曆十月 **(November 8th – December 6th)** 己亥
There is a likelihood of a loss of wealth as a result of fraud or theft this month. Internal injuries will be a problem to those who are already in poor health, so if you are prone to health conditions, this is not the month to be reckless and push your body to its limits. Make health your number one priority instead. Speculative investments in financial instruments should result in good profits this month.

農曆十一月 **(December 7th – January 5th 2012)** 庚子
Elderly men using this bedroom should be careful of lung problems this month. This is a difficult time for parents as their sons might challenge their authority – a change of room may be of benefit in order to tame and calm their sons' rebellious spirits. The possibility of recognition, rewards and advancement is likely in the workplace, and you may have the chance of being appointed to positions of power. This is your time to shine, so put your best foot forward!

農曆十二月 **(January 6th – February 3rd 2012)** 辛丑
It would be best to avoid important business decisions this month if you sleep in the North bedroom, as disputes and slander are possible. Those in business should toe a conservative line this month as any stepping out of line could result in demotion. It will be best for you to play by the rules and leave the risk-taking for another month. Couples using this bedroom this month must be patient and tolerant as both parties will listen to other people but not each other.

Main Door	Southwest	Bedroom Sector	Northwest

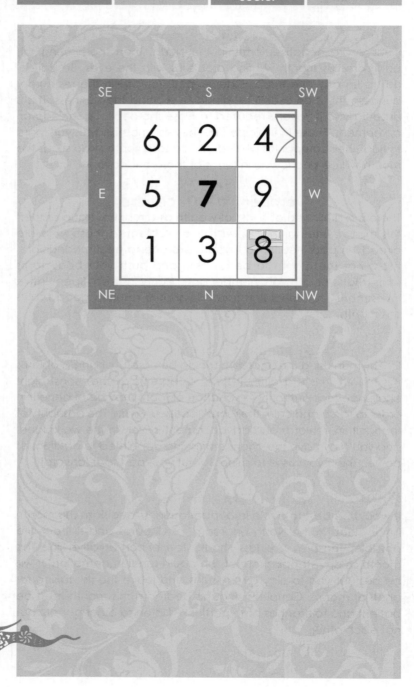

農曆正月 (February 4th – March 5th) 庚寅

Don't be too easily swayed by any romantic interludes you encounter this month. Chances are they will only turn out to be short-term flings, no matter how passionate they may seem. Look forward instead to being rewarded for your diligent efforts at work, in the form of a promotion and salary increment. Indeed, this promises to be a month of good tidings, celebrations and happy events for those using the Northwest bedroom.

農曆二月 (March 6th – April 4th) 辛卯

Wealth luck smiles upon you this month, although you'll need to be both diligent and persevering to enjoy the fruits of your labour at the end of the day. In fact, there will be substantial profits to be made by investing in long-term real estate or property deals. Just ensure that they are viable and proceed carefully! Watch out for disputes with your partner or spouse as well, and deal with any tacky situation swiftly and tactfully, to prevent it from getting out of hand.

農曆三月 (April 5th – May 5th) 壬辰

Those in logistics or the travel industry will have improved profits this month. Couples using this bedroom will have a happy month together, and if they are considering starting a new family, then they should do so this month. Bladder-related ailments will be a problem to those using this bedroom this month, and this will be especially true for elderly folks in the Northwest bedroom.

農曆四月 (May 6th – June 5th) 癸巳

You will receive recognition for something you have succeeded in, and promotion is likely as a result. This will be a month of celebrations, good news, and happy activities for those who use the Northwest bedroom this month. Short-term flings and passionate romances await those who use this bedroom, so be prepared for some romantic intrigue and keep your life spicy by being open-minded to new developments.

Southwest Sector Main Door

農曆五月 (June 6th – July 6th) 甲午

Profitable, long-term deals in real estate and property will be most advantageous this month and produce increased profits. If you're in these industries, ensure that you go after possible opportunities with renewed gusto. Personal relationships come under strain this month and it will require a concentrated effort to keep things stable. Watch out for rivals at work as they will try to plot your downfall, and things could turn ugly as a result.

農曆六月 (July 7th – August 7th) 乙未

Couples who work hard at their relationship will be rewarded with a harmonious month even though there may be a few arguments to occasionally disrupt the peace. Windfall gains are possible this month so look to realize these profits in your portfolio but it is important that you bank the money rather than let it slip through your fingers. Lung infections could be a problem for those who have negative structures located in the Northwest sector.

農曆七月 (August 8th – September 7th) 丙申

If you are in the banking industry, you can look forward to an increase in your salary package this month due to the hard work that you put in that is finally noticed by your superiors. However, this may be a lonely month for females using this bedroom. Professional sportspeople who show their talents to the world will receive recognition and fame as they draw attention to their abilities.

農曆八月 (September 8th – October 7th) 丁酉

Relationships will be harmonious and thriving this month. Why not seek to foster even closer ties with your business partners, co-workers and loved ones? There will also be substantial gains to be made from property investments, especially if there's a body of water located just outside the Northwest. Females using this sector should guard against acquiring any chronic abdominal problems or ailments.

農曆九月 (October 8th – November 7th) 戊戌

Do not let superiors take advantage of you and end up making gains at your expense. You will need to watch your back and safeguard your own interests. Those in management and consulting will do well to expand their businesses this month, as both profits and clients abound. Improved health is in the cards so if you are in need of recovery or recuperation from a health ailment, then you should try to use this bedroom this month.

農曆十月 (November 8th – December 6th) 己亥

There are big changes expected this month that should help revive stagnant careers. It would be best to keep young children out of this room this month, as they may end up being hurt with sharp metal objects or dangerous metal implements. Adults using this sector should focus on academic activities or self-cultivation that should result in personal growth and maturation.

農曆十一月 (December 7th – January 5th 2012) 庚子

Older women who use this bedroom this month should not dismiss minor stomach ailments offhand, as these could develop into something more serious. It will be best to get any issues or problems checked out by a doctor. Those in authority or of high social status will find things are in their favour this month so take advantage of any opportunity that comes your way. Lucrative property deals present themselves and you should be ready to take advantage of these as soon as they appear.

農曆十二月 (January 6th – February 3rd 2012) 辛丑

Those using the Northwest bedroom will be blessed with good health this month. So use this to your advantage, as you go about planning stratagems to advance in your career, especially if you happen to specialize in the paper, packaging or psychology field. Meanwhile, those in the services industry should seek to widen their network of contacts, if they wish to achieve their ambitions in their chosen profession.

Main Door	Southwest	Bedroom Sector	West

SE	S	SW
6	2	4
5 (E)	**7**	9 (W)
1	3	8
NE	N	NW

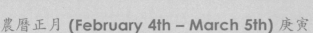
農曆正月 (February 4th – March 5th) 庚寅

Romance luck may well be on your side this month, but take care so as not to be too blinded by the beauty or charms of your potential partner, and in the process, overlook the more important virtues of this person. Perhaps then it's ironic enough that eye and problems affecting one's vision could be pose problems for those using the West room this month. Those involved in speculative property investments and in the equities market will enjoy considerable gains on their ventures.

農曆二月 (March 6th – April 4th) 辛卯

Good progress will be made insofar as personal and professional relationships are concerned this month. Take the opportunity to consolidate your ties with others. There will also be rewards in the form of recognition and a possible promotion for those using the West bedroom, but with more power, comes more responsibility. Be prepared for the initial adjustment to a more demanding schedule.

農曆三月 (April 5th – May 5th) 壬辰

Use the West room for meditative, spiritual or religious pursuits this month. Also, you'll find that any travels to the west will bring about significant rewards, especially if you're in the midst of finalizing deals in the precious metals' industry. Likewise, new inroads will be paved for those in the media, marketing and consultancy businesses, with possible offers by financial intermediaries to provide you with the capital required.

農曆四月 (May 6th – June 5th) 癸巳

Good news and celebrations await those using the West, especially politicians and civil servants who have worked hard, and deserve to be promoted to a higher position by virtue of their efforts. Similarly, if you're in a committed relationship, now's a good time to take your relationship to the next level or formalise it. There will also be financial gains to be made by those speculating in properties or real estate.

Southwest Sector Main Door

| Main Door | Southwest | Bedroom Sector | West |

農曆五月 **(June 6th – July 6th)** 甲午

Those using the West room may expect to be transferred within their organization where work is concerned, but on more favourable terms and perks due to their hard work. Likewise, speculative investments in the metal and equities markets will yield favourable outcomes this month; just don't get overzealous in pouring in your hard-earned cash in every high-risk portfolio you come across. Take care of your health and don't overlook minor ailments.

農曆六月 **(July 7th – August 7th)** 乙未

Business-related travels will prove to be favourable for you this month, so pack your bags, and get ready to make money. Be mindful of disgruntled employees, though, as their actions will cause you plenty of trouble, if you let your guard down. All in all, this promises to be a favourable month, where those using the West stand to reap the fruits of their labour soon enough.

農曆七月 **(August 8th – September 7th)** 丙申

Don't let work-related stress get the better of you. Instead, plan your schedule and manage your lifestyle, so as to strike a work-life balance. In any case, refrain from engaging in any speculative investments or gambling this month, as you only risk incurring huge financial losses if you do so! Pregnant women are also advised not to use the West room to prevent any complications that could even result in a miscarriage.

農曆八月 **(September 8th – October 7th)** 丁酉

This is a good month to invest your hard-earned cash into the financial markets, as any viable investments made will tend to be profitable. In addition, students sitting for exams soon will find the energies of the West to be beneficial to their endeavours. This is also a good sector for couples seeking harmony and romance in their relationship, as the goodwill and intimacy flows easily between both partners.

農曆九月 (October 8th – November 7th) 戊戌

Those using the West room may have to travel to generate their income this month, but what's a little travel-lag compared to the gains you stand to make? Scrutinise all legal documents carefully before committing yourself to them this month to mitigate the possibility of any legal complications later on. Couples looking to conceive should use the West room for positive results.

農曆十月 (November 8th – December 6th) 己亥

Those of you who have been dabbling in speculative property investments and the equities market will find that you will enjoy good profits and make some gains that will prove to be substantial. It's also a good month for love for those using the West room, but it will be important to evaluate potential partners reasonably and not get too carried away on the waves of infatuation.

農曆十一月 (December 7th – January 5th 2012) 庚子

This month, go ahead and apply for that grant you've been eyeing, though, as you will find the energies of the West room conducive enough in allowing you to promote and commercialize your ideas, with the aid of the necessary financial backing for your research. This is the time to make the most of your opportunities, so do all you can to "sell" your ideas to the right people.

農曆十二月 (January 6th – February 3rd 2012) 辛丑

People in the media and marketing industries and fields will have a good month, especially in terms of finances. There will be sponsors or partners stepping up to provide the capital you need for your ventures. Those using the West room will also find it a good month to focus on religious or contemplative pursuits. It will help you quiet your thoughts and develop your concentration.

South Sector
Main Door

Main Door	South	Bedroom Sector	South

This section contains the monthly outlook for all 12 months of the year, for different bedrooms in a property with a South Main Door.

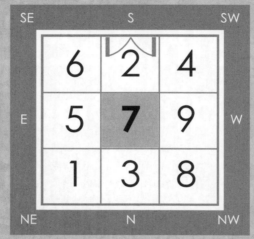

Ground Floor

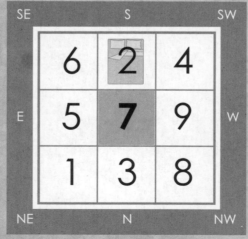

First Floor

農曆正月 (February 4th – March 5th) 庚寅

Just when you least expect them, legal entanglements rear their ugly heads. The more tangible outcomes include speeding summons, or worse still, complicated lawsuits. Still, not all hope is lost: Be proactive by looking out for any negative features outside your Main Door and readying the necessary contingency plans. And if you've a son or sons using the South bedroom, don't be surprised to find them becoming more argumentative and difficult to handle this month. Instead of losing your patience with your kids, why not move them out of the South, at least until the month is over? After all, it seems that the Qi in this sector is the harbinger of trouble insofar as relationships are concerned because even disputes and petty bickering involving elderly women are amongst the outcome for those using the South this month.

農曆二月 (March 6th – April 4th) 辛卯

You stand a good chance of generating substantial financial gains by investing in real estate or property as long as you remember to vet through each and every deal carefully before committing yourself to it. As a matter of precaution, do not engage in any property deals should you notice a significant body of water outside the South sector, as this is a likely indicator of impending heavy losses. Ladies using a South bedroom will tend to behave in a more domineering and assertive manner this month, although they should also mind their health, as they are particularly susceptible to stomach-related ailments.

農曆三月 (April 5th – May 5th) 壬辰

Postpone that real estate deal you've been eyeing, at least, until the month is over. There's a time for everything, and this is not a suitable period to involve yourself in such dealings. You might actually need to expend your energy and time on mediating any discord on the domestic front - no thanks to misunderstandings that enmesh relatives and family members in disputes. And expectant mothers should avoid using the South bedroom this month, as there's a very high possibility of miscarriage or premature delivery for pregnant women using this room.

South Sector Main Door

Main Door	South	Bedroom Sector	South

農曆四月 (May 6th – June 5th) 癸巳

Any dealings pertaining to real estate or properties would probably result in losses; so obviously, this is not an ideal time to invest in real estate. You may also want to keep an eye open for potential eye afflictions this month. Consult your physician at the first indication of trouble, as a stitch in time saves nine. On the domestic front, you might find the elder ladies in your household behaving in a more adamant and possibly, foolhardy manner than usual. Be patient and seek to understand their viewpoint and disgruntlement by sitting down and talking to them where possible.

農曆五月 (June 6th – July 6th) 甲午

If you happen to be suffering from a chronic illness of any sort, be sure to mind your health this month. The risk of your ailment rearing its ugly head again is very likely, so adopt a healthy lifestyle and consult your doctor at the first sign of trouble. And be mindful of any negative landform features in the South, as these are possible indicators of trouble involving older or elderly women! Look on the bright side of things though: Any property or real estate dealings will probably land you substantial financial gains.

農曆六月 (July 7th – August 7th) 乙未

Have a qualified electrician or personnel check the wiring and electrical apparatus in your home or office, more so if you notice the presence of any negative features outside your Main Door. It would also be advisable to monitor the interaction between the women in your household or amongst your staff, as the probability of misunderstandings and discord is very likely amongst members of the fairer sex this month. Last but not least, couples looking to start a family are advised to avoid using the South bedroom this month, as you will only be undermining your own objective by doing so.

農曆七月 (August 8th – September 7th) 丙申

This is especially for those who are religious, superstitious, or simply believe in the paranormal or supernatural: Refrain from using the South bedroom this month to avoid any unwanted 'interludes' of the supernatural kind. And keep your eyes peeled for any negative structures or features outside your Main Door; otherwise, you could well find your money being siphoned away from you! The good news is, if you heed these advisories, this month promises to be a relatively comfortable and smooth-sailing one for you.

農曆八月 (September 8th – October 7th) 丁酉

Rein in any temptation to speculate or engage in any high-risk ventures this month, as you would probably end up poorer at the end of the day. Obviously, this is not the time to commit yourself to any major or significant deals - not if you wish to benefit from your endeavors. Older or elderly ladies, in particular, should guard against acquiring any abdominal ailments this month, and seek immediate medical treatment at the first sign of trouble.

農曆九月 (October 8th – November 7th) 戊戌

Older women of the household should be careful of injuries resulting from sharp metal objects or any metal-based implements. You will also have to be careful of a potential risk of fire, particularly if there is negative Sha in the South. Those involved in athletics or competitive sports will do well if they use this bedroom this month.

農曆十月 (November 8th – December 6th) 己亥

There is a possibility of mental and emotional strain, which may cause stress or even hallucinations for you this month. Try not to let stress get to you too much or your mental health will suffer. Make sure that any deals concluded this month does not rely on capital, as this may end in losses that could be potentially serious. Employees will find that no matter how hard they work this month, they will find it difficult to make money.

農曆十一月 (December 7th – January 5th 2012) 庚子

There is a chance of superior property deals this month if you do your homework well, but don't neglect to tie up all loose ends as these may result in legal issues later. Those using this bedroom this month may suffer from serious illnesses this month. If there is a need to sign legal documents, be particularly careful this month, exercising extreme caution and double-checking all that you sign.

農曆十二月 (January 6th – February 3rd 2012) 辛丑

Those in the literary field will find that it's their time to shine this month, as they will receive awards and achievements and be recognised for their efforts. Money can be made from real estate-related fields this month so long as the deals have been thoroughly worked out. There will be strife and disharmony between in-laws this month so extra patience will be required to make the relationship work. Exercise tolerance as well as it can go a long way!

Main Door	South	Bedroom Sector	Southeast

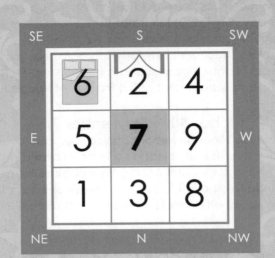

農曆正月 (February 4th – March 5th) 庚寅

Lawyers and professionals dabbling in the legal field will find their services much sought-after this month. In any case, you should also be on the look out for disputes and office politics in the form of power struggles. But stay out of them to avoid running into any legal entanglements later on. And don't give your heart away too easily because chances are, any romantic fling will remain what it is. So, don't expect anything solid or long-term to develop out of it.

農曆二月 (March 6th – April 4th) 辛卯

Pack your suitcase, and get ready to hit the road. There's money to be made from your travels. Employees, especially those working in the media and travel industries, will also find their career prospects greatly heightened this month with a possible pay-rise just lurking around the corner. And sportspersons and athletes will excel in competitions and tournaments this month!

農曆三月 (April 5th – May 5th) 壬辰

Unfortunately, this is not a very favorable or positive month, regardless of whatever your endeavor may be. For one, disloyal or greedy employees will betray or con you, causing you to incur considerable financial losses and even face lawsuits. That's life, but now that you've been forewarned, you might want to keep a closer eye on those working under your purview. And for some reason or other, you also run the risk of suffering from mental agony and stress, which could subsequently lead to the advent of headaches and migraines. And as if prevailing circumstances aren't bad enough, your family members won't exactly give you any peace of mind at home. Instead of losing your patience with them, let them be, as this is not the time to thrash it out with anyone in particular!

農曆四月 (May 6th – June 5th) 癸巳

You're just an employee, so why should you bother with trivial disputes or arguments, which could fester into legal complications, if blown out of proportion? So ignore all those backstabbers and your rivals at work and concentrate on your job! That aside, this is a good month to forge closer ties in both your personal and professional relationships, so expend your energy on more rewarding enterprises. Those who are actively involved in the trading of stocks and shares will be pleased to know that there will be gains to be made from their transactions.

農曆五月 (June 6th – July 6th) 甲午

Engineers, technicians and those involved in the technical and engineering professions will find their career prospects looking more promising this month. Keep up your good work if you wish to taste success in due time. Nevertheless, investment deals, especially risky ones, are a big no-no - unless you want to end up with legal problems on your hands. Athletes and sportspersons should also guard against any sports-inflicted injuries, particularly those affecting their legs and feet.

農曆六月 (July 7th – August 7th) 乙未

Manufacturers and players in the manufacturing industry will find production to be efficient and at its peak this month with minimal labor-related problems and maximum profits being the outcomes of the day. Those who are keen on spiritual or religious pursuits should use the Southeast bedroom more frequently this month if you wish to make any progress in your endeavors. The Southeast, however, is unsuitable for anyone already suffering from a mental or emotional problem, as the energies present therein will only further aggravate the patient's condition.

農曆七月 (August 8th – September 7th) 丙申

Those using a Southeast bedroom will find themselves to be in the pink of health and their relationships thriving harmoniously. So take advantage of a good thing, and see if you can extend your run of good luck! What's more, long-term investments will finally yield considerable profits for those using the Southeast. In addition, your prowess and capabilities at work will also gain the respect and recognition of your superiors, who might just be tempted enough to reward you for your exertions!

農曆八月 (September 8th – October 7th) 丁酉

Defer any important decision-making as far as personal and professional relationships are concerned, to a more suitable time. It's hard to be rational and logical when emotions are running high! And move any elderly family members out of the Southeast this month, lest they become more susceptible to heart disease or even a stroke. This is generally not a good month for those in the entertainment and electrical and electronic industries as well, as demand will not be very encouraging, particularly if you happen to be a market player born in the Year of the Horse.

農曆九月 (October 8th – November 7th) 戊戌

You will receive the accolades, recognition, advancement and financial rewards you've worked so hard to achieve, except if you happen to be born in the Year of the Goat. Investment and merchant bankers who specialize in stocks, equities and corporate deals and mergers also stand to make substantial monetary gains on-the-job, so double your efforts if you want more. Meanwhile, couples using the Southeast bedroom will be blessed with a harmonious relationship this month!

農曆十月 (November 8th – December 6th) 己亥

Lawyers and professionals dabbling in the legal field will find their services much sought-after this month. In any case, you should also be on the look out for disputes and office politics in the form of power struggles. But stay out of them to avoid running into any legal entanglements later on. And don't give your heart away too easily because chances are, any romantic fling will remain what it is. So don't expect anything solid or long-term to develop out of it.

農曆十一月 (December 7th – January 5th 2012) 庚子

Pack your suitcase and get ready to hit the road. There's money to be made from your travels. Employees, especially those working in the media and travel industries, will also find their career prospects greatly heightened this month with a possible pay-rise just lurking around the corner. And sportspersons and athletes will excel in competitions and tournaments this month!

農曆十二月 (January 6th – February 3rd 2012) 辛丑

Unfortunately, this is not a very favorable or positive month, regardless of whatever your endeavor may be. For one, disloyal or greedy employees will betray or con you, causing you to incur considerable financial losses and even face lawsuits. That's life, but now that you've been forewarned, you might want to keep a closer eye on those working under your purview. And for some reason or other, you also run the risk of suffering from mental agony and stress, which could subsequently lead to the advent of headaches and migraines. And as if prevailing circumstances aren't bad enough, your family members won't exactly give you any peace of mind at home. Instead of losing your patience with them, let them be, as this is not the time to thrash it out with anyone in particular!

South Sector Main Door

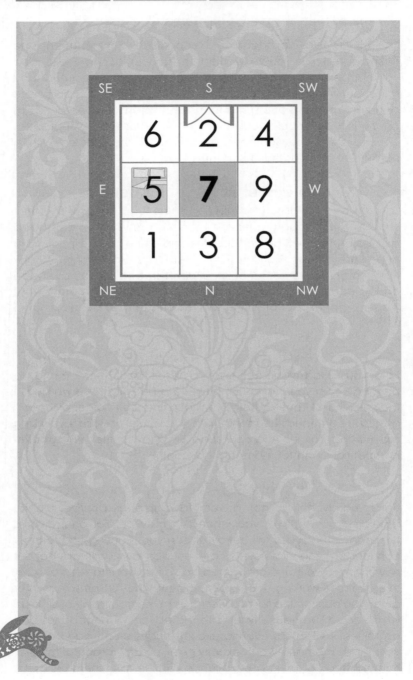

農曆正月 (February 4th – March 5th) 庚寅

If you are due to sit for an important examination soon and do not wish to be distracted, then it would be wise to avoid using the East bedroom this month. There will also be the possibility of suffering from a head injury or lung ailment during this month. Those in the communications and public relations industries will also find miscommunication to be rather problematic. But instead of getting upset, see if you can straighten the record and seek to communicate more coherently with other parties. Wealth Luck is generally poor for those using the East, so refrain from making any investments for the time being.

農曆二月 (March 6th – April 4th) 辛卯

Pregnant women, where possible, should not use the East bedroom this month to prevent complications with your pregnancy. From a general viewpoint, this is not a favorable month for most, if not all, important activities. So, don't approach your boss yet to request for that promotion or raise you've been eyeing. Meanwhile, businesspersons are advised to shelve all major business deals for a more favorable period in time.

農曆三月 (April 5th – May 5th) 壬辰

Lawyers will have a difficult month as they have trouble trying to put their case across. Miscommunication will be a problem for you this month, and those in the cell phone and IT industry will find that losses may be incurred. Throat and mouth cancer may be a problem for those using the East bedroom this month.

農曆四月 (May 6th – June 5th) 癸巳

It is best to avoid investment decisions this month and where possible, you should stall or delay deals for conclusion until next month. Health-wise, liver and leg-related injuries and illness will be a problem, so you will need to be careful and keep an eye out for anything amiss. Miscommunications are likely to plague the public relations industry this month.

| Main Door | South | Bedroom Sector | East |

農曆五月 (June 6th – July 6th) 甲午

Ambitious or optimistic as you may be, this is simply not the right time to embark on a new enterprise or venture as the probability of tasting early success is very low. Instead, wait for a more suitable time to make your move. Likewise, resist the temptation to gamble and/or engage in any form of speculative investment as you may end up poorer than when you first started. And where possible, relocate your Mum or any elderly ladies from the East sector this month, as they run the risk of acquiring oral disease or even appendicitis should they stay put.

農曆六月 (July 7th – August 7th) 乙未

Stay away from casual relationships this month, as these may result in sexually-transmitted diseases. Be careful when travelling, however, as this could result in accidents that may require hospitalisation. Ladies using the East bedroom may find that they suffer from liver problems this month.

農曆七月 (August 8th – September 7th) 丙申

Avoid ventures and projects that require the support of your staff, as this is not a month to rely on employees, who are likely to create more trouble than they are worth. If possible, postpone any major projects that require lots of teamwork and collaboration. It is also wise to postpone important financial deals until a better time, as any deals concluded this month would end up being unprofitable. Tolerance and patience will be the key to surviving the turbulent energies of this sector this month, as it is not conducive to good relationships. Therefore, this is not a time to push any arguments.

農曆八月 (September 8th – October 7th) 丁酉

Invest carefully in conservative, long-term property deals, and you stand to reap the benefits of your investments, in time to come. Now, if you happen to run a family-owned business, you might want to monitor your employees more closely this month, to hedge the risk of being betrayed or 'played out' by disloyal staff. In addition, those using a East bedroom should watch what they do, and how they move about, as they are particularly susceptible to injuring their nerves or tendons.

農曆九月 (October 8th – November 7th) 戊戌

Get a qualified electrician or technician to check the wiring of your property. And if you are an advocate and solicitor, you might find it hard to put your points across this month in presenting your case in court. Don't be unduly frustrated though. Keep your wits about you, and remain calm and patient as you go about executing your duties. Married couples or couples in a committed relationship will also be put to the test this month. But surely, don't you think it foolish to allow a bad patch in your relationship to be the factor that splits you and your loved one apart?

農曆十月 (November 8th – December 6th) 己亥

Religious enthusiasm could end up in fanaticism for those using the East bedroom this month. Monetary issues and relationship problems may cause added stress this month. Those in the political arena will find that friends and acquaintances will be around this month to help them with their political aspirations.

農曆十一月 (December 7th – January 5th 2012) 庚子

Good profits can be made from conservative property deals but to benefit you will need to watch the markets carefully. Avoid taking any untoward financial risks. Younger children in the home may have health problems this month in the form of ligament, muscles and tendon injuries. Relationships are not good this month, and those using these rooms should be patient with their loved ones. Avoid getting impatient and losing your temper because it will only make things worse.

農曆十二月 (January 6th – February 3rd 2012) 辛丑

Unless you're prepared to face up to the consequences or repercussions of a casual fling - no thanks to a night of binging - do not overindulge in alcohol, or spend too many an evening at your local pub or 'watering hole'. Also, those suffering from poor health should seriously consider moving out of the East bedroom to mitigate the risk of having their health worsened by a skin or liver ailment. This month promises to be a challenging one at work as well, where rivals and competitors will be baying for your blood. The key to riding this storm out is to remain patient and calm instead of simply allowing others to push your 'pressure buttons' at their whims and fancies.

| Main Door | South | Bedroom Sector | Northeast |

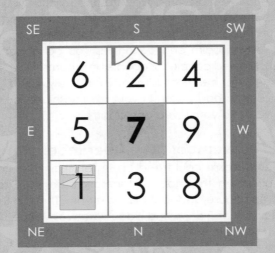

SE	S	SW
6	2	4
E 5	7	9 W
NE 1	3	8
NE	N	NW

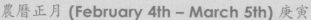

農曆正月 (February 4th – March 5th) 庚寅

Do not deal in shares and equities this month, as you may face some tough challenges ahead. Avoid making any important personal or financial decisions this month, as you will not be able to see the situation clearly and may end up making wrong choices that you will regret. Pregnant women should avoid using the Northeast bedroom this month. There is a risk of complications in the pregnancy or accidents when travelling.

農曆二月 (March 6th – April 4th) 辛卯

Those in academia will find that they receive recognition for their works and writing this month if they use this room. Be careful if you are involved in any joint ventures and partnerships because these just may have hidden legal entanglements. Romantic relationships will be on the upswing this month for those using the Northeast bedroom, but you need to be careful if there is water outside this sector.

農曆三月 (April 5th – May 5th) 壬辰

Overseas and offshore business opportunities will enhance the bottom line this month. Those in the furniture business will find that financial gains will be made this month. However, a loss of wealth and legal problems are possible this month as a result of betrayals and rumours spread about your business. You may need to watch your back and safeguard your interests as much as possible.

農曆四月 (May 6th – June 5th) 癸巳

If you're married, you should be careful of third-party gossip causing you some amount of tension in your relationship. There is a chance of miscarriage for pregnant women using this sector this month. Those in the real estate business will find that property deals return good profits this month, and you are likely to enjoy some good financial gains.

農曆五月 (June 6th – July 6th) 甲午

Use your inner talents of wisdom and knowledge to gain the promotion you deserve. If you're involved in professional, competitive sports, you will do well in international competitions this month if you use the Northeast bedroom. Elderly people should be careful of head injuries especially if there is negative Sha outside this sector.

農曆六月 (July 7th – August 7th) 乙未

Those aspiring to achieve literary success should showcase their talents this month. If you're in professional or competitive sports, you will do well this month, and you should maximise efforts while the going is good. Mental instability and emotional stress are problems this month for those using the Northeast bedroom.

農曆七月 (August 8th – September 7th) 丙申

Water-related industries such as tourism, travel, logistics and the spa industry will have some positive publicity and should return favourable profits as a result. Spouses may feel a bit neglected this month, as one partner is busy making money while the other is being sidelined. Look into property investments this month, as there are good deals to be had with good financial rewards.

農曆八月 (September 8th – October 7th) 丁酉

Health is weak in the Northeast this month, and problems with the head and mouth are likely. You might need to stay away from romance, as it will only end in a tarnished reputation and lowered spirits. Avoid speculative investments this month, as they are likely to turn sour as a result of miscommunication.

農曆九月 (October 8th – November 7th) 戊戌

This is a good month to make progress with your personal reputation in your field or industry, or even to gain recognition at work. So accept the credit given to you, and enjoy it with good grace! Complicated relationships or estrangements can be smoothed out and amicably resolved if you are using the Northeast room this month. Joint venture opportunities will arise at this point and should be followed-up, as they should end in good profits in the long-term.

農曆十月 **(November 8th – December 6th)** 己亥

Be wary of some tough challenges when dealing in shares and equities. Best to avoid them this month. You may be making the wrong choices that you will regret later when it comes to important personal or financial decisions this month, especially when you are unable to see the situation clearly. Expectant women should avoid using the Northeast bedroom as there is a risk of complications in the pregnancy or accidents when travelling.

農曆十一月 **(December 7th – January 5th 2012)** 庚子

Romance is in the air this month for those using the Northeast bedroom, though you need to be careful if there is water outside this sector. If you are involved in any joint ventures and partnerships, be careful of any hidden legal entanglements. However. Those in academia will receive a much-deserved recognition for their works and writing this month.

農曆十二月 **(January 6th – February 3rd 2012)** 辛丑

Good news for those in the overseas and offshore business as opportunities will enhance the bottom line this month. The same goes for those in the furniture business as well. However, you may need to watch your back and safeguard your interests as much as possible as there's a high chance for legal problems or loss of wealth due to betrayals and rumours spreading about your business.

South Sector Main Door

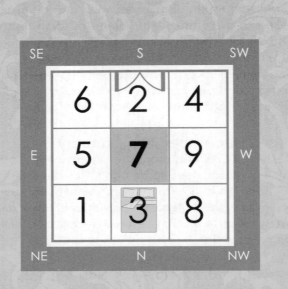

	SE	S	SW	
	6	2	4	
E	5	**7**	9	W
	1	3	8	
	NE	N	NW	

農曆正月 (February 4th – March 5th) 庚寅

Monitor your employees or staff closely this month, as there's a chance that a dishonest individual or two might be up to some hanky-panky at work, or have their hands in the company's 'money jar'. It's always wise to err on the side of caution, although this does not mean that you should mistrust or distrust those who work under your purview, automatically. Now, if you happen to make a living from the literary, creative or artistic fields, you will be pleased to know that good tidings await you this month, in the form of fame, wider repute and above all, a fatter bank account. Nevertheless, those suffering from depression or any mental problems might want to consider moving out of their West bedroom for the duration of the month, to prevent aggravating their condition.

農曆二月 (March 6th – April 4th) 辛卯

You only risk losing your share of the market or even niche market, by failing to keep abreast of current trends and stay on top of your 'game'. Pay particular attention to communication, as lack thereof could potentially undermine your endeavors. At the same time, have your finger on the pulse of the atmosphere at home. There's a likelihood of disputes brewing within the family, and you really want to arrest such a situation before it festers into something more serious. And last but not least, prioritize personal safety this month, to prevent yourself being robbed or mugged.

農曆三月 (April 5th – May 5th) 壬辰

Couples using this room must be patient and tolerant, as both parties will listen to other people but not to each other. Avoid playing the blame game and pointing fingers, as this will only make the situation worse. Stay away from gambling this month, as the result will be a loss of wealth. Those in poor health should avoid using this bedroom this month as illness could take a turn for the worse.

農曆四月 (May 6th – June 5th) 癸巳

Underhand transactions are on the increase this month, and you would be well advised to be on the lookout for the possibility of fraud. Those who suffer from emotional issues or depression should be careful when using the North room this month. It might be a good idea to find alternate accommodation until things improve. There is a possibility of fame, enhanced reputation and an increase in wealth for those in the company this month.

農曆五月 (June 6th – July 6th) 甲午

Personal safety should be made a priority this month, as there is a possibility of being robbed or mugged. Analysts and scientific researchers will benefit from the good energies of this room this month, provided that there is a good quality mountain outside the North sector. Do not be drawn into family arguments and disagreements, as these could end up in lawsuits, dividing the family into factions as a result. Where possible, work to improve on the family ties.

農曆六月 (July 7th – August 7th) 乙未

This is a good time to expand your enterprise, more so if you happen to be dabbling in the fashion or clothing-retail business! You may have to travel to seal your deals, but what's a bit of jetlag compared to the profits you stand to make from them? Scholars, academics and those in the literary and artistic fields will also benefit from the Qi in the North this month. And if you're looking for the right time to pop 'the Question' to your darling partner, here's your cue to do so!

農曆七月 (August 8th – September 7th) 丙申

If you've been feeling poorly of late, you need to be extra vigilant this month, and guard against acquiring any internal form of injury. Seek the advice and treatment of a physician at the first sign of trouble; otherwise your health will only decline to a more serious level. Also, ensure that the necessary internal controls and procedures are in place, to negate the risk of fraud or theft as much as possible. Nothing's absolutely certain, but you can always play your part in hedging such risks. The good news is, there will be windfall gains for those involved in business ventures with overseas or offshore partners!

農曆八月 (September 8th – October 7th) 丁酉

Where possible, avoid traveling for business-related purposes, as the outcomes from such trips will not be favorable to you. If you've been toiling at your job and sense that a promotion is just waiting for you, you might just be hitting the nail right on its head! And if it comes, you will be elevated to a position with more power, status and authority, which is well-deserved. Now, those with male teenage kids using a North bedroom might want to consider relocating them to another room this month, unless you wish to put up with their more-rebellious-than-normal attitude.

South Sector Main Door

農曆九月 (October 8th – November 7th) 戊戌

Resist the temptation to gamble and indulge in any form of speculative investments this month, unless you wish to risk accumulating huge financial losses. And if you've been doing well financially of late, thanks to profitable business transactions of late, it would be advisable for you to remain discreet and prudent on your financial status. In other words, you wouldn't want to have your newly-acquired wealth robbed or stolen from you, would you? Last but not least, be mindful of health problems in the form of ulcers, gallstones or liver-related ailments; and have these treated at the first sign of trouble.

農曆十月 (November 8th – December 6th) 己亥

Fraud and embezzlement by friends and family members will result in a feeling of betrayal for those who use this bedroom this month. Those working with heavy machinery should be extra careful this month, as there is an increased risk of injury while at work. Exercise more caution than you typically would. Employees will find that petty politics raises its head at this point in time and should not be tempted into arguments and disputes as these could end up in legal problems.

農曆十一月 (December 7th – January 5th 2012) 庚子

There is an increased risk of car accidents this month so limit your travel to necessities only. Where possible, walk! If this is difficult, be more cautious when using your car on the roads. The possibility of recognition, reward and advancement is likely, with the possibility of you being appointed to positions of power. Disagreements with superiors or fathers are likely for those using this bedroom, so family tensions should be diffused as much as possible.

農曆十二月 (January 6th – February 3rd 2012) 辛丑

If you've elderly women living in a North bedroom in your household, you might want to temporarily relocate them to another room, as they're at risk of suffering from depression or other forms of mental illness. That aside, your business and personal negotiations with other parties will proceed smoothly, and reward you financially at the end of the day. Lawyers, advocates, solicitors and those in the legal field will equally benefit from their persuasive abilities; thereby solidifying their reputation in the process.

Main Door	South	Bedroom Sector	Northwest

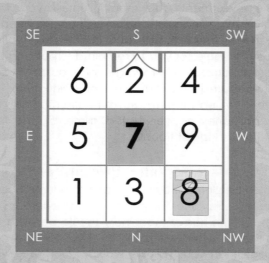

農曆正月 (February 4th – March 5th) 庚寅

Looking to go on bended knee and pop `the Question' to your darling beloved? Well, now's a good time to take that all-important leap! In addition, couples looking to conceive should use the Northwest bedroom this month as well. All in all, this is a favorable time of the year for both personal and professional endeavors, as career advancement, promotion, recognition and financial rewards beckon to those who deserve them.

農曆二月 (March 6th – April 4th) 辛卯

Speculative investments in real estate will provide handsome profits this month but make sure that all the details have been taken care of by lawyers. Don't leave any legal stone unturned, or it may cause some problems in the future. Those in authority or of high social status will find that things are in their favour this month so take advantage of any opportunity that comes your way. Older women who use this room this month should not dismiss minor stomach ailments, as these could develop into something more serious. At the first sign of something amiss, a visit to the doctor as a precautionary measure will be better.

農曆三月 (April 5th – May 5th) 壬辰

Health luck smiles upon those using the Northwest this month, and couples using a bedroom in this sector will find their relationship to be harmonious and happy. Furthermore, students due to write important examinations soon will also benefit from the positive energies of the Northwest, so use this bedroom for good results. You'll probably make a good profit from your investments in shares and equities, but it would be wiser for you to invest whatever profits you've amassed to generate even more profit in the future. As they say, 'money makes money'.

農曆四月 (May 6th – June 5th) 癸巳

Good news and celebrations await those using the Northwest room this month. You will receive recognition for something you have succeeded in and promotion is likely as a result. You will finally feel rewarded for all the hard work you've put in. Those wishing to get married should take advantage of the good energies this month and go ahead with the preparations.

農曆五月 (June 6th – July 6th) 甲午

Sportspersons, especially professional athletes, should watch how you move about and what you do, as the risk of pulling a muscle or tearing a tendon threatens to plague your career, this month. This is also not a suitable time to engage in real estate or property deals, as they will tend to be loss-making or worse still, cause you to be robbed. Nevertheless, it would still be more advisable to concentrate on your career and work, rather than be tempted to party and socialize frequently throughout the month.

農曆六月 (July 7th – August 7th) 乙未

It's only normal for salaried employees to feel that they are being exploited by their superiors at work, who are only out to make financial gains at the expense of their staff. Know when and where to draw the line, and negotiate deadlines and workloads where necessary. Still, journalists, reporters and individuals who harbor literary or artistic ambitions will find this to be a good time of the year to pursue their dreams. After all, nothing ventured, nothing gained. As a matter of precaution, be mindful of the presence of negative features outside the Northwest sector, as these are the harbingers of potential back or joint problems.

農曆七月 (August 8th – September 7th) 丙申

Postpone or avoid altogether engaging in important business negotiations this month, unless you wish to risk getting entangled in a legal dispute, later. Generally speaking, this is a stressful time of the year for both professional and personal relationships, so resist the temptation to commit yourself to any major decision about the future. And you might also want to consider temporarily relocating young boys or your infant sons to another bedroom this month; as they may suffer from leg injuries or cuts from a mishap by remaining in the Northwest.

農曆八月 (September 8th – October 7th) 丁酉

There will be a slow down this month and managers should use this time to motivate and inspire staff for the months ahead. You should focus on your career this month rather than on romance, as it will be quiet on the relationship front. This is a good time to plan and put your goals for your career in action without having to worry about relationship issues. Be careful of dislocating limbs or tearing ligaments this month.

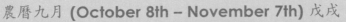

| Main Door | South | Bedroom Sector | Northwest |

South Sector Main Door

農曆九月 (October 8th – November 7th) 戊戌

This is a profitable month for those in the forestry, dairy or agriculture business. However, be careful that you do not let your superiors take advantage of you and end up making gains at your expense. Keep your back up and protect your own interests. Possible improved health is on the cards this month.

農曆十月 (November 8th – December 6th) 己亥

Big changes will help revive stagnant careers and businesses this month. Try to approach things with a fresh perspective and relegate old ways out the window if they don't give you good results. If would be best to keep young children out of this room this month, as they may be prone to injury by sharp metal objects and any metal implements. Do not let your arguments with anyone get out of hand, as these could end in lawsuits.

農曆十一月 (December 7th – January 5th 2012) 庚子

You will be pleased to know that those who are single-and-searching will not be short of potential partners this month! In any case, remember that success breeds contempt and jealousy. Nevertheless, what else can you do, except ignore the plots hatched by such individuals to undermine you? By giving them your time of the day, you give them victory as well. On the property and real estate front, go ahead and invest prudently. Your investments, however, should be made with a view to generate long-term income.

農曆十二月 (January 6th – February 3rd 2012) 辛丑

Marital relations prove to be harmonious and rewarding for those using the Northwest bedroom this month. Those in the construction and engineering business will find that business picks up this month and there will be a chance to make good investments abroad. If you're required to travel for business, you should jump at the chance! This is a good month for those who have taken investment positions in the preceding months or who work as fund managers in the futures markets to realise their financial gains.

South Sector Main Door

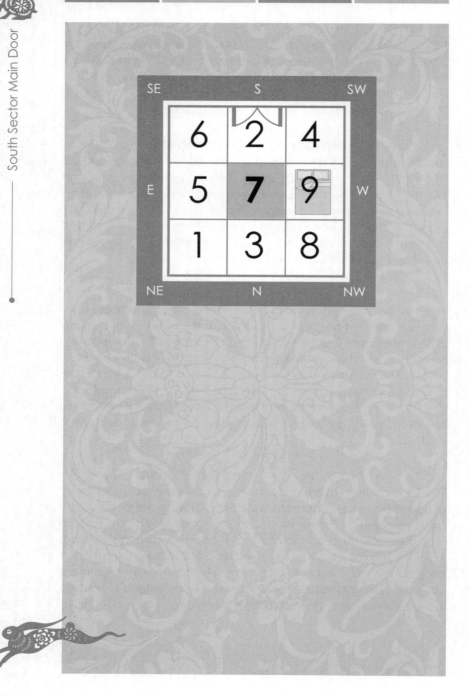

SE	S	SW
6	2	4
5 (E)	**7**	9 (W)
1	3	8
NE	N	NW

農曆正月 (February 4th – March 5th) 庚寅

You might well be feeling rather hostile, aggressive or irritable lately. Keep a tight rein on your emotions, as any altercations with the law or confrontation with other parties would only land you in hot soup. That aside, this is a suitable month to widen your network of contacts, especially if you're working in the communications industry, as you only stand to gain by doing so. And if you're an inventor, use the positive Qi of the West this month to let inspiration overtake you, and don't be afraid to take that all-important step in marketing your latest gadget!

農曆二月 (March 6th – April 4th) 辛卯

This could well turn out to be a month of 'fire-fighting' at the workplace for you, what with disgruntled employees throwing the occasional spanner in the works. It's important to stay focused, and nip every problem in the bud, before it spins out of control. Take heart in the fact that relationship and health luck will be favorable this month, so make the most of both these luck prospects and bend them to your advantage. And as opportunity never knocks twice, those dabbling in the futures, equities and stock trading industries should be vigilant, in seizing any opportunities that come by.

農曆三月 (April 5th – May 5th) 壬辰

Couples using a West bedroom need to be more cognizant and sensitive of each other's feelings, as chances are, you will both tend to be temperamental and moody this month. Be patient, and employ tact and understanding in dealing with your partner. Look out for the presence of any negative features or structures outside the West as well to safe yourself the misery of acquiring food poisoning! Business-wise, this is not an ideal month to conclude major investment deals, as they would more likely be loss-generating than profitable.

農曆四月 (May 6th – June 5th) 癸巳

This is not an ideal month to place elderly or sickly folk in the West bedroom, as the energies present there would only further aggravate their health problems. In fact, they would be particularly susceptible to liver problems. Now, if you happen to be involved in the education business, look out for competition from industrial rivals. The good news is, you stand to profit from your endeavors as long as you execute any business plans carefully and shrewdly. Ladies using the West will also benefit at work, especially those in the public relations and marketing fields, so make the most of this opportunity to advance your career even further!

Main Door	South	Bedroom Sector	West

農曆五月 (June 6th – July 6th) 甲午

Fortune favors the wise and prudent, so invest wisely. They might also be domestic or family-related problems, but see if you can solve them quickly, to prevent things from festering into a more serious situation. And if you happen to counsel or provide others psychiatric or psychological treatment, you will be pleased to know that your beneficiaries will appreciate the wisdom, advice and knowledge you share with them.

農曆六月 (July 7th – August 7th) 乙未

Expectant mothers using the West bedroom might want to relocate yourself to another room, at least until the month is over, to mitigate the risk of pregnancy complications. Nevertheless, those who are single-and-searching for Mr. or Ms. Right will find the energies in the West to be a boon in their search for romance. So, don't be shy or hesitate to take the initiative! All in all, career luck will be favorable throughout the month with possible promotion and advancement prospects for those who have worked hard.

農曆七月 (August 8th – September 7th) 丙申

Go ahead and pack your suitcase: Travel opportunities in the name of business beckon with positive financial gains being the outcome of the day. Definitely a good month to ensure that your passport and other travel documents are valid and in order! Players in the services and entertainment industries will also experience a boon in their business with more customers patronizing their joints. And if you're married, why not take the opportunity to go on that long-planned vacation with your spouse, as this is an extremely ideal time to foster even closer ties with your loved one.

農曆八月 (September 8th – October 7th) 丁酉

Look out for any negative features or structures outside the West sector of your home or office this month, as these indicate the possibility of a fire hazard. You know what to do in the event that such a feature is present: Have a qualified electrician check the wiring and electrical systems and apparatus in your property promptly. Those working in the fashion industry might need to travel this month but good things await you in the form of more revenue! Now, if you've been inclined to pursue all matters spiritual or religious recently, this would be a good time of the year to embark on a spiritual or meditative retreat to cleanse your thoughts and get away from the hullabaloo that is life.

農曆九月 (October 8th – November 7th) 戊戌

Are you working in the public/civil service, or is politics your chosen profession? Then double your efforts, as this is a favorable month to attain that promotion, career or status advancement, or salary increment that you've been eyeing all this while. Budding entrepreneurs looking to establish a joint-venture or partnership with another party should also seize the opportunity to do so. On the domestic front, happy events and celebrations are very likely, so why not pop that bottle of champagne if the occasion calls for it?

農曆十月 (November 8th – December 6th) 己亥

Be wary with any altercations with the law or confrontation with other parties that would only land you in hot soup as your emotions is rather hostile, aggressive or irritable of late. But if you're working in the communications industry, this is a great time to widen your network of contacts as you stand to gain by doing so. Take note, inventors: Positive Qi from the West will inspire you and give you the push to make that crucial first step in marketing your latest creation.

農曆十一月 (December 7th – January 5th 2012) 庚子

Not a good month at the workplace for you as may be dealing with a lot of disgruntled employees throwing the occasional spanner in the wheel. Remember: Stay focus and nip every problem in the bud before it escalates into something bigger. However, the relationship and health front looks favourable this month. So make the most of these luck prospects and bend them to your advantage. Those dabbling in the futures, equities and stock trading industries need to be vigilant in seizing any opportunities that comes a-knocking.

農曆十二月 (January 6th – February 3rd 2012) 辛丑

Patience and tact is required when dealing with your partner this month. Though couples using the West bedroom may tend to be temperamental and moody this month, it is best to be more cognizant and sensitive of each other's feelings to iron matters out. Take note for the presence of any negative features or structures outside the West as well as you may be prone to food poisoning. This is not an ideal month to conclude major investment deals as loss of wealth will likely to occur.

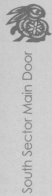

South Sector Main Door

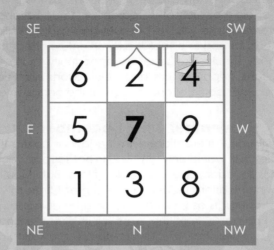

SE	S	SW
6	2	4
5 (E)	**7**	9 (W)
1	3	8
NE	N	NW

農曆正月 (February 4th – March 5th) 庚寅

Actively involved in the real estate and property field, and wish to realize your returns on investment? Then this is the month to do so! Professionals and enthusiasts dabbling in the metaphysical and esoteric fields will also benefit from the energies of the Southwest, so seek growth this month. However, if you happen to be a married woman sleeping in a Southwest bedroom, don't be surprised to find your relationship with your mother-in-law to be slightly tense this month, especially if you both live under the same roof. Don't give in to your emotions, and where possible, avoid contact with your in-law to sidestep any unnecessary misunderstandings.

農曆二月 (March 6th – April 4th) 辛卯

If you are a specialist in the media or consultation industry, and seek fame, publicity and recognition for your efforts and capabilities, this is the month to let your talents shine for all to see! And if you're a couple seeking to enhance that 'loving feeling' with your partner, use the Southwest sector. But you need to also be on the look out for any significant water feature outside this sector, as it could indicate the possibility of one partner straying, and engaging in an extra-marital affair. In any case, the Southwest is a good place to be, for students facing major exams, or academics or intellectuals conducting research as part of their job-scope.

農曆三月 (April 5th – May 5th) 壬辰

A good month to consider expanding your business, particularly for those specializing in the management and consultation industries. Similarly, professionals in the literary and media fields will also do well this month, with inspiration never in short supply. However, couples using a Southwest bedroom might find their relationship to be slightly more tense or strained than usual. Why not go on a vacation together, to clear your minds and forget all your worries?

農曆四月 (May 6th – June 5th) 癸巳

Equity and share dealings will turn a good profit this month, although you might find that concluding the deal will be laborious and require much effort and patience on your behalf – especially when dealing with difficult clients! Relationships take on a new level of commitment this month, whilst harmonious energies of the sector will generally prevail.

農曆五月 (June 6th – July 6th) 甲午

Couples using this bedroom will find this a month of happiness and growth in partnership. Those of you who are looking to build stronger bonds may find this a good month to get things going! Those who are in marketing and consulting will have the opportunity to excel and make a name for themselves through publishing papers or doing some form of intellectual research. This is a good month for leisure travel, so consider booking your holiday tickets early!

農曆六月 (July 7th – August 7th) 乙未

Those who are artistic and creative will do well this month, especially if they market themselves abroad. If you're one of them, going to other places will bring in greater profits and critical acclaim for your work. Be careful of office politics this month, as there will be unfriendly rivalries that could escalate out of control and become extremely unhealthy. Children using this sector could be encouraged by peer pressure to get involved in rebellious activities, so parents may need to keep a closer eye on them.

農曆七月 (August 8th – September 7th) 丙申

This is a good month for those in the metaphysical fields, as they will find this a good month to embark on new studies in this field. Offshore business dealings may result in misunderstandings that could end up jeopardising future business relationships. Stomach upsets, ulcers and gastronomical problems will plague females using the Southwest bedroom this month, so you may need to take extra care of your health.

農曆八月 (September 8th – October 7th) 丁酉

Couples using this room should find it a happy situation that is conducive to good relationships, but if there is water in the Southwest, this could cause infidelity and scandals. Those in the academic world will find this a good month for delivering papers or speeches, and you can expect a good reception to your work. Those involved in the engineering and mining industries should use this month to engage in new deals, as it will be beneficial for them.

農曆九月 (October 8th – November 7th) 戊戌

Watch your back and what you say. Malicious people are out for your blood this month, so don't arm them with anything they could use against you. Health-wise, look out for head or brain-related injuries. This is obviously not something to be taken lightly, or shrugged off easily! In any case, those involved in the artistic and creative fields will enjoy success this month, although they might have to travel to earn their income.

農曆十月 (November 8th – December 6th) 己亥

This is a good month for property acquisitions, but these will produce even better financial rewards if you are required to travel to conclude the deal. Travel can bring about greater profits, so consider doing it if possible. Older women might have problems with strokes and migraines. Those of you in forestry and dairy farming will find that business demands increase the need for your products.

農曆十一月 (December 7th – January 5th 2012) 庚子

Serious disagreements are possible for couples using this sector and where estrangement is already present, divorce is likely. Address any severe issues first, as this can help you minimise the troubles ahead. Workmen using machinery with sharp blades should be extra cautious this month, as it may result in injury. Legal documents should be scrutinised carefully so that legal obligations are thoroughly checked before concluding the relevant deals.

農曆十二月 (January 6th – February 3rd 2012) 辛丑

Female employees might not find support from their superiors to be forthcoming or readily available this month. Don't despair; instead, plan your workload and schedule carefully to mitigate the risk of any hiccups on the job. The Southwest is also not a good sector for students scheduled to sit for important examinations soon, as the energies there will probably yield unfavorable outcomes for those using this sector. Nevertheless, there will be positive results from any joint-ventures undertaken in the financial world, so use this opportunity to forge an even closer alliance with your business partners!

Southeast
Sector
Main Door

Main Door	Southeast	Bedroom Sector	Southeast

This section contains the monthly outlook for all 12 months of the year, for different bedrooms in a property with a Southeast Main Door.

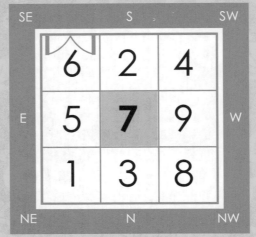

Ground Floor

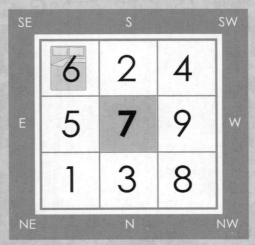

First Floor

農曆正月 (February 4th – March 5th) 庚寅

Watch out for the 6-7 Flying Stars combination in your bedroom, which spells intense business rivalry, accompanied by backstabbing and jealousy at work. Given the negative situation you are in, a confrontation or argument of any sort could well blow-up into epic proportions. So keep your emotions under control and be tactful. Politicians will, however, find their policies and stances popular amongst the masses, this month. You might also want to monitor your health closely and keep an eye open for kidney-related trouble.

農曆二月 (March 6th – April 4th) 辛卯

Make an appointment with your boss to ask for that promotion and salary increment that you deserve. Jealous rivals may, however, plot to bring you down. If you happen to be working in the banking, equities or financial industries, you'll find things gradually picking up after a slow start at the beginning of the month. Those born in the Year of the Rabbit will be susceptible to flu or any illnesses attacking your respiratory system this month. Hence, maintain a healthy lifestyle, and consult your doctor if necessary.

農曆三月 (April 5th – May 5th) 壬辰

This is a good month for property or gilt investments so don't be afraid to stick your neck out, as you will make good financial gains! Newly-married couples will find this a very good month for harmonious relationships and you will be able to enjoy many happy moments together. As an employee waiting for recognition and promotion, you will find that this month will bring you what you have been waiting for.

農曆四月 (May 6th – June 5th) 癸巳

Competitors will challenge you in the work place and if you do not take a backseat, things could very swiftly get out of hand. Rivalries will intensify and colleagues will be jealous this month, resulting in squabbles. If these get out of hand, it will most likely end up in legal problems. Those who work on heavy machinery should be careful of injury while on duty. Couples using this will have difficulties and face quite a few troubles, as arguments will continue for months.

| Main Door | Southeast | Bedroom Sector | Southeast |

農曆五月 (June 6th – July 6th) 甲午

People involved in competitive sports will find this a good month to obtain good results in competitions. Faithful employees will find that those long-awaited rewards within the company will materialise, and those months of effort will come to fruition this month. Elderly members of the household will become stubborn when it comes to health issues this month.

農曆六月 (July 7th – August 7th) 乙未

Manufacturers and producers should make the most of your resources this month to maximize their profits. While a bedroom in the North sector augurs well for spiritual or religious pursuits, be mindful of any negative (environmental) forms outside the room. These could be the harbingers of urinary-tract or blood-circulation problems.

農曆七月 (August 8th – September 7th) 丙申

Pack your bags, and get ready to embark on your business trips. There will be good returns to be enjoyed from them. However, if you are involved in the financial world of stocks, bonds, and anything that involves monetary management, maintain a low profile this month. On the domestic front, things aren't, unfortunately, looking too good; what with constant bickering amongst family members that might even lead to legal entanglements! If you happen to be a chronic migraine or headache sufferer, then there's very little you can do but stay clear of these disputes until you're fit enough to deal with them.

農曆八月 (September 8th – October 7th) 丁酉

Employees in the engineering field will benefit from gaining the support of their superiors this month, which is likely to result in financial rewards. There is an increase in tension between father and son and it would be better to keep children out of this sector this month.

農曆九月 (October 8th – November 7th) 戊戌

Speculative investments in the defense industry will produce good profits, especially for those who do their homework and research on the ins and outs of the industry. Mental and emotional instability will plague those using this bedroom this month, and if this is already a problem then alternate arrangements should be sought. The 'well to do' will find things going well for them this month with a life that is free of troubles and generally comfortable.

農曆十月 (November 8th – December 6th) 己亥

Those in the logistics, courier and tourism businesses should benefit from increased profits this month. Health and relationships are stable this month, so you can expect little problems on those fronts. If your job involves strategic thinking or analysis, you will find that you have the chance to advance your career and gain a name for yourself this month.

農曆十一月 (December 7th – January 5th 2012) 庚子

Employers should be careful with labour relations this month, as workers will be prone to challenging authority and will be somewhat difficult to manage. Older men should watch their health, especially with regards to blood and lung disease. Those in the entertainment and electrical industry will find that this is a good month for them financially with the executives as the forefront of the gains.

農曆十二月 (January 6th – February 3rd 2012) 辛丑

Be careful how you handle any staff retrenchment or dismissal this month unless you want to end up with these staff taking you to a court of law for your actions. And if you happen to be sitting in a managerial position, keep a sharp eye open for a possible act of betrayal or fraud by your subordinates. Where romance is concerned, however, bachelors and bachelorettes should take the opportunity to play the field this month. Who knows, your perfect partner could be just waiting for you somewhere out there. It would also be advisable to temporarily relocate elderly family members from this bedroom for the duration of the month to prevent them from suffering from any lung-related ailments.

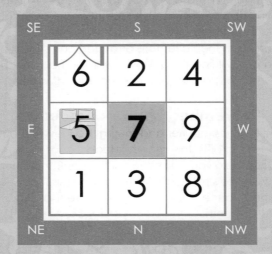

農曆正月 (February 4th – March 5th) 庚寅

Those in the entertainment business, or the operator of a pub, disco or bistro might want to keep a closer eye on your finances this month, especially when it comes to dealing with third parties. Your relationships will also be stormy and troubled. Health-wise, you'll find yourself prone to leg injuries, liver ailments and/or other forms of illnesses.

農曆二月 (March 6th – April 4th) 辛卯

Do not engage in any high-risk ventures this month, especially where property and real estate are concerned. The chances of incurring huge amounts of losses are very high! And by `high-risk' ventures, we are also talking about gambling, games of chance and speculative investments. You would be better off taking care of your own health, and seeking immediate treatment from your doctor at the first sign of an illness.

農曆三月 (April 5th – May 5th) 壬辰

If you happen to be a person involved in the tourism, travel and/or media business, this might be a challenging month for you. As such, refrain from making any major decisions this month. Chances are, you would already be in a confused and irritable state of mind, and this doesn't augur well for your sense of reasoning and judgment. Expectant mothers should not use the East bedroom as well, as this will only result in pregnancy complications!

農曆四月 (May 6th – June 5th) 癸巳

Those using the East bedroom might encounter health problems affecting your kidneys or blood circulatory system. Your relationship with your partner will also be affected, due to a possible interference by a third party, and this will lead to major quarrels at home. And if you happen to be involved in the tourism, courier and logistics industries, you'll find yourself having to double your efforts this month. Help or support from friends, superiors and mentors will not be forthcoming, but don't give up easily.

Main Door	Southeast	Bedroom Sector	East

農曆五月 (June 6th – July 6th) 甲午

Do not use the East bedroom, especially if you are due to sit for a major examination anytime soon. It is equally ill-advised to use a East bedroom, and engage in any significant investments this month – since these will only burn a big hole in your financial books.

農曆六月 (July 7th – August 7th) 乙未

Miscommunication seems to be the order of the day, and indeed, it can spell trouble for both personal and professional relationships. Hence, those whose jobs require them to utilize their communicative skills on a daily basis will be most affected. Lawyers and legal counselors, especially those born in the Year of the Snake, might want to consider delaying or postponing any litigation cases, as your argumentative and persuasive powers are weak this month.

農曆七月 (August 8th – September 7th) 丙申

If you happen to be sleeping in the East bedroom, then be sure to look out for office politics this month. No one seems to be talking to each other and everyone is out to `get' someone else. And if you're an employer or business owner, there is a chance that you might be betrayed by your own employees/subordinates. Look out as well for health issues, particularly lung problems and joint pains. Consult your physician at once should you find yourself feeling poorly.

農曆八月 (September 8th – October 7th) 丁酉

Those in the political arena will find that friends and acquaintances will be around this month to help them with their political aspirations. Tensions will mount between colleagues, and between staff members and superiors, as a result of stress in the workplace. Speculative investments, positions on the stock exchange or even gambling will return potential heavy losses this month.

農曆九月 (October 8th – November 7th) 戊戌

Conservative property deals will bring financial gains this month but extreme caution needs to be exercised throughout the deals. Younger children in the home may have health problems this month in the form of muscle and tendon injuries, so parents may need to keep a watchful eye. Relationships don't fare very well, and those using these bedrooms should be extra patient with their loved ones and exercise a greater a sense of tolerance.

農曆十月 (November 8th – December 6th) 己亥

Lawyers will have a tough month, as they will have trouble putting their case across. Communication is at an all time low this month so couples using this bedroom should be careful about what is said, and also what is done, as this could exacerbate this issue and prolong it for an indefinite length of time. Miscommunications will be a problem this month and those in the cell phone and IT industry will find that losses may be incurred.

農曆十一月 (December 7th – January 5th 2012) 庚子

Disloyal employees will use underhanded tactics and deceit to try to undermine their employers this month. If you own or manage a company, you will need to be careful and pre-empt any such attempts. Head injuries and bone problems will plague those in the East bedroom this month, particularly the elderly. Avoid investment decisions this month. Instead, you should maintain a more hands-on approach within the company.

農曆十二月 (January 6th – February 3rd 2012) 辛丑

No important decisions or investments should be made this month, as these will result in a loss of wealth. Those in the travel and logistics industry should keep a low profile this month, as things are difficult at best. This is not a month to ask for a promotion or a raise, as the outcome will be unfavourable.

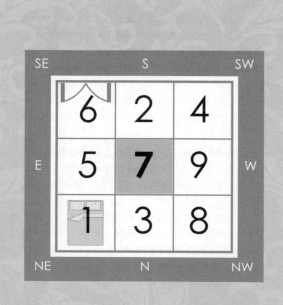

Main Door	Southeast	Bedroom Sector	Northeast

SE	S	SW
6	2	4
5 (E)	**7**	9 (W)
1	3	8
NE	N	NW

農曆正月 (February 4th – March 5th) 庚寅

Business owners will find it hard to make progress in anything, so if you own a business you need to keep a back seat and consolidate your position instead. Couples using this bedroom will find that jealousy may cause discord this month, so they should avoid this room, as should pregnant women, who might find that complications may arise.

農曆二月 (March 6th – April 4th) 辛卯

This is a good room for children to use as a study if they are facing important examinations this month. It generally bodes well for academics and exam preparations. Those involved in ports and transportation will do well financially this month, as deals increase to provide more profits. This should be a good room for couples this month, particularly if there is a good mountain located outside the Northeast.

農曆三月 (April 5th – May 5th) 壬辰

Business booms for those in the furniture or publishing industry this month. Look for overseas and offshore business opportunities in particular, as those will enhance the bottom line even more. Couples using this room may experience some marital discord this month so patience will be the best option in order not to further aggravate the tension in the relationship.

農曆四月 (May 6th – June 5th) 癸巳

Offload property from your property portfolio, as it will result in good financial gains. If you are pregnant, however, it would be best to avoid this room this month. Do not accept remarks or information at face value because at this point in time, you are surrounded by people looking after themselves first. You won't be getting the most accurate answer.

農曆五月 (June 6th – July 6th) 甲午

This is a good month for those in the creative industries, as there is a chance for you to make a name for yourself and get into the limelight and make solid financial profits. Those in committed relationships should be careful of temptation this month, as this will lead to tension with your partner. There are many mentors and helpful people around you this month, so you need to take advantage of the good energies of this sector at this point to take on ambitious endeavours that are certain to be a success.

農曆六月 (July 7th – August 7th) 乙未

Those who are in the entertainment industry, or who are running or employed by health clubs, will do well to sleep in the Northeast sector this month. Be proactive and ask for an increase in salary and for a new position with more authority and status. This month should prove to be a boon for restaurant owners, as there is a chance of profits.

農曆七月 (August 8th – September 7th) 丙申

This is a good month for relationships so investing time in this partnership will bring its own rewards. It's also a good time to sell some favourable property investments, as these will realise into exceptional financial gains. Bankers and financial institution employees will see positive career development this month, and this will be most likely in the form of a pay raise.

農曆八月 (September 8th – October 7th) 丁酉

Romance is on the cards this month, but you should expect short-term passionate flings rather than anything lasting. There should be an improvement in interpersonal relationships amongst family members and friends, so use this time to strengthen your ties. This is a month to mind your own business because if you meddle in other people's affairs, arguments and ill will rather than gratitude is likely.

農曆九月 (October 8th – November 7th) 戊戌

Politicians and public servants will have a good month enjoying excellent public support and may even find themselves rising up the ranks in government or in their parties. The Nobleman star will help you achieve your aims this month, although at the same time you need to bear in mind that there might be people out to get you this month. Those of you involved in professional sports will do well this month in your respective fields or disciplines of sport.

農曆十月 (November 8th – December 6th) 己亥

This month is not a good time for progressing your business. If you do own a business, best to stay in the back seat for now and consolidate your position. Envy is the cause of much friction with couples using this bedroom this month and therefore, they should avoid this room. Expectant women should also avoid this room as they might find that complications may arise.

農曆十一月 (December 7th – January 5th 2012) 庚子

The Northeast room bodes well for academics and exam preparations this month, and would make a good choice for children who use this room to study. Those in the ports and transportation industry will do well financially this month as they can see an increase of profits. This would also make a good room for couples, especially if there is a good mountain located outside the Northeast.

農曆十二月 (January 6th – February 3rd 2012) 辛丑

Expect business to be booming for those in the furniture or publishing industry. It is recommended to look for overseas and offshore business opportunities as it will help to enhance the bottom line more. Couples sleeping in the Northeast room may experience some marital friction this month so it is best to practice patience to ease any tension in the relationship.

Southeast Sector Main Door

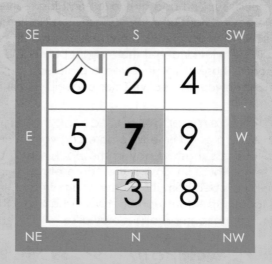

農曆正月 (February 4th – March 5th) 庚寅

It's always wise to listen to good, sound financial advice. So lend others your ears, and listen very carefully as they dispense positive tips on how you can make your money work for you. This, however, does not mean that you can afford to let your guard down, unless you wish to fall victim to conmen or fraudsters. And don't feel too bad if you find yourself feeling a bit down this month. It's quite natural to feel depressed or sad once in a while, but seek professional advice if such symptoms continue.

農曆二月 (March 6th – April 4th) 辛卯

If you happen to be suffering from asthma or any respiratory ailment, do not use the North bedroom this month, as your condition will only worsen. It would, in fact, be a good idea to continue your medical treatment, or seek the advice of your physician if you find yourself feeling poorly. Petty-minded, malicious people seem intent on making your life difficult. Meanwhile, gossips and conflicts may also lead to legal disputes or entanglements. Keep a cool head, and think before you act! All in all, there will be some turbulence this month in your life, but always look forward to better times!

農曆三月 (April 5th – May 5th) 壬辰

A good month to conclude any sales or purchase of properties/real estate. Just be careful, though, to read the small print before you put your signature on that dotted line, to avoid future legal complications. And have your electrical wiring and appliances checked immediately by a qualified electrician, as nobody wants a fire hazard in his/her house! It would equally be advisable to keep a tight rein on your emotions, especially if you find your relationships with others a bit strained this month. Don't rush into committing yourself where decisions are concerned. Instead, wait and see how things unfold, provided you employ tact in your interaction with others, of course.

Main Door	Southeast	Bedroom Sector	North

農曆四月 (May 6th – June 5th) 癸巳

If you happen to be in the legal profession or your work requires you to persuade others, this is a good month for you. Nevertheless, do not rush into making decisions, especially personal ones. Think carefully, before you act. Watch your steps in whatever you do, and wherever you go. You really don't want to fall victim to an accident, no matter how minor, do you?

農曆五月 (June 6th – July 6th) 甲午

Plan carefully and seize every opportunity that comes your way! With the proper timing and stratagem, your efforts will yield satisfactory financial rewards. The energies of the month augur well for thinking and intellectual pursuits, so once you've allotted enough thought to a decision, go for it. And if you have kids, you will be pleased to know that the Wood-Fire combination in this bedroom will be favorable for their academic and educational activities. Hence, this is where they should be studying this month, especially if they will be sitting for exams anytime soon.

農曆六月 (July 7th – August 7th) 乙未

Speculative investments, especially in the property market, will return good investments this month. Relationships should improve so take advantage of this good month to take your spouse away for a treat or a vacation together. People involved in professional sports should be careful of injuries to legs and feet.

農曆七月 (August 8th – September 7th) 丙申

Those in the oil and gas business should take advantage of good business deals offered to them this month. Printing and publishing houses will do well this month with profits coming mostly from overseas sales. This is a tough month for relationships.

農曆八月 (September 8th – October 7th) 丁酉

A financially challenging month awaits you with the possibility of betrayals and loss of wealth. However, those using this room should expect the unexpected, as changes are likely to bring good fortune for those using this bedroom. Good news will come to those who use this bedroom this month so long as they are involved in travel and travel-related activities.

Southeast Sector Main Door

農曆九月 (October 8th – November 7th) 戊戌

Watch out for certain older people who will try to bring you down this month because they are envious of your success. Those in real estate will find that they close better deals than usual this month, resulting in increased turnover. The retail side of fashion and clothing will make excellent gains this month, so if you're involved in those industries you can expect to enjoy some good profits.

農曆十月 (November 8th – December 6th) 己亥

Theft and fraud is a problem this month especially by close friends and family members. It would be advisable to put extra financial controls in place. Windfall gains can be attained from deals made with offshore partners. Health problems, especially ligament tears and tendon injuries, are especially prevalent this month.

農曆十一月 (December 7th – January 5th 2012) 庚子

There is an increased chance of car accidents and travelling mishaps this month. The chances of career advancement resulting in added power and authority is very likely. Male teenagers using this bedroom this month may be more rebellious than normal and should consider using a different room.

農曆十二月 (January 6th – February 3rd 2012) 辛丑

Those who have had profitable months should keep this information to themselves, and refrain from making their newfound wealth gains known to all, as there is a chance of robbery and theft for those using the North bedroom. Health problems in the form of liver troubles could be an issue this month. Property investments will return exceptional profits at this point.

Main Door	Southeast	Bedroom Sector	Northwest

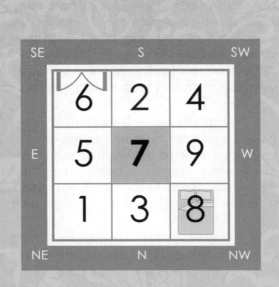

	SE	S	SW
	6	2	4
E	5	**7**	9	W
	1	3	8
	NE	N	NW

農曆正月 (February 4th – March 5th) 庚寅

Those looking to propose to their loved ones, or couples trying to conceive should tap into the positive energies of the Northwest bedroom this month. Now, if you've worked hard all along and believe that you deserve a promotion and salary increment, go ahead and ask your boss for one. Just remember to catch your boss at a good time though.

農曆二月 (March 6th – April 4th) 辛卯

Property dealers and real estate agents will make financial gains this month especially if there is natural water outside the Northwest sector. Older women sleeping in the Northwest sector may have niggling stomach issues this month, so they will need to take extra care of their health and be alert for any potential health issues that arise. Rivals, subordinates and colleagues look to undermine you this month especially if you are born in the Year of the Goat.

農曆三月 (April 5th – May 5th) 壬辰

Those involved in the communications, public relations and any other industry that requires networking will find this month to be a particularly rewarding one. Your network of business contacts expands quickly, with new opportunities for you to explore. And parents will also find their kids developing a sense of independence and responsibility, resulting in better academic performances.

農曆四月 (May 6th – June 5th) 癸巳

Couples looking to start a family should make use of the good energies of this bedroom this month. This is the month when you will receive recognition for something you have done, for example, publishing a paper in the field of psychology. Short-term flings and passionate romances await those who use this bedroom this month.

| Main Door | Southeast | Bedroom Sector | Northwest |

農曆五月 (June 6th – July 6th) 甲午

Business-owners should not overemphasize the need to arrest any decline in profit margins because you'd only be stressing-out and de-motivating your employees unnecessarily. Instead, sit down with them, and come out with a realistic business plan to improve the fortunes of your company. Likewise, romance luck won't exactly be on your side this month, so spend your energy on other more rewarding endeavors.

農曆六月 (July 7th – August 7th) 乙未

Excellent commercial opportunities beckon to those involved in the marketing and consultation industries with corresponding financial gains to be made by the shrewd, prudent businessperson. And if you also happen to own a portfolio of properties, this would be a suitable month to sell or divest a part of your portfolio, to cash in on the profits from your investments. Academic luck features strongly for those using an Northwest bedroom, so go ahead and enroll for that self-improvement or any other course that will add to your existing repertoire of skills!

農曆七月 (August 8th – September 7th) 丙申

Those in banking and the finance industries using the Northwest room will find reward and recognition from superiors this month. People in competitive sports will find success in their international activities, resulting in possible fame and recognition this month. You will need to be careful of illness, with kidney problems being the most likely health issues plaguing you.

農曆八月 (September 8th – October 7th) 丁酉

Athletes and long-distance runners should take care of their joints this month, as injury is possible, especially through over-exertion. Employees will find that they are stressed at this point in time, as superiors step up the pressure for them to perform and increase their expectations. This is a difficult month to make profits, so a more conservative approach to wealth management and investment should be adopted.

農曆九月 (October 8th – November 7th) 戊戌

This promises to be a pleasant and productive month for those using an Northwest bedroom. There will be substantial profits to be made from the travel or construction business. Also, this is a good time of the year to engage in speculative investments, if you wish to make a quick buck. You need to know, however, when to stop engaging in such investments, to gain from them. Couples using the Northwest bedroom this month will find their relationship harmonious and thriving.

農曆十月 (November 8th – December 6th) 己亥

Young boys using this sector should stay away from any sort of machinery, as there could be injuries to their legs. This is a stressful month for relationships so do not make any important decisions about the future. If possible, hold off all important relationship talks and decisions to the next month. Big changes and bold new steps will be needed to revive stagnant careers and floundering investments.

農曆十一月 (December 7th – January 5th 2012) 庚子

You may be disappointed to find that your efforts are not bearing the results expected. This is the time to consider whether you've been doing things right and the right things as well! Similarly, this is an ideal month to engage in property deals, but ensure that proper planning has been undertaken if you wish to profit from your investments. You may also find your personal relationships to be more strained and tense than usual this month. Be tactful, sensitive and patient to preserve harmony in your relationships.

農曆十二月 (January 6th – February 3rd 2012) 辛丑

Take advantage of speculative investments this month, as these will provide short-term gains. However, you need to be careful of being too greedy or it will end up costing you dearly. Marital relations prove to be harmonious and rewarding this month for those in the Northwest bedroom. This is a good month for those who have taken investment positions in the preceding months or who work as fund managers in the futures markets to realise their financial gains and make some profit out of it.

Southeast Sector Main Door

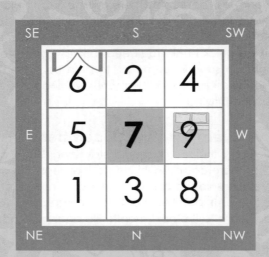

農曆正月 (February 4th – March 5th) 庚寅

Looking to expand your business or diversify your area of commercial operations? Then use the West bedroom, work hard, expand your network of contacts, and you should be able to enjoy the rewards of your labors in due time. What's more, do take every opportunity to travel as much as possible, as those who do so will enjoy favorable wealth luck this month. Look out, though, for any sharp or negative features outside the West sector. The presence of such features only increases the risk of heart disease or eye problems.

農曆二月 (March 6th – April 4th) 辛卯

If you are a salesperson or someone whose work involves intensive sales and marketing, double your efforts, and pursue every business opportunity that comes your way! And to attain a balanced life, use a West bedroom or room for meditative or spiritual pursuits. The Qi present in the West this month also augurs well for academic luck, so children or students whose exams are just around the corner should use this bedroom to sleep in to enjoy maximum results.

農曆三月 (April 5th – May 5th) 壬辰

Much good news and happiness will come to those using this bedroom this month. Financial gain is also on the cards, especially if you are in property development or real estate.

農曆四月 (May 6th – June 5th) 癸巳

This is perhaps the best time to keep a close eye on what your competitors are doing. Otherwise, you may well find your company the target of a hostile takeover. So be vigilant, although this should not prevent you from promoting your products or services aggressively, or embarking on an intensive marketing campaign of your company, as the mass media will provide you with the desired positive exposure. Married men or guys in a committed relationship are advised to be faithful to your Other Half and instead of giving in to temptation!

Main Door	Southeast	Bedroom Sector	West

農曆五月 (June 6th – July 6th) 甲午

Your earlier investments will yield substantial gains this month, so now's the time to cash in on them. If you are a boss or employer, expect your subordinates to challenge or question your authority this month. Nevertheless, seek first to understand the grievances of your staff, before you make yourself understood. Drive carefully this month and ensure that the necessary insurance policies are up-to-date, as there's a possibility of a travel-related mishap.

農曆六月 (July 7th – August 7th) 乙未

Nothing good seems to come out of using the West bedroom this month. For one, tempers will flare, and those involved in speculative activities will suffer from mental agony, anxiety and financial loss from using this bedroom. Expectant mothers should refrain from using the West bedroom as much as possible, as it could result in a miscarriage or pregnancy complications!

農曆七月 (August 8th – September 7th) 丙申

You find your diligence and commitment to your job earning the recognition of your superiors and colleagues. So use this to your advantage by expanding your network of contacts to bring you financial and monetary rewards. Women, in particular, who dabble in the marketing, public relations and sales industries will find it to be a most rewarding month. The fact that you're a successful career woman though does not justify your dominating or treating your partner or spouse poorly.

農曆八月 (September 8th – October 7th) 丁酉

You may need to be a little more patient in expecting any career advancement that is due you, especially if your employer's been undergoing a financially-challenging period lately. Students due to sit for important examinations soon should, however, use a West bedroom to study and sleep in, as the Qi present there will be favorable to their endeavors. Beware of the presence of any significant body of water within or beyond the West sector, though, as it might cause couples to stray or be tempted by another party outside their relationship.

農曆九月 (October 8th – November 7th) 戊戌

Use the West bedroom more frequently this month and chances are, you stand to benefit from your efforts and capabilities being recognized by others. Those involved in the travel, tourism or engineering industries will find this month to be a relatively profitable one, so make hay while the sun shines. And if you happen to be in a steady, committed relationship and wish to foster even closer ties with your loved one, use the West bedroom more often this month.

農曆十月 (November 8th – December 6th) 己亥

It's a good month to ask for a promotion or seek to advance your career further this month. Academic Luck is also good for those using this sector as a bedroom. Relationships will be positive and harmonious, as long as there is no natural water formation outside this sector.

農曆十一月 (December 7th – January 5th 2012) 庚子

You may be aggressive and temperamental this month if you are using the West bedroom - mind your own behaviour while you are in public or at work as it may land you in trouble if you don't control yourself. Watch out for fire hazards caused by wiring or short-circuits in this sector this month.

農曆十二月 (January 6th – February 3rd 2012) 辛丑

A good month for those in the diplomatic service or corps using the West bedroom - things proceed smoothly for you at work. Those who have credit card debts must be careful they don't add more zeros to the amount they already owe this month.

| Main Door | Southeast | Bedroom Sector | Southwest |

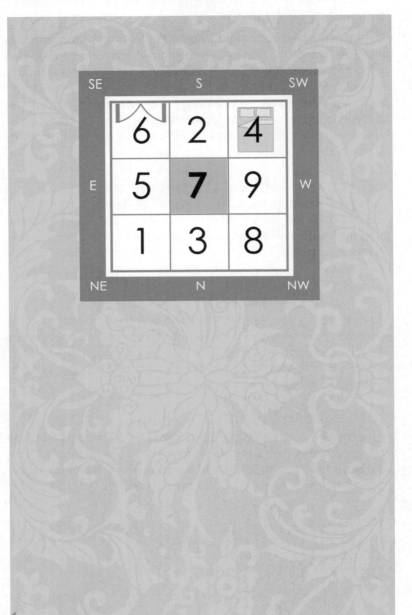

農曆正月 (February 4th – March 5th) 庚寅

Not a very good month for most, if not all, endeavors, unfortunately. Marital bliss won't exactly be there for married couples to enjoy, so give each other some breathing space this month, and be patient. And keep a sharp eye open for any negative features in the Southwest that result in negative Qi. These indicate the risk of acquiring an infection or worse still, liver or breast cancer. Hold on to your money as well, and do not invest in real estate or property at least for the duration of the month, as you'll only stand to suffer losses from such investments.

農曆二月 (March 6th – April 4th) 辛卯

Be careful of being cut whilst handling blades or sharp instruments. If you work on heavy machinery, care should be taken not to injure yourself on duty. This is not the time to get careless! Women in frail health should be careful of respiratory problems and spinal injuries. Those in the furniture and paper and packaging businesses will do well this month, but you will just need to be extra vigilant when signing documents, as this could have legal implications.

農曆三月 (April 5th – May 5th) 壬辰

If your kids seem to be more prone to picking fights with others, you might want to consider relocating them to another bedroom. You certainly don't need them to be continuously engaged in some form of unfriendly or unhealthy rivalry! Nevertheless, those seeking a new romantic interest will find this month to be ideal enough to pursue the person who's caught their eye. Artistic and creative people will also benefit from using the Southwest, particularly if they are seeking to market their skills abroad.

農曆四月 (May 6th – June 5th) 癸巳

Relationships will be strained this month so it would be better if partners could allow each other space and be tolerant of any tension caused by the other party. Do not play the stock market, as the volatility could result in potentially severe financial losses. Women using this room should check for breast cancer.

| Main Door | Southeast | Bedroom Sector | Southwest |

農曆五月 (June 6th – July 6th) 甲午

Publishing a new research paper or academic work and wish your efforts to be recognized and acknowledged? Then use the Southwest bedroom more frequently this month. You will also find this month to be a favorable one when it comes to finalizing new deals, especially if you're working in the engineering or mining industry. Romantic interludes will also meet with success. Still, one should be mindful of the presence of any significant water forms or features outside the Southwest, as these could be the harbingers of trouble.

農曆六月 (July 7th – August 7th) 乙未

Be careful of office politics, as there will be unfriendly and unhealthy rivalries that could escalate out of control. Those using this sector should be careful of head and brain injuries. Marital relations will be strained this month so tolerance will have to be exercised by those involved.

農曆七月 (August 8th – September 7th) 丙申

Those looking to sell their house or buy one should tap into the positive energies of the Southwest bedroom to optimize their chances. This sector also augurs well for students or anyone due to sit for important exams soon. Now, if you happen to be involved in the literary, media or engineering industry, take every opportunity to travel as much as possible. You'll find the outcomes from your travels to be financially rewarding.

農曆八月 (September 8th – October 7th) 丁酉

This is a good month for married couples and newly-weds who use this bedroom, as their relationships become very cozy and harmonious. If you are in the literary field, you should look for publishers in order to put out new work this month, as it could very well result in fame and fortune for you. Scholars approaching important examinations this month should use this room to sleep in or to study in order to benefit from the good energies.

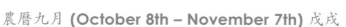
農曆九月 (October 8th – November 7th) 戊戌

Those in a committed relationship will find this a good month to formalize your partnership. Your good reputation and honour will be enhanced this month so you should use this time to promote yourself aggressively, but not too aggressively that you turn people off! A modicum of good grace will always help. If you are expecting to conclude deals in the entertainment industry this month, you should take advantage of this as the outcomes will move in your favour.

農曆十月 (November 8th – December 6th) 己亥

Those in agriculture, forestry or dairy farming will have a bumper month and should use it to further their name in that particular field or even buy new farms. The elderly using this room will face the risk of stroke or arterial blockage related to circulation this month, so they will need to exercise extra caution. Marital problems are likely to affect couples using this sector so spouses should try to travel more to give each other more space.

農曆十一月 (December 7th – January 5th 2012) 庚子

Expectant mothers should avoid using a Southwest bedroom this month to minimize the risk of pregnancy complications or worse still, miscarriage. Ladies, if you believe yourself to be prepared to fall head over heels in love again, select your potential partner carefully. After all, you certainly wouldn't want to fall for a guy with a shady personality, would you? And if you make a living from your artistic or creative talents, you may need to travel this month to earn your keep. It will, however, be worth your while, ultimately.

農曆十二月 (January 6th – February 3rd 2012) 辛丑

Professional sports players and journalists will have a good month this month but it will be more beneficial to their fame than their income. So you can expect to see your moment in the limelight grow larger! Those in the financial industry will do well to conclude deals that require travel abroad, especially if the investment is in real estate. Pregnant women should try to avoid long-distance travel this month, as accidents are likely whilst on the move. This is particularly true if they use the Southwest bedroom.

Southeast Sector Main Door

Main Door	Southeast	Bedroom Sector	South

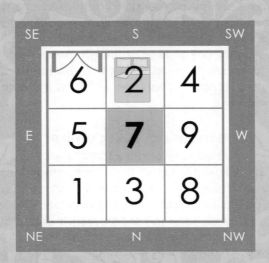

Southeast Sector Main Door

Main Door	Southeast	Bedroom Sector	South

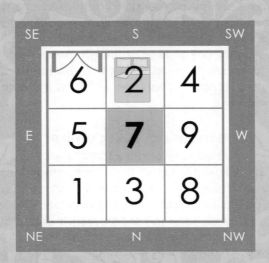

農曆正月 (February 4th – March 5th) 庚寅

Your real estate and property deals will net you handsome gains. On the downside though, you might find your relationship with your partner rather strained and tense this month, so be sensitive and tactful in dealing with him or her. Drive safely this month, as there's a risk of getting involved in a traffic accident due to reckless driving.

農曆二月 (March 6th – April 4th) 辛卯

This is a good month to invest in property or real estate, so go ahead and select the best property that will guarantee you maximum Returns-on-Investment (ROI). However, if you're sitting for important exams this month, sleeping in a South bedroom is a big no-no, as is the case for pregnant women. As a candidate, you would not want to settle for a result that is less than you deserve. And if you're an expectant mother, you certainly wouldn't want any complications during your pregnancy.

農曆三月 (April 5th – May 5th) 壬辰

Not everything that glitters is gold, especially if someone makes you an offer that appears too good to be true! Play it safe. Refrain from putting your signature to any legal documents or contracts this month, so that you'll not end up worse-off than you first started. Students sitting for exams this month should not use this bedroom to study or revise as well. The Qi present in this sector throughout the month will affect one's capability to think. Hence, do not make any important decisions if you happen to be using a South bedroom.

Southeast Sector Main Door

農曆四月 (May 6th – June 5th) 癸巳

That much-awaited promotion might just be yours soon. However, the bad news is, you might find yourself susceptible to respiratory ailments this month, so do what it takes to prevent yourself from falling ill. Likewise, this health alert goes out to all expectant mothers who are currently sleeping in South bedrooms. You might want to relocate to another bedroom this month to avoid even the remotest possibility of a miscarriage or pregnancy complications. However, this is not an entirely inauspicious month for everyone and everything. Take the opportunity to network more and expand your list of contacts. It might just pave the way for that business 'opening' that you've been eyeing.

農曆五月 (June 6th – July 6th) 甲午

Good opportunities and openings to make money beckon to you this month. The crucial key to success lies in not allowing yourself to get carried away and eventually succumb to stress. Romance is in the air for singles this month. However, you also need to also keep an eye on your business to avoid being unduly distracted from the other important facets of your life.

農曆六月 (July 7th – August 7th) 乙未

Be careful of business dealings this month as things are not what they seem and rivals are out to deceive you into deals which will not be financially sound. Couples need to watch for potential discords in marriage, arguments and family disharmony. Do not be deceived by appearances this month and evaluate all new deals conclusively; otherwise, these could end up costing quite a bit of money.

農曆七月 (August 8th – September 7th) 丙申

Eye problems will cause health issues for those using this bedroom this month. Avoid partnerships and joint ventures, as things are not good this month and will not have favourable outcomes. Stubbornness and a lack of logical thinking will cause employees to make some bad decisions that are likely to result in financial losses.

農曆八月 **(September 8th – October 7th)** 丁酉

This is a month to make large investments in property and real estate, as the returns will be extremely good. Those in the upper-social circles of society will find that this month brings with it plenty of opportunities to rub shoulders with the rich and famous. Those of you who are married should be careful that your spouse is not seduced by wealthy people who are out to only have a good time.

農曆九月 **(October 8th – November 7th)** 戊戌

Parents who are involved in their careers while their children are left to their own devices are likely to bring trouble and difficulties for unsupervised children. Surgeons will find that there will be an increased demand for their services this month. There will be increased competition at work that is caused primarily by women, and this could result in arguments and disputes.

農曆十月 **(November 8th – December 6th)** 己亥

Mental and emotional problems are prevalent this month and care should be taken not to exacerbate the problem for those who already suffer from these issues. Those who have a tendency towards apparitions and spiritual activities might have a problem this month. Real estate ventures may produce beneficial results but it will inevitably take its toll in the form of stress.

農曆十一月 **(December 7th – January 5th 2012)** 庚子

No investment or business deals should be concluded this month as these will end up with major losses. Those who use this bedroom this month may find that there is a chance of appendicitis or complications with pregnancy. No matter how conservatively you run your business, there will be obstructions in all areas. Don't worry, and consider lying low to let the worst of it pass you by.

農曆十二月 **(January 6th – February 3rd 2012)** 辛丑

There will be strife and disharmony between in-laws this month so extra patience will be required to make the relationship work. If there is negative Sha at the South this month, there is likely to be spleen and internal organ trouble for the women of the family. This is a time for self-cultivation, and if the opportunity arises, you should consider taking a course that will help develop the self.

Northwest Sector Main Door

Main Door	Northwest	Bedroom Sector	Northwest

This section contains the monthly outlook for all 12 months of the year, for different bedrooms in a property with a Northwest Main Door.

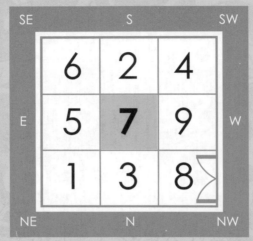

Ground Floor

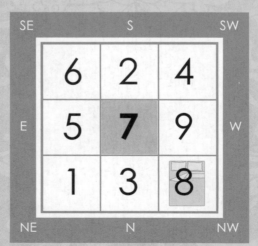

First Floor

| Main Door | Northwest | Bedroom Sector | Northwest |

農曆正月 (February 4th – March 5th) 庚寅

Expect good news and happy events to those using the Northwest this month. Likewise, couples looking to start a family should use the Northwest bedroom this month. This is also a suitable time to seek the recognition you deserve; perhaps by publishing that paper or thesis you've labored on for some time.

農曆二月 (March 6th – April 4th) 辛卯

Singles, take note: It's a good time to play the field this month. Be forewarned though. Any flings you encounter will remain what they are; so don't expect them to develop into anything long-term or solid. If you and your Other Half happen to be using the Northwest bedroom, be more sensitive towards each other's feelings to preserve domestic harmony and prevent arguments from escalating. There may be profits to be realized from real estate or property investments. But then again, the scales of fortune could just as easily tip against you.

農曆三月 (April 5th – May 5th) 壬辰

There's no harm in buying a lottery or lotto ticket; this might just be your lucky month. Just be reminded not to gamble off your savings, as this doesn't necessarily guarantee an absolute win. This month also promises substantial returns-on-investment, especially for those involved in the communications industry. Similarly, young and budding entrepreneurs should take the opportunity to foray into the market this month, as chances are, you'll be off to a good start.

農曆四月 (May 6th – June 5th) 癸巳

Mentors, life coaches and professionals in the self-help and motivational fields will find their advice benefiting others this month, especially if they make the effort to initiate changes in their own personal lives. Hardworking employees will finally see their efforts paid off at work, attaining a higher position and an increased of income. However, they need to be equally mindful of jealous colleagues who are only out to sabotage their efforts. Those interested in starting up their own business should try to do so this month by tapping into the energies of the Northwest.

| Main Door | Northwest | Bedroom Sector | Northwest |

農曆五月 (June 6th – July 6th) 甲午

Wealth luck smiles upon those using the Northwest this month and the presence of any water forms in this sector will only enhance your wealth prospects even further. So, why not consider engaging in some form of speculative but viable investment? Couples using the Northwest will also find their relationship to be harmonious and smooth sailing. However, salaried workers and employees may find themselves feeling stressed or even exhausted due to the increased amount of pressure to perform imposed upon them by their superiors. Keep in mind to manage your work-life balance carefully.

農曆六月 (July 7th – August 7th) 乙未

Have you been eyeing that dream home that recently caught your attention? Then this could be a good month to invest in property so that you may enjoy your new home in no time. Don't be impatient in concluding other types of deals, as you need all the facts and information at your disposal before you can make the final decision. Salaried employees should be mindful of superiors, who are out to profit at their productivity and expense by exploiting them.

農曆七月 (August 8th – September 7th) 丙申

Where possible, postpone all deals to a more suitable period in time as chances are your dealings this month will be less than profitable. In fact, chaos and unexpected changes may plague your business or venture this month resulting in unbudgeted losses. However, stagnant careers and flailing enterprises may still be revived or resuscitated if you're prepared to make drastic changes to your business where necessary.

農曆八月 (September 8th – October 7th) 丁酉

Elderly women using the Northwest should guard against acquiring any potentially chronic stomach ailments this month. Seek the advice of your doctor at the first sign of trouble. On the other hand, the energies of the Northwest bode well for those who desire to take their relationship to the next level; so tap into them accordingly if that's what you seek. Be vigilant for any lucrative property deals headed your way. When opportunity comes a-knocking, seize them at once!

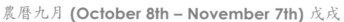

農曆九月 (October 8th – November 7th) 戊戌

Couples using the Northwest will find their relationship to be easygoing and harmonious. As such, those looking to conceive should seize this sector more frequently! Professionals in the travel and construction industries will find their profit margins significantly improved this month. This is indeed an ideal month for fund/investment managers or those dabbling in investment portfolios to cash in on their investments as well.

農曆十月 (November 8th – December 6th) 己亥

Children should be careful of injuries to limbs caused by sharp metal objects and implements. Adults using this bedroom sector should focus on academic activities or self-improvement that is likely to result in personal growth. Do not make any important business decisions this month, as at best, these will not be in your favour and at worst, may end in losses.

農曆十一月 (December 7th – January 5th 2012) 庚子

Older women who use this sector this month should not dismiss any minor stomach ailments because these could develop into something more serious. There should be success for those in real estate resulting in superior profits. This is especially the case if there is water in the Northwest. Those who wish to take their relationship to the next level should do so this month and make use of its favourable energies.

農曆十二月 (January 6th – February 3rd 2012) 辛丑

This is a good month for those who have taken investment positions in the preceding months, or work as fund managers in the futures markets, to realise their financial gains. Couples using this bedroom will have a happy month together. If they are keen to start a family, then they could do so this month as the outlook is good. Those in the oil and gas industry will make good money this month as financial gains are on the upswing.

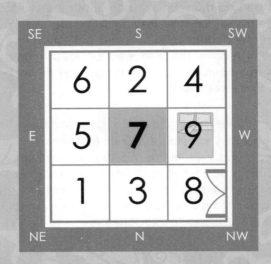

農曆正月 (February 4th – March 5th) 庚寅

It would be wise to stay away from discos, nightclubs and places of ill-repute as your visits there will affect your relationship with your loved ones negatively. Pregnant women using the West bedroom should also take good care of their health to minimize the risk of miscarriage. This will be an emotional month, where frayed tempers and impatience threaten to wreck your relationships and dealings with others. Keep your wits about you and use your head to handle yourself.

農曆二月 (March 6th – April 4th) 辛卯

Professionals involved in the services industry will be pleased to find their customer base increasing this month with substantial financial returns following suit. This is also a good time of the year to embark on your business trips as their outcomes will very likely turn out to be profitable and successful. Auspicious news and celebrations are the order of the day, more so if your child excels with flying colours in his or her examinations.

農曆三月 (April 5th – May 5th) 壬辰

Use the energies of the West, especially if you wish to develop yourself spiritually, mentally or religiously this month. Budding politicians and seasoned ones should also take this opportunity to take on their rivals or opponents and make their cause known to the highest powers in the government. This is an ideal time to engage in speculative deals, especially those in the inflammable liquids/chemicals business.

農曆四月 (May 6th – June 5th) 癸巳

Ladies should avoid using the West this month, as they are particularly susceptible to eye problems and/or gallstones if they do so. While every relationship undergoes the occasional rough patch, this is no excuse to indulge in an illicit or extra-marital affair! Those specialising in the fashion and hairdressing businesses should capitalise on the publicity given to them in the mass media to promote their services and skills to generate more revenue.

| Main Door | Northwest | Bedroom Sector | West |

農曆五月 (June 6th – July 6th) 甲午

You'll do well to hold your tongue instead of talking non-stop about the affairs of others. There's no point in giving unsolicited advice, which will not be appreciated. Watch out for your health as respiratory problems and hemorrhoids may afflict those using the West this month. Those finding it necessary to travel in order to conclude their deals will stand to reap the rewards of their efforts in due time.

農曆六月 (July 7th – August 7th) 乙未

Maintain a low profile in both the professional and personal aspects of your life. Otherwise, you only cause yourself problems and heartache. Expectant mothers are advised to consult their gynecologist as well as the energies of the West could give rise to certain pregnancy complications. Obviously, this is not the best of time to engage in speculative investments as they will bring about anxiety, mental stress and financial losses.

農曆七月 (August 8th – September 7th) 丙申

Your thoughts and reasoning ability will be affected by the energies of the West, so refrain from making any important decisions this month. Those sleeping in the West bedroom will find themselves more temperamental and aggressive towards others. As such, be sure to exercise patience and think before you act or say anything. Guard against acquiring food poisoning as well, especially if you notice any negative features or structures in the West.

農曆八月 (September 8th – October 7th) 丁酉

Couples will find their relationships going well this month due to the positive energies of the West. Similarly, those sitting for major examinations soon should use this sector if they wish to achieve good results. Nevertheless, be forewarned that the Qi of the West could also pose health problems in the form of eye or heart ailments or even strokes. Hence, look out for the presence of a negative feature outside this sector.

農曆九月 (October 8th – November 7th) 戊戌

Travel is on the cards for those using the West this month; so are you ready for the adventure of the lifetime? The West is also a good sector to use for couples looking to conceive. Meanwhile, counsellors, coaches and mentors will find their skills and advice highly sought-after this month. Share your wisdom and knowledge well so that others may benefit from them.

農曆十月 (November 8th – December 6th) 己亥

A good month for those in the academic or scholarly research fields. There is the possibility of commercialising an idea or your research this month, or you will be successful in applying for a grant for your research.

農曆十一月 (December 7th – January 5th 2012) 庚子

you sleep in the West bedroom, use this month to make decisions about your investment portfolio or those that involve financial matters as thinking will be lucid. Those in the fashion industry will find that travel brings about positive outcomes this month.

農曆十二月 (January 6th – February 3rd 2012) 辛丑

A good month for those looking to undertake bold ambitious plans at work. Relationship-wise, look to take things to the next level. Couples using this bedroom could expect happy news this month.

Main Door	Northwest	Bedroom Sector	Southwest

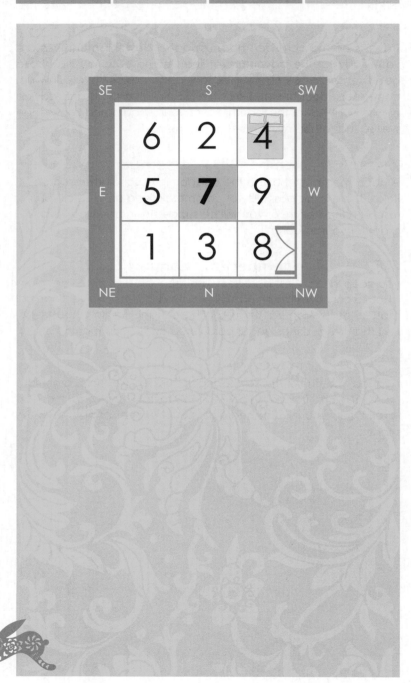

農曆正月 (February 4th – March 5th) 庚寅

If you're in agriculture, forestry or dairy farming, you can expect to have a bumper month. You should use this month to further your name in your particular field, as you are likely to receive the proper recognition. If you have written a book, you should try to find a publisher this month as it will bring good reputation and financial gain. While you may not be The Next Big Thing, a certain amount of success can be expected! If you want to buy or sell your house and are using a Southwest bedroom, this is a beneficial time to do this.

農曆二月 (March 6th – April 4th) 辛卯

If meditation or spiritual development is your interest, then using this bedroom this month will be favourable for further progress. Those in the furniture business will do well, but you need to be extra vigilant when signing documents as this could have legal implications that might come back to haunt you in the future. So it is better to be safe than sorry right now. Workmen on worksites should be very careful of sustaining injuries from sharp metal objects.

農曆三月 (April 5th – May 5th) 壬辰

By all means, make the most of favourable wealth luck, especially if you're involved in the food and beverage business. Just be careful not to violate any health laws though, as these could cause you financial losses. Recognition, promotion and career advancement will also be yours, but bear in mind that they do come with additional responsibilities and greater stress levels. In fact, your colleagues might just be the root of your problems at work this month; no thanks to their backstabbing and the underhand tactics used against you.

農曆四月 (May 6th – June 5th) 癸巳

This appears to be a stressful, even depressing, month for those using the Southwest, especially with stomach ailments and ulcers likely to affect your health. You might even encounter problems communicating with your in-laws. Hence, for the meantime, it's best to minimize any form of contact with them whilst exercising patience in dealing with them. If you're traveling this month, ensure that all the necessary insurance policies are in order, in case you encounter unexpected hiccups during your travels.

農曆五月 (June 6th – July 6th) 甲午

Singles will find this a good month to play the field, although chances are, any flings you encounter will not likely develop into anything long-term or serious. However, couples using the Southwest should find the energies of this sector conducive to their relationship. Take note that the presence of any water in the Southwest could cause infidelity and scandals! That aside, those in the mining and engineering industries should be able to reap substantial profits this month.

農曆六月 (July 7th – August 7th) 乙未

Those in the services and property industries will find this time of the year to be ideal enough to seek the promotion and recognition they've worked so hard for all along. The fact that your relationships will be thriving and smooth-sailing this month only augurs well for all efforts that require networking and the support of others. So, if you're looking to embark on a joint venture, go for it, as you stand to give your enterprise a good start! Another plus: Any deal concluded this month will also be beneficial in terms of the lucrative investment potential it presents.

農曆七月 (August 8th – September 7th) 丙申

Seeking the fame, promotion, recognition and advancement you've toiled for all this while? Then tap into the energies of the Southwest this month. Similarly, management consultants and professionals in the real estate and property fields will find the energies of the Southwest conducive towards generating revenue from their business. You need to know, though, that this sector is also the harbinger of health issues such as back and spinal problems!

農曆八月 (September 8th – October 7th) 丁酉

Serious disputes and misunderstandings threaten to flare up between couples, so be mindful of your partner's feelings to prevent your relationship from falling apart. You're also advised to scrutinize all legal documents carefully before committing yourself to them, to sidestep the possibility of any legal complications later on. Also, those working on industrial or construction sites should prioritize safety and guard against injuring their limbs at work.

農曆九月 (October 8th – November 7th) 戊戌

Athletes and sportspersons involved in competitions or tournaments should find this a promising month in their quest for gold. Better still, your relationships will be elevated to the next level as the energies of the Southwest bode well for fostering closer ties with other parties. You may, however, need to be just a little patient in concluding your share or equities deals, as difficult clients may delay your chances of tasting immediate success. Don't worry though, as what's yours will ultimately be yours!

農曆十月 (November 8th – December 6th) 己亥

Ladies might want to go for a full medical check-up or even a mammogram this month, as there's a risk of acquiring breast cancer due to the energies of the Southwest. Avoid indulging in gambling or any form of speculative investment as you could well end up losing all you have! Business owners should also ensure that all their dealings are above-board, as they stand to incur huge losses in addition to violating the law by engaging in any illegal deals.

農曆十一月 (December 7th – January 5th 2012) 庚子

Asthma, bronchitis and health problems affecting the lungs and respiratory system may well be the bane of those using the Southwest bedroom this month. Seek medical advice and treatment at the first sign of trouble. Those using this sector to study for their exams or engage in other IQ-related or academic endeavors will find their efforts yielding positive outcomes. Businesswomen should try to venture abroad in securing their deals, as chances are, these will bring them considerable profits in time to come.

農曆十二月 (January 6th – February 3rd 2012) 辛丑

By all means, make the most of favourable wealth luck, especially if you're involved in the food and beverage business. Just be careful not to violate any health laws though, as these could cause you financial losses! Recognition, promotion and career advancement will also be yours, but bear in mind that they do come with additional responsibilities and greater stress levels. In fact, your colleagues might just be the cause of your problems at work this month, no thanks to their backstabbing and the underhand tactics used against you.

Northwest Sector Main Door

Main Door	Northwest	Bedroom Sector	South

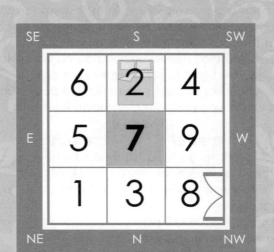

農曆正月 (February 4th – March 5th) 庚寅

This is a good month to make financial gains from the sale of property, but it will take its toll on your stress levels. Those of you involved in religious pursuits or gaining spiritual knowledge should use this bedroom, as the outcome is likely to be good. If you have a tendency towards mental instability, then it would be best to change bedrooms this month.

農曆二月 (March 6th – April 4th) 辛卯

Any business issues that arise this month should be dealt with after careful consideration or even after obtaining some help from lawyers. There is a chance of great fortune and financial gain but you will need to know what you are doing to realise these gains. Couples who use this bedroom this month may find that their relationships are under severe stress that is likely to result in divorce.

農曆三月 (April 5th – May 5th) 壬辰

This is a good time for self-cultivation and if the opportunity arises, they should take a course that will develop the self. Academics and scholars will benefit from the good energies of the South this month if they are facing important examinations. Those who use their intelligence to make money from property-related fields will reap the rewards in the months to come.

農曆四月 (May 6th – June 5th) 癸巳

This is a good sector for those who wish to become involved in religious or spiritual endeavours. Ensure that all traffic fines and outstanding taxes are up-to-date. Otherwise, you will be overwhelmed by the revenue offices throughout the rest of the month. If you're a parent with a son using this bedroom, you will have to be prepared for him to be more difficult and argumentative this month.

Main Door	Northwest	Bedroom Sector	South

農曆五月 (June 6th – July 6th) 甲午

Those using the South are particularly susceptible to head and brain problems, so consider relocating yourself from this sector this month. Ladies should not be tempted to indulge in illicit or scandalous affairs as these will only sully your reputation when what you previously thought you could hide becomes public knowledge! That aside, real estate and property developers stand to acquire great wealth from their investments this month.

農曆六月 (July 7th – August 7th) 乙未

Envious parties threaten to undermine or sabotage whatever good efforts you've put in at work. Do your best to resist any attempts by such malicious people to provoke you into an argument or dispute, which will only obscure all the good work you've done so far. There is, however, some extra cash to be made from side investments. Doctors and physicians will also find their skills much sought-after, thanks to their reputation and good name, rather than the incidence of more people falling ill this month.

農曆七月 (August 8th – September 7th) 丙申

The affluent and wealthy will find life to be a breeze and hassle-free this month. So, make the most of this opportunity to prepare for the inevitable rainy day. On the other hand, salaried employees will find it difficult to make money, as the going will be tough regardless of how much effort they put into their work. Don't give up easily, but instead, work hard and work smart. Meanwhile, those who're already prone to mental disorders may want to consider using a sector other than the South this month, as you could find yourself 'spiritually disturbed' by ignoring this advisory.

農曆八月 (September 8th – October 7th) 丁酉

Those expecting to be promoted to positions of authority and high social status could find these desires being fulfilled this month. People using the South sector may be more inclined towards spiritual and religious pursuits. Opportunities will present themselves this month resulting in an upturn in fortunes and an increased financial income for those involved.

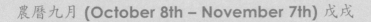

農曆九月 (October 8th – November 7th) 戊戌

The energies of the South will promise growth and self-improvement. Why not take the chance to taking up something that interests you? Unsurprisingly, those involved in the media, publicity and writing/journalistic fields will find this a good time of the year to generate as much income as possible from their endeavors. Use your wisdom and experience while investing in real estate and property this month to reap the rewards due you in time to come.

農曆十月 (November 8th – December 6th) 己亥

Use the South, especially if you're religiously or spiritually inclined, for such pursuits. Nevertheless, be forewarned that marital problems could arise if you use the South too frequently this month. If you're a salaried worker, be careful about being drawn into a dispute or argument at work, which could result in legal entanglements.

農曆十一月 (December 7th – January 5th 2012) 庚子

If you're the gambling type, there's no harm in buying a lottery ticket or playing the sweepstakes this month. Just don't use up every penny at your disposal to win big. The ladies of the household will find themselves more susceptible to stomach and other ailments plaguing their digestive system. Seek immediate medical treatment at the first sign of trouble. Medical practitioners will, however, find their skills much sought-after this month.

農曆十二月 (January 6th – February 3rd 2012) 辛丑

Couples using the South bedroom may find their relationship strained and tense this month. It is advisable to exercise tolerance and patience with each other and remember that this is only a temporary bad patch. Expectant mothers may want to rethink using the South, as the risk of running into pregnancy complications is heightened by the energies present in this sector at this time of the year. That aside, competitive sportspersons and athletes should go for gold this month, as the energies of the South are on your side.

Main Door	Northwest	Bedroom Sector	Southeast

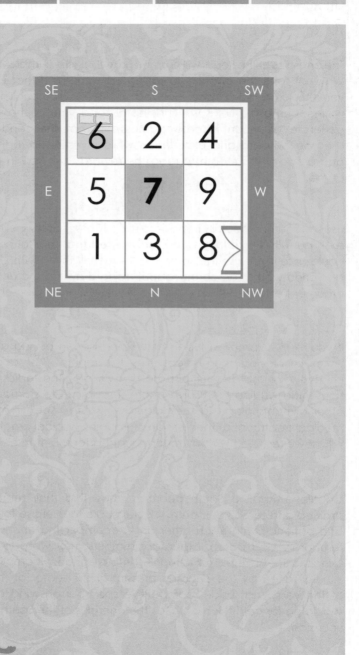

SE	S	SW
6	2	4
5	**7**	9
1	3	8
NE	N	NW

農曆正月 (February 4th – March 5th) 庚寅

Prioritise safety if you work with machinery on a regular or daily basis. You risk injuring yourself at work by neglecting this aspect. The workplace could also prove to be a hornet's nest this month, particularly with the incessant power-struggles and jostling for authority amongst employees and management personnel. Stay out of such a scenario if possible. Look on the bright side of things: The skills and talents of those dabbling in the academic or legal field will be acknowledged and highly sought-after this month.

農曆二月 (March 6th – April 4th) 辛卯

Cut-throat competition resulting in price wars will only bring in a market where nobody wins and any party that raises its prices will lose out in the end. This looks set to be a stressful and challenging month, but things will eventually sort themselves out as long as you're prepared to spend and do what it takes to neutralize the opposition. The energies of the Southeast will, however, bode well for professional athletes and sportspersons participating in competitions and tournaments in their quest for gold!

農曆三月 (April 5th – May 5th) 壬辰

There is a risk of endeavours meeting with failure this month so put on hold any grand plans for business expansion or to seek a promotion or even take on an ambitious project. Business owners must especially be careful of legal problems this month. Health-wise, watch out for stress-induced headaches and migraines.

農曆四月 (May 6th – June 5th) 癸巳

With the added complication of negative environmental forms, arguments could break out at work if the situation is not well-controlled. Diffuse the tension by refusing to join in the petty backbiting. Politicians will find that they are able to promote their policies this month and end up with support from those around them. This should be a good month for those in the legal fields with strong demand for their skills, but you need to be careful of unwanted gossip.

| Main Door | Northwest | Bedroom Sector | Southeast |

農曆五月 (June 6th – July 6th) 甲午

Business owners should stay away from wheeling-dealing this month and those who are employed should not change jobs as well. There may be some tension between fathers and sons this time around, especially if either is using the Southeast bedroom.

農曆六月 (July 7th – August 7th) 乙未

Property investments will yield good gains this month and those in the real estate industry will also have a good month. If there are negative forms outside the Southeast sector, be careful of heart attacks or heart problems within this period.

農曆七月 (August 8th – September 7th) 丙申

Those in speculative investments or stocks and equities will make good profits this month if they use this bedroom. If you are looking to improve either your personal or professional relationships, you will find this a good month to do so. It also bodes well for travel in both leisure and business environment, especially if you are doing a fact-finding mission or are involved in research and development.

農曆八月 (September 8th – October 7th) 丁酉

Be aware of travel-related problems this month that could result in injury to the limbs. The elderly should take care of their health this month and see a doctor rather than dismiss minor ailments as unimportant. Prevention is always better than cure! Parents of teenagers might find this a difficult month to deal with their offspring if they are using the Southeast sector.

農曆九月 (October 8th – November 7th) 戊戌

Those using the Southeast are particularly susceptible to head and brain problems, so consider relocating yourself from this sector this month. Ladies should not be tempted to indulge in illicit or scandalous affairs, as these will only sully your reputation when what you previously thought you could hide becomes public knowledge! That aside, real estate and property developers stand to reap great wealth from their investments this month.

農曆十月 (November 8th – December 6th) 己亥

Jealous parties threaten to undermine or sabotage whatever good efforts you've put in at work. Do your best to resist any attempts by such malicious people to provoke you into an argument or dispute, which will only cloud all the good work you've done so far. There is, however, some extra cash to be made from side investments. Doctors and physicians will also find their skills much sought-after, thanks to their reputation and good name, rather than the incidence of more people falling ill this month.

農曆十一月 (December 7th – January 5th 2012) 庚子

Couples should be tolerant of each other and will need to put more effort into their relationships. Exercise tolerance and patience as it will help to dispel any potential tension. Avoid putting children in this bedroom this month, as they will be rebellious and difficult to control. Employers should be careful with labour relations this month as workers will challenge authority and become difficult to manage.

農曆十二月 (January 6th – February 3rd 2012) 辛丑

Employers should monitor your staff closely and beware of dishonest and disloyal employees, who are out to defraud or steal from you this month. Couples using the Southeast will also find their relationship tense and strained. Exercise patience and tact in dealing with each other as much as possible. Athletes and professional sportspersons need to be extra careful in training or while competing, as they risk serious injuries to their head!

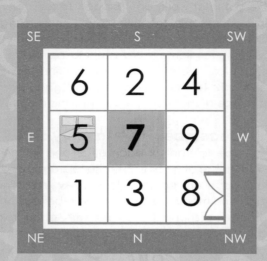

	SE	S	SW	
	6	2	4	
E	5	**7**	9	W
	1	3	8	
	NE	N	NW	

農曆正月 (February 4th – March 5th) 庚寅

Avoid all investment deals this month. Chances are you'll only end up poorer than when you first started off by pouring your money into such ventures. Instead, monitor your employees closely as disloyal subordinates could try to undermine your efforts every turn of the way. Health-wise, the elderly are particularly prone to head injuries and bone problems this month. It may hence be wise to have them undergo a full medical check-up if they happen to be using the East bedroom.

農曆二月 (March 6th – April 4th) 辛卯

Conservative property deals will bring financial gains this month but extreme caution needs to be exercised throughout the deals. Business is also likely to be slow and thus, this is not the time for any business expansion but rather, a time for business owners to consolidate their position. Pay extra attention to customers and clients as disloyalty amongst employees is rife and this might affect your business in significant ways.

農曆三月 (April 5th – May 5th) 壬辰

There will be a slowdown in the communications and entertainment industries this month. As a result, profits will experience a sharp decline so plan strategically for the future. Don't be overly disheartened if you find your business plagued by problems. Instead, persevere and see if you can get to the root of your problems no matter how long it may take. Mind your health as well to ward off the possibility of getting a skin disease or liver infection!

農曆四月 (May 6th – June 5th) 癸巳

People in competitive sports will find competitions an uphill battle this month and should rather use the time to physically improve themselves. Stress and depression might cause a worsening mental instability this month, especially if negative Sha is located in the East sector. Those in new relationships should ease off a little this month. Otherwise, they might find the romantic fires cooling off much sooner than expected.

| Main Door | Northwest | Bedroom Sector | East |

農曆五月 (June 6th – July 6th) 甲午

Do not engage in any major personal endeavors just yet. Instead, wait and act only when the right moment presents itself. Indeed, this is not a good time for any important decision-making. Keep a close eye on your eldest daughter as well, as she's particularly susceptible to ill health due to the energies of the East this month. Be mindful of disputes and acts of negligence, which could prove to be costly, especially to those dabbling in real estate and properties.

農曆六月 (July 7th – August 7th) 乙未

Avoid gambling this month, as there is a strong possibility of losing property or even your entire fortune! Those in ill health should watch out for kidney problems, especially if cancer-related. If you have made profits from investments, it would be wise to cash in on these gains at this point in time.

農曆七月 (August 8th – September 7th) 丙申

You may be dismayed to find the stress and pressures of life taking their toll on your relationships this month. Manage your lifestyle carefully and seek a work-life balance in everything you do. Look out as well for eye ailments and the possibility of suffering from a stroke if you happen to be using the East bedroom. Get a qualified electrician to check the wiring and electrical appliances in the East sector of your property as well, more so if your premises have been around for quite a while.

農曆八月 (September 8th – October 7th) 丁酉

This is not the time to start new ventures or businesses as the possibility of success is limited. Those of you who are in the property and real estate fields and are in the know should be able to make quick, beneficial financial gains this month. Mothers and older women will find that their relationships are under strain this month.

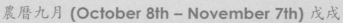

農曆九月 (October 8th – November 7th) 戊戌

Watch out for any miscommunication, especially if you specialize in the mobile or IT industry, to mitigate the risk of losses due to disputes and misunderstandings. Lawyers and legal professionals will also find it hard to put their cases across, as will those who rely on their vocal abilities/prowess for a livelihood such as motivational speakers. Don't worry unduly as this is only a temporary bad patch.

農曆十月 (November 8th – December 6th) 己亥

Religious enthusiasm could end in fanaticism for those using the East bedroom this month. Mentors and superiors are around to help you and offer some guidance and advice. As a result, you will find contracts more readily available at this point. Speculative investments, positions on the stock exchange, or even gambling will return heavy losses this month.

農曆十一月 (December 7th – January 5th 2012) 庚子

Those sleeping in the East bedroom will have good Peach Blossom Luck but the romantic prospects thrown up are likely to be best for a short fling or a date or two at best. So don't take the relationship too seriously. Health-wise, watch out for asthma attacks, bronchitis, rheumatism and joint problems.

農曆十二月 (January 6th – February 3rd 2012) 辛丑

A difficult month for those sleeping in the East bedroom – your emotional or mental state may be a little vulnerable or rocky. Children using this bedroom could be egged on by peer pressure to engage in rebellious activities or even shoplifting. At work, watch out for embezzlement, fraud and deceptions this month.

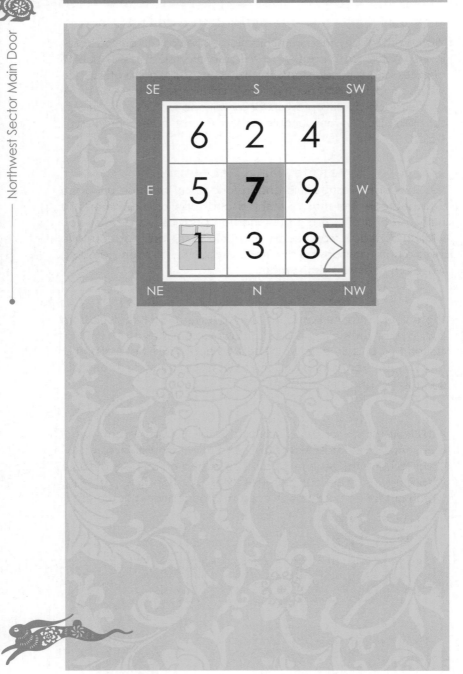

| Main Door | Northwest | Bedroom Sector | Northeast |

農曆正月 (February 4th – March 5th) 庚寅

It will be difficult to make progress in anything this month so it would be best to take the back seat and consolidate your position. Pregnant women should avoid using this bedroom this month, as they may end up with complications or even a possible miscarriage. Where possible, they will need to use another room. Turnover will be affected for those in the travel, courier and logistics businesses. Best to lie low and work through the tough month and you are likely to emerge unscathed.

農曆二月 (March 6th – April 4th) 辛卯

Asset acquisition will be successful this month, especially if it involves overseas travel. Romance will bloom for those using the Northeast sector as a bedroom. Take advantage of this good time to seek out prospective partners if you are single. Engineering-related businesses will have a good month as media attention will bring in new customers.

農曆三月 (April 5th – May 5th) 壬辰

Take extra care with present disputes as these may escalate into full legal problems. Look for overseas or offshore business opportunities in particular, as these are likely to enhance the bottom line. Tension enters into relationships, so extreme patience will be required throughout the month.

農曆四月 (May 6th – June 5th) 癸巳

Those who are in the entertainment industry or are running or employed in health centers, clubs and discos, as well as those sleeping in a Northeast sector bedroom will do well financially this month. Married couples are recommended to go on a holiday together at this time.

| Main Door | Northwest | Bedroom Sector | Northeast |

農曆五月 (June 6th – July 6th) 甲午

This is a good month for those in the creative industries as you will be in the limelight with a chance for you to make a name for yourself. Resist temptation leading you astray if you use this bedroom this month, as this may cause trouble with your present partner. This is a good time to throw out the old and bring in the new. It is generally a month of improvements.

農曆六月 (July 7th – August 7th) 乙未

This is a month to ask for the promotion you wanted especially if you are in the food and beverage or media industries. Business owners in the restaurant business or entertainment industry will see a boom this month. In addition, there might also be a risk of heart and eye-related problems this particular time.

農曆七月 (August 8th – September 7th) 丙申

Business owners will make money and employees will experience career advancement, especially if they are in the oil and gas or the mining industries. Those in the jewelry or jade business can expect good profits this month if they are using the Northeast bedroom. Travelling brings positive benefits, including new investors into the business or open up new venture possibilities.

農曆八月 (September 8th – October 7th) 丁酉

A month to avoid making important personal or financial decisions as you will find you are not able to make a clear one. Couples using a Northeast bedroom should be tolerant of each other this month as there is a risk of communications leading to conflicts.

農曆九月 (October 8th – November 7th) 戊戌

A good month for those in the media business - there will be fame, recognition and some publicity. Couples using this bedroom will be very lovey-dovey this month. However, if there is water outside this sector, be wary of extra-marital dalliances. Car accidents are also possible, so be careful on the road.

農曆十月 **(November 8th – December 6th)** 己亥

Professional and personal relationships may be tainted by gossip and hearsay. You should stay above the fray to prevent things from getting out of hand.

農曆十一月 **(December 7th – January 5th 2012)** 庚子

A month to be suspicious of colleagues who seem too good to be true; there may well be some ulterior motives in play, especially for those who may have to contend with being bullied or pressured by colleagues at work. Negative features outside this sector could aggravate health problems this month, especially those who have diabetes or pregnant, and sleep in the Northeast.

農曆十二月 **(January 6th – February 3rd 2012)** 辛丑

Romantic temptation will be aplenty for those using the Northeast bedroom; singles can have some fun but married couples should be careful. Pregnant women should, if possible, avoid this bedroom this month as there is a risk of miscarriage or premature birth.

Northwest Sector Main Door

Northwest Sector Main Door

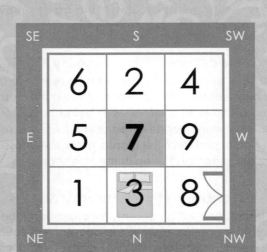

SE   S   SW

6	2	4
5	**7**	9
1	3	8

E   W

NE   N   NW

農曆正月 (February 4th – March 5th) 庚寅

Avoid travelling if possible this month, as your journeys will tend to be problematic. Those using the North will also find themselves prone to emotional and psychological disturbances and this could lead to depression if left unchecked. There will be good financial prospects for professionals in the literary, arts and other creative fields with your newfound fame and enhanced reputation contributing to your wealth luck.

農曆二月 (March 6th – April 4th) 辛卯

It would be wise to avoid unsavory spots and places of ill-repute especially this month, as your outings could result in arguments. Worse still, you might even sustain bodily harm and end up facing a lawsuit. In any case, specialists in the analytical and scientific fields will benefit from the energies of the North with a breakthrough, the likely outcome of their efforts. Those involved in the communications, public relations and research and development industries will be able to pave inroads into markets traditionally dominated by their competitors this month.

農曆三月 (April 5th – May 5th) 壬辰

Legal issues arising from financial disputes or problems could well result in a loss of wealth this month if left unmonitored. Couples using the North bedroom also need to be more patient with each other to preserve harmony in their relationship. Where possible, utilise your network of contacts to pave new ways for your business as such a step will bring about favorable results.

農曆四月 (May 6th – June 5th) 癸巳

This is a good month to make that career move or embark on that new venture you've always wanted to do. So plan wisely before you act. Negotiators, lawyers and those who rely on their powers of persuasion will also find their skills in great demand this month. Couples using the North bedroom will find their relationship tense and strained this month. So exercise patience and tolerance with each other to minimize unnecessary friction.

農曆五月 (June 6th – July 6th) 甲午

Personal safety should be made a priority this month, as there is a chance of being robbed and mugged. A lack of communication will cause problems in relationships, so endeavour to try and be more open with your partner. Analysts and scientific researchers will benefit from the good energies of this room this month provided that there is a good quality mountain outside the North sector.

農曆六月 (July 7th – August 7th) 乙未

Those who trade at markets or manage restaurants will find this to be a financially rewarding month. If you have outstanding fines or taxes owing, you may be in trouble with the law and should pay all outstanding penalties as soon as possible. Illnesses affecting the stomach and intestines will be a significant problem this month.

農曆七月 (August 8th – September 7th) 丙申

Mentors and counsellors will find that they are inundated by new clients looking for help and support. Those artistically inclined, especially sculptors and carvers, will find that they attract increased commissions for their work. This is a favourable month for those in the construction industry especially if you are required to travel to conclude deals.

農曆八月 (September 8th – October 7th) 丁酉

A financially challenging month awaits you with betrayals and loss of wealth being very likely. Profits being realised this month should be invested wisely by those who cash in their gains. Good news will come to those who use this bedroom so long as they are involved in travel.

農曆九月 (October 8th – November 7th) 戊戌

Negotiations and discussions will tend to be heated and difficult this month so avoid trying to close or conclude any deals. Merchant bankers and equity dealers will find that they close better deals than usual, resulting in increased turnover and better profits. If there are negative features outside the North, prepare for the likelihood of health problems cropping up in the form of kidney trouble.

農曆十月 (November 8th – December 6th) 己亥

Fraud and theft is a problem this month, especially by close friends and family members. It would be advisable to put extra financial controls in place. People involved in deals with overseas partners can make windfall gains this month. People who are already in poor health should be careful of sustaining internal injuries.

農曆十一月 (December 7th – January 5th 2012) 庚子

This is not a favourable month to travel for business as the journey will be plagued by problems throughout. However, it is a good month for contractors to submit the tender for that 'job of a lifetime' as the outcome is likely to be positive. This is a difficult time for parents as sons challenge their authority. A change of room may be beneficial, especially if he is born in the Year of the Goat.

農曆十二月 (January 6th – February 3rd 2012) 辛丑

Avoid all investment opportunities this month as these are likely to turn sour. If this is unavoidable, then all contracts should be carefully scrutinised by a legal team. Women should have the necessary breast examinations and check-ups this month as malignancy is possible. Couples using this bedroom must be patient and tolerant, as both parties will listen to other people but not to each other resulting in frustration and resentment.

About Joey Yap

Joey Yap is the founder of the Mastery Academy of Chinese Metaphysics, a global organization devoted to the teaching of Feng Shui, BaZi, Mian Xiang and other Chinese Metaphysics subjects. He is also the Chief Consultant of Yap Global Consulting, an international consulting firm specialising in Feng Shui and Chinese Astrology services and audits.

Joey Yap is the bestselling author of over 30 books on Feng Shui, Chinese Astrology, Face Reading and Yi Jing, many of which have topped the Malaysian and Singaporean MPH bookstores' bestseller lists.

Thousands of students from all around the world have learnt and mastered Classical Feng Shui, Chinese Astrology, and other Chinese Metaphysics subjects through Joey Yap's structured learning programs, books and online training. Joey Yap's courses are currently taught by over 30 instructors worldwide.

Every year Joey Yap conducts his 'Feng Shui and Astrology' seminar to a crowd of more than 3500 people at the Kuala Lumpur Convention Center. He also takes this annual seminar on a world tour to Frankfurt, San Francisco, New York, Toronto, London, Sydney and Singapore.

In addition to being a regular guest on various radio and TV shows, Joey Yap has also written columns for The New Straits Times and The Star - Malaysia's two leading newspapers. He has also been featured in many popular global publications and networks like Time International, Forbes International, the International Herald Tribune and Bloomberg.

He has also hosted his own TV series, 'Discover Feng Shui with Joey Yap', on 8TV, a local Malaysian network in 2005; and 'Walking The Dragons with Joey Yap' on Astro Wah Lai Toi, Malaysia's cable network in 2008.

Joey Yap has worked with HSBC, Bloomberg, Microsoft, Samsung, IBM, HP, Alliance, Great Eastern, Citibank, Standard Chartered, OCBC, SIME UEP, Mah Sing, Auto Bavaria, Volvo, AXA, Singtel, ABN Amro, CIMB, Hong-Leong, Manulife and others.

Author's personal website :www.joeyyap.com

Joey Yap on Facebook:

 www.facebook.com/JoeyYapFB

EDUCATION
The Mastery Academy of Chinese Metaphysics:
the first choice for practitioners and aspiring students of the
art and science of Chinese Classical Feng Shui and Astrology.

For thousands of years, Eastern knowledge has been passed from one generation to another through the system of discipleship. A venerated master would accept suitable individuals at a young age as his disciples, and informally through the years, pass on his knowledge and skills to them. His disciples in turn, would take on their own disciples, as a means to perpetuate knowledge or skills.

This system served the purpose of restricting the transfer of knowledge to only worthy honourable individuals and ensuring that outsiders or Westerners would not have access to thousands of years of Eastern knowledge, learning and research.

However, the disciple system has also resulted in Chinese Metaphysics and Classical Studies lacking systematic teaching methods. Knowledge garnered over the years has not been accumulated in a concise, systematic manner, but scattered amongst practitioners, each practicing his/her knowledge, art and science, in isolation.

The disciple system, out of place in today's modern world, endangers the advancement of these classical fields that continue to have great relevance and application today.

At the Mastery Academy of Chinese Metaphysics, our Mission is to bring Eastern Classical knowledge in the fields of metaphysics, Feng Shui and Astrology sciences and the arts to the world. These Classical teachings and knowledge, previously shrouded in secrecy and passed on only through the discipleship system, are adapted into structured learning, which can easily be understood, learnt and mastered. Through modern learning methods, these renowned ancient arts, sciences and practices can be perpetuated while facilitating more extensive application and understanding of these classical subjects.

The Mastery Academy espouses an educational philosophy that draws from the best of the East and West. It is the world's premier educational institution for the study of Chinese Metaphysics Studies offering a wide range and variety of courses, ensuring that students have the opportunity to pursue their preferred field of study and enabling existing practitioners and professionals to gain cross-disciplinary knowledge that complements their current field of practice.

Courses at the Mastery Academy have been carefully designed to ensure a comprehensive yet compact syllabus. The modular nature of the courses enables students to immediately begin to put their knowledge into practice while pursuing continued study of their field and complementary fields. Students thus have the benefit of developing and gaining practical experience in tandem with the expansion and advancement of their theoretical knowledge.

Students can also choose from a variety of study options, from a distance learning program, the Homestudy Series, that enables study at one's own pace or intensive foundation courses and compact lecture-based courses, held in various cities around the world by Joey Yap or our licensed instructors. The Mastery Academy's faculty and make-up is international in nature, thus ensuring that prospective students can attend courses at destinations nearest to their country of origin or with a licensed Mastery Academy instructor in their home country.

The Mastery Academy provides 24x7 support to students through its Online Community, with a variety of tools, documents, forums and e-learning materials to help students stay at the forefront of research in their fields and gain invaluable assistance from peers and mentoring from their instructors.

TM

MASTERY ACADEMY
OF CHINESE METAPHYSICS

www.masteryacademy.com

MALAYSIA
19-3, The Boulevard
Mid Valley City
59200 Kuala Lumpur, Malaysia
Tel : +603-2284 8080
Fax : +603-2284 1218
Email : info@masteryacademy.com

Australia, Austria, Canada, China, Croatia, Cyprus, Czech Republic, Denmark, France, Germany, Greece, Hungary, India, Italy, Kazakhstan, Malaysia, Netherlands (Holland), New Zealand, Philippines, Poland, Russian Federation, Singapore, Slovenia, South Africa, Switzerland, Turkey, U.S.A., Ukraine, United Kingdom

Introducing...
The Mastery Academy's E-Learning Center!

The Mastery Academy's goal has always been to share authentic knowledge of Chinese Metaphysics with the whole world.

Nevertheless, we do recognize that distance, time, and hotel and traveling costs – amongst many other factors – could actually hinder people from enrolling for a classroom-based course. But with the advent and amazing advance of IT today, NOT any more!

With this in mind, we have invested heavily in IT, to conceive what is probably the first and only E-Learning Center in the world today that offers a full range of studies in the field of Chinese Metaphysics.

| Convenient | Study from Your Own Home | Easy Enrollment |

The Mastery Academy's E-Learning Center

Now, armed with your trusty computer or laptop, and Internet access, knowledge of classical Feng Shui, BaZi (Destiny Analysis) and Mian Xiang (Face Reading) are but a literal click away!

Study at your own pace, and interact with your Instructor and fellow students worldwide, from anywhere in the world. With our E-Learning Center, knowledge of Chinese Metaphysics is brought DIRECTLY to you in all its clarity – topic-by-topic, and lesson-by-lesson; with illustrated presentations and comprehensive notes expediting your learning curve!

Your education journey through our E-Learning Center may be done via any of the following approaches:

1. Online Courses

There are 3 Programs available: our Online Feng Shui Program, Online BaZi Program, and Online Mian Xiang Program. Each Program consists of several Levels, with each Level consisting of many Lessons in turn. Each Lesson contains a pre-recorded video session on the topic at hand, accompanied by presentation-slides and graphics as well as downloadable tutorial notes that you can print and file for future reference.

Video Lecture

Presentation Slide

Downloadable Notes

2. MA Live!

MA Live!, as its name implies, enables LIVE broadcasts of Joey Yap's courses and seminars – right to your computer screen. Students will not only get to see and hear Joey talk on real-time `live', but also participate and more importantly, TALK to Joey via the MA Live! interface. All the benefits of a live class, minus the hassle of actually having to attend one!

How It Works

Our Live Classes   You at Home

3. Video-On-Demand (VOD)

Get immediate streaming-downloads of the Mastery Academy's wide range of educational DVDs, right on your computer screen. No more shipping costs and waiting time to be incurred!

Instant VOD Online

Choose From Our list of Available VODs!   Click "Play" on Your PC

Welcome to **www.maelearning.com**; the web portal of our E-Learning Center, and YOUR virtual gateway to Chinese Metaphysics!

Mastery Academy around the world

Canada

United States

Denmark

United Kingdom

Czech Republic
Austria

Switzerland

Poland

Netherlands
France
Italy
Cyprus

Germany
Slovenia
Croatia
Greece
Hungary

Russian
Federation

Ukraine

Turkey

Kazakhstan

India

South Africa

China

Philippines
Kuala Lumpur
Malaysia

Singapore

Australia

New Zealand

YAP GLOBAL CONSULTING

Joey Yap & Yap Global Consulting

Headed by Joey Yap, Yap Global Consulting (YGC) is a leading international consulting firm specializing in Feng Shui, Mian Xiang (Face Reading) and BaZi (Destiny Analysis) consulting services worldwide. Joey Yap - an internationally renowned Master Trainer, Consultant, Speaker and best-selling Author - has dedicated his life to the art and science of Chinese Metaphysics.

YGC has its main office in Kuala Lumpur, and draws upon its diverse reservoir of strength from a group of dedicated and experienced consultants based in more than 30 countries, worldwide.

As the pioneer in blending established, classical Chinese Metaphysics techniques with the latest approach in consultation practices, YGC has built its reputation on the principles of professionalism and only the highest standards of service. This allows us to retain the cutting edge in delivering Feng Shui and Destiny consultation services to both corporate and personal clients, in a simple and direct manner, without compromising on quality.

Across Industries: Our Portfolio of Clients

Our diverse portfolio of both corporate and individual clients from all around the world bears testimony to our experience and capabilities.

Virtually every industry imaginable has benefited from our services - ranging from academic and financial institutions, real-estate developers and multinational corporations, to those in the leisure and tourism industry. Our services are also engaged by professionals, prominent business personalities, celebrities, high-profile politicians and people from all walks of life.

YAP GLOBAL CONSULTING

e (Mr./Mrs./Ms.):_____

:act Details

_____ Fax:_____

ile :_____

ail:_____

t Type of Consultation Are You Interested In?
□ eng Shui   □ BaZi   □ Date Selection   □ Yi Jing

e tick if applicable:
are you a Property Developer looking to engage Yap Global
onsulting?

are you a Property Investor looking for tailor-made pack-
ges to suit your investment requirements?

> Please attach your name card here.

Thank you for completing this form. Please fax it back to us at:

Malaysia & the rest of the world
Fax : +603-2284 2213   Tel : +603-2284 1213

---

www.joeyyap.com

Feng Shui Consultations

For Residential Properties
- Initial Land/Property Assessment
- Residential Feng Shui Consultations
- Residential Land Selection
- End-to-End Residential Consultation

For Commercial Properties
- Initial Land/Property Assessment
- Commercial Feng Shui Consultations
- Commercial Land Selection
- End-to-End Commercial Consultation

For Property Developers
- End-to-End Consultation
- Post-Consultation Advisory Services
- Panel Feng Shui Consultant

For Property Investors
- Your Personal Feng Shui Consultant
- Tailor-Made Packages

For Memorial Parks & Burial Sites
- Yin House Feng Shui

BaZi Consultations

Personal Destiny Analysis
- Personal Destiny Analysis for Individuals
- Children's BaZi Analysis
- Family BaZi Analysis

Strategic Analysis for Corporate Organizations
- Corporate BaZi Consultations
- BaZi Analysis for Human Resource Management

Entrepreneurs & Business Owners
- BaZi Analysis for Entrepreneurs

Career Pursuits
- BaZi Career Analysis

Relationships
- Marriage and Compatibility Analysis
- Partnership Analysis

For Everyone
- Annual BaZi Forecast
- Your Personal BaZi Coach

Date Selection Consultations

- **Marriage Date Selection**
- **Caesarean Birth Date Selection**
- **House-Moving Date Selection**
- **Renovation & Groundbreaking Dates**

- **Signing of Contracts**
- **Official Openings**
- **Product Launches**

Yi Jing Assessment

A Time-Tested, Accurate Science

- With a history predating 4 millennia, the Yi Jing - or Classic of Change - is one of the oldest Chinese texts surviving today. Its purpose as an oracle, in predicting the outcome of things, is based on the variables of Time, Space and Specific Events.

- A Yi Jing Assessment provides specific answers to any specific questions you may have about a specific event or endeavor. This is something that a Destiny Analysis would not be able to give you.

Basically, what a Yi Jing Assessment does is focus on only ONE aspect or item at a particular point in your life, and give you a calculated prediction of the details that will follow suit, if you undertake a particular action. It gives you an insight into a situation, and what course of action to take in order to arrive at a satisfactory outcome at the end of the day.

Please Contact YGC for a personalized Yi Jing Assessment!

INVITING US TO YOUR CORPORATE EVENTS

Many reputable organizations and institutions have worked closely with YGC to build a synergistic business relationship by engaging our team of consultants, led by Joey Yap, as speakers at their corporate events. Our seminars and short talks are always packed with audiences consisting of clients and associates of multinational and public-listed companies as well as key stakeholders of financial institutions.

We tailor our seminars and talks to suit the anticipated or pertinent group of audience. Be it a department, subsidiary, your clients or even the entire corporation, we aim to fit your requirements in delivering the intended message(s).

Tel: +603-2284 1213   Email: consultation@joeyyap.com

CHINESE METAPHYSICS REFERENCE SERIES

The Chinese Metaphysics Reference Series is a collection of reference texts, source material, and educational textbooks to be used as supplementary guides by scholars, students, researchers, teachers and practitioners of Chinese Metaphysics.

These comprehensive and structured books provide fast, easy reference to aid in the study and practice of various Chinese Metaphysics subjects including Feng Shui, BaZi, Yi Jing, Zi Wei, Liu Ren, Ze Ri, Ta Yi, Qi Men and Mian Xiang.

The Chinese Metaphysics Compendium

At over 1,000 pages, the *Chinese Metaphysics Compendium* is a unique one-volume reference book that compiles all the formulas relating to Feng Shui, BaZi (Four Pillars of Destiny), Zi Wei (Purple Star Astrology), Yi Jing (I-Ching), Qi Men (Mystical Doorways), Ze Ri (Date Selection), Mian Xiang (Face Reading) and other sources of Chinese Metaphysics.

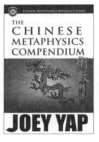

It is presented in the form of easy-to-read tables, diagrams and reference charts, all of which are compiled into one handy book. This first-of-its-kind compendium is presented in both English and the original Chinese, so that none of the meanings and contexts of the technical terminologies are lost.

The only essential and comprehensive reference on Chinese Metaphysics, and an absolute must-have for all students, scholars, and practitioners of Chinese Metaphysics.

The Ten Thousand Year Calendar

Dong Gong Date Selection

The Date Selection Compendium

Plum Blossoms Divination Reference Book

San Yuan Dragon Gate Eight Formations Water Method

Xuan Kong Da Gua Ten Thousand Year Calendar

Xuan Kong Da Gua Structures Reference Book

Xuan Kong Da Gua 64 Gua Transformation Analysis

Xuan Kong Purple White Script

Earth Study Discern Truth Second Edition

Bazi Structures and Structural Useful Gods - Wood

Bazi Structures and Structural Useful Gods - Fire

Bazi Structures and Structural Useful Gods - Earth

Bazi Structures and Structural Useful Gods - Metal

Bazi Structures and Structural Useful Gods - Water

Educational Tools & Software

Xuan Kong Flying Stars Feng Shui Software
The Essential Application for Enthusiasts and Professionals

The Xuan Kong Flying Stars Feng Shui Software is a brand-new application by Joey Yap that will assist you in the practice of Xuan Kong Feng Shui with minimum fuss and maximum effectiveness. Superimpose the Flying Stars charts over your house plans (or those of your clients) to clearly demarcate the 9 Palaces. Use it to help you create fast and sophisticated chart drawings and presentations, as well as to assist professional practitioners in the report-writing process before presenting the final reports for your clients. Students can use it to practice their Xuan Kong Feng Shui skills and knowledge, and it can even be used by designers and architects!

Some of the highlights of the software include:
- Natal Flying Stars
- Monthly Flying Stars
- 81 Flying Stars Combinations
- Dual-View Format
- Annual Flying Stars
- Flying Stars Integration
- 24 Mountains

All charts will be are printable and configurable, and can be saved for future editing. Also, you'll be able to export your charts into most image file formats like jpeg, bmp, and gif.

The Xuan Kong Flying Stars Feng Shui Software can make your Feng Shui practice simpler and more effective, garnering you amazing results with less effort!

Mini Feng Shui Compass

This Mini Feng Shui Compass with the accompanying Companion Booklet written by leading Feng Shui and Chinese Astrology Master Trainer Joey Yap is a must-have for any Feng Shui enthusiast.

The Mini Feng Shui Compass is a self-aligning compass that is not only light at 100gms but also built sturdily to ensure it will be convenient to use anywhere. The rings on the Mini Feng Shui Compass are bi-lingual and incorporate the 24 Mountain Rings that is used in your traditional Luo Pan.

The comprehensive booklet included will guide you in applying the 24 Mountain Directions on your Mini Feng Shui Compass effectively and the 8 Mansions Feng Shui to locate the most auspicious locations within your home, office and surroundings. You can also use the Mini Feng Shui Compass when measuring the direction of your property for the purpose of applying Flying Stars Feng Shui.

Educational Tools & Software

BaZi Ming Pan Software Version 2.0
Professional Four Pillars Calculator for Destiny Analysis

The BaZi Ming Pan Version 2.0 Professional Four Pillars Calculator for Destiny Analysis is the most technically advanced software of its kind in the world today. It allows even those without any knowledge of BaZi to generate their own BaZi Charts, and provides virtually every detail required to undertake a comprehensive Destiny Analysis.

This Professional Four Pillars Calculator allows you to even undertake a day-to-day analysis of your Destiny. What's more, all BaZi Charts generated by this software are fully printable and configurable! Designed for both enthusiasts and professional practitioners, this state-of-the-art software blends details with simplicity, and is capable of generating 4 different types of BaZi charts: **BaZi Professional Charts, BaZi Annual Analysis Charts, BaZi Pillar Analysis Charts and BaZi Family Relationship Charts.**

Additional references, configurable to cater to all levels of BaZi knowledge and usage, include:
• Dual Age & Bilingual Option (Western & Chinese) • Na Yin narrations • 12 Life Stages evaluation • Death & Emptiness • Gods & Killings • Special Days • Heavenly Virtue Nobles

This software also comes with a Client Management feature that allows you to save and trace clients' records instantly, navigate effortlessly between BaZi charts, and file your clients' information in an organized manner.

The BaZi Ming Pan Version 2.0 Calculator sets a new standard by combining the best of BaZi and technology.

Joey Yap Feng Shui Template Set

Directions are the cornerstone of any successful Feng Shui audit or application. The **Joey Yap Feng Shui Template Set** is a set of three templates to simplify the process of taking directions and determining locations and positions, whether it's for a building, a house, or an open area such as a plot of land, all with just a floor plan or area map.

The Set comprises 3 basic templates: The Basic Feng Shui Template, 8 Mansions Feng Shui Template, and the Flying Stars Feng Shui Template.

With bi-lingual notations for these directions; both in English and the original Chinese, the **Joey Yap Feng Shui Template Set** comes with its own Booklet that gives simple yet detailed instructions on how to make use of the 3 templates within.

• Easy-to-use, simple, and straightforward
• Small and portable; each template measuring only 5" x 5"
• Additional 8 Mansions and Flying Stars Reference Rings
• Handy companion booklet with usage tips and examples

Accelerate Your Face Reading Skills With
Joey Yap's Face Reading Revealed DVD Series

Mian Xiang, the Chinese art of Face Reading, is an ancient form of physiognomy and entails the use of the face and facial characteristics to evaluate key aspects of a person's life, luck and destiny. In his Face Reading DVDs series, Joey Yap shows you how the facial features reveal a wealth of information about a person's luck, destiny and personality.

Mian Xiang also tell us the talents, quirks and personality of an individual. Do you know that just by looking at a person's face, you can ascertain his or her health, wealth, relationships and career? Let Joey Yap show you how the 12 Palaces can be utilised to reveal a person's inner talents, characteristics and much more.

Each facial feature on the face represents one year in a person's life. Your face is a 100-year map of your life and each position reveals your fortune and destiny at a particular age as well as insights and information about your personality, skills, abilities and destiny.

Using Mian Xiang, you will also be able to plan your life ahead by identifying, for example, the right business partner and knowing the sort of person that you need to avoid. By knowing their characteristics through the facial features, you will be able to gauge their intentions and gain an upper hand in negotiations.

Do you know what moles signify? Do they bring good or bad luck? Do you want to build better relationships with your partner or family members or have your ever wondered why you seem to be always bogged down by trivial problems in your life?

In these highly entertaining DVDs, Joey will help you answer all these questions and more. You will be able to ascertain the underlying meaning of moles, birthmarks or even the type of your hair in Face Reading. Joey will also reveal the guidelines to help you foster better and stronger relationships with your loved ones through Mian Xiang.

Feng Shui for Homebuyers DVD Series

Best-selling Author, and international Master Trainer and Consultant Joey Yap reveals in these DVDs the significant Feng Shui features that every homebuyer should know when evaluating a property.

Joey will guide you on how to customise your home to maximise the Feng Shui potential of your property and gain the full benefit of improving your health, wealth and love life using the 9 Palace Grid. He will show you how to go about applying the classical applications of the Life Gua and House Gua techniques to get attuned to your Sheng Qi (positive energies).

In these DVDs, you will also learn how to identify properties with good Feng Shui features that will help you promote a fulfilling life and achieve your full potential. Discover how to avoid properties with negative Feng Shui that can bring about detrimental effects to your health, wealth and relationships.

Joey will also elaborate on how to fix the various aspects of your home that may have an impact on the Feng Shui of your property and give pointers on how to tap into the positive energies to support your goals.

Discover Feng Shui with Joey Yap (TV Series)

Discover Feng Shui with Joey Yap: Set of 4 DVDs

Informative and entertaining, classical Feng Shui comes alive in *Discover Feng Shui with Joey Yap!*

Dying to know how you can use Feng Shui to improve your house or office, but simply too busy attend for formal classes?

You have the questions. Now let Joey personally answer them in this 4-set DVD compilation! Learn how to ensure the viability of your residence or workplace, Feng Shui-wise, without having to convert it into a Chinese antiques' shop. Classical Feng Shui is about harnessing the natural power of your environment to improve quality of life. It's a systematic and subtle metaphysical science.

And that's not all. Joey also debunks many a myth about classical Feng Shui, and shares with viewers Face Reading tips as well!

Own the series that national channel 8TV did a re-run of in 2005, today!

Continue Your Journey with Joey Yap's Books

Pure Feng Shui

Pure Feng Shui is Joey Yap's debut with an international publisher, CICO Books, and is a refreshing and elegant look at the intricacies of Classical Feng Shui – now compiled in a useful manner for modern-day readers. This book is a comprehensive introduction to all the important precepts and techniques of Feng Shui practice.

He reveals how to use Feng Shui to bring prosperity, good relationships, and success into one's life the simple and genuine way – without having to resort to symbols or figurines! He shows readers how to work with what they have and make simple and sustainable changes that can have significant Feng Shui effect. The principles of Classical Feng Shui and Chinese Astrology inform his teachings and explanations, so all that the readers need are a compass, a pencil, some paper, and an open mind!

Joey Yap's Art of Face Reading

The Art of Face Reading is Joey Yap's second effort with CICO Books, and takes a lighter, more practical approach to Face Reading. This book does not so much focus on the individual features as it does on reading the entire face. It is about identifying common personality types and characters.

Joey shows readers how to identify successful career faces, or faces that are most likely to be able to do well financially. He also explores Face Reading in the context of health. He uses examples of real people - famous and ordinary folk - to allow readers to better understand what these facial features look like on an actual face. Readers will learn how to identify faces in Career, Wealth, Relationships, and Health (eg. 'The Salesperson Face,' 'The Politician Face,' 'The Unfaithful One,' 'The Shopaholic One,' and plenty more.)

Continue Your Journey with Joey Yap's Books

Easy Guide on Face Reading (English & Chinese versions)

The Face Reading Essentials series of books comprise 5 individual books on the key features of the face – Eyes, Eyebrows, Ears, Nose, and Mouth. Each book provides a detailed illustration and a simple yet descriptive explanation on the individual types of the features.

The books are equally useful and effective for beginners, enthusiasts, and the curious. The series is designed to enable people who are new to Face Reading to make the most of first impressions and learn to apply Face Reading skills to understand the personality and character of friends, family, co-workers, and even business associates.

 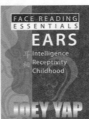  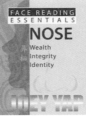 

BaZi Essentials Series (English & Chinese versions)

The BaZi Essentials series of books comprise 10 individual books that focus on the individual Day Masters in BaZi (Four Pillars of Destiny, or Chinese Astrology) study and analysis. With each book focusing on one particular Day Master, Joey explains why the Day Master is the fundamental starting point for BaZi analysis, and is the true essence of one's character traits and basic identity.

With these concise and entertaining books that are designed to be both informative and entertaining, Joey shows how each person is different and unique, yet share similar traits, according to his or her respective Day Master. These 10 guides will provide crucial insight into why people behave in the various different ways they do.

    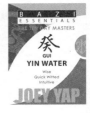

Continue Your Journey with Joey Yap's Books

Walking the Dragons

Walking the Dragons is a guided tour through the classical landform Feng Shui of ancient China, an enchanting collection of deeply-researched yet entertaining essays rich in historical detail.

Compiled in one book for the first time from Joey Yap's Feng Shui Mastery Excursion Series, the book highlights China's extensive, vibrant history with astute observations on the Feng Shui of important sites and places. Learn the landform formations of Yin Houses (tombs and burial places), as well as mountains, temples, castles, and villages.

It demonstrates complex Feng Shui theories and principles in easy-to-understand, entertaining language and is the perfect addition to the bookshelf of a Feng Shui or history lover. Anyone, whether experienced in Feng Shui or new to the practice, will be able to enjoy the insights shared in this book. Complete with gorgeous full-colour pictures of all the amazing sights and scenery, it's the next best thing to having been there yourself!

Your Aquarium Here

Your Aquarium Here is a simple, practical, hands-on Feng Shui book that teaches you how to incorporate a Water feature – an aquarium – for optimal Feng Shui benefit, whether for personal relationships, wealth, or career. Designed to be comprehensive yet simple enough for a novice or beginner, *Your Aquarium Here* provides historical and factual information about the role of Water in Feng Shui, and provides a step-by-step guide to installing and using an aquarium.

The book is the first in the **Fengshuilogy Series**, a series of matter-of-fact and useful Feng Shui books designed for the person who wants to do fuss-free Feng Shui. Not everyone who wants to use Feng Shui is an expert or a scholar! This series of books are just the kind you'd want on your bookshelf to gain basic, practical knowledge of the subject. Go ahead and Feng Shui-It-Yourself – *Your Aquarium Here* eliminates all the fuss and bother, but maintains all the fun and excitement, of authentic Feng Shui application!

The Art of Date Selection: Personal Date Selection

In today's modern world, it is not good enough to just do things effectively – we need to do them efficiently, as well. From the signing of business contracts and moving into a new home, to launching a product or even tying the knot; everything has to move, and move very quickly too. There is a premium on Time, where mistakes can indeed be costly.

The notion of doing the Right Thing, at the Right Time and in the Right Place is the very backbone of Date Selection. Because by selecting a suitable date specially tailored to a specific activity or endeavor, we infuse it with the most positive energies prevalent in our environment during that particular point in time; and that could well make the difference between `make-and-break'! With the *Art of Date Selection: Personal Date Selection*, learn simple, practical methods you can employ to select not just good dates, but personalized good dates. Whether it's a personal activity such as a marriage or professional endeavor such as launching a business, signing a contract or even acquiring assets, this book will show you how to pick the good dates and tailor them to suit the activity in question, as well as avoid the negative ones too!

The Art of Date Selection: Feng Shui Date Selection

Date Selection is the Art of selecting the most suitable date, where the energies present on the day support the specific activities or endeavors we choose to undertake on that day. Feng Shui is the Chinese Metaphysical study of the Physiognomy of the Land – landforms and the Qi they produce, circulate and conduct. Hence, anything that exists on this Earth is invariably subject to the laws of Feng Shui. So what do we get when Date Selection and Feng Shui converge?

Feng Shui Date Selection, of course! Say you wish to renovate your home, or maybe buy or rent one. Or perhaps, you're a developer, and wish to know WHEN is the best date possible to commence construction works on your project. In any case – and all cases – you certainly wish to ensure that your endeavors are well supported by the positive energies present on a good day, won't you? And this is where Date Selection supplements the practice of Feng Shui. At the end of the day, it's all about making the most of what's good, and minimizing what's bad.

(Available Soon)

Continue Your Journey with Joey Yap's Books

Feng Shui For Homebuyers - Exterior (English & Chinese versions)

Best selling Author and international Feng Shui Consultant, Joey Yap, will guide you on the various important features in your external environment that have a bearing on the Feng Shui of your home. For homeowners, those looking to build their own home or even investors who are looking to apply Feng Shui to their homes, this book provides valuable information from the classical Feng Shui theories and applications.

This book will assist you in screening and eliminating unsuitable options with negative FSQ (Feng Shui Quotient) should you acquire your own land or if you are purchasing a newly built home. It will also help you in determining which plot of land to select and which to avoid when purchasing an empty parcel of land.

Feng Shui for Homebuyers - Interior (English & Chinese versions)

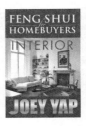

A book every homeowner or potential house buyer should have. The Feng Shui for Homebuyers (Interior) is an informative reference book and invaluable guide written by best selling Author and international Feng Shui Consultant, Joey Yap.

This book provides answers to the important questions of what really does matter when looking at the internal Feng Shui of a home or office. It teaches you how to analyze your home or office floor plans and how to improve their Feng Shui. It will answer all your questions about the positive and negative flow of Qi within your home and ways to utilize them to your maximum benefit.

Providing you with a guide to calculating your Life Gua and House Gua to fine-tune your Feng Shui within your property, Joey Yap focuses on practical, easily applicable ideas on what you can implement internally in a property.

Feng Shui for Apartment Buyers - Home Owners

Finding a good apartment or condominium is never an easy task but who do you ensure that is also has good Feng Shui? And how exactly do you apply Feng Shui to an apartment or condominium or high-rise residence?

These questions and more are answered by renowned Feng Shui Consultant and Master Trainer Joey Yap in **Feng Shui for Apartment Buyers - Home Owners**. Joey answers the key questions about Feng Shui and apartments, then guides you through the bare basics like taking a direction and super-imposing a Flying Stars chart onto a floor plan. Joey also walks you through the process of finding an apartment with favorable Feng Shui, sharing with you some of the key methods and techniques that are employed by professional Feng Shui consultants in assesing apartment Feng Shui.

In his trademark straight-to-the-point manner, Joey shares with you the Feng Shui do's and dont's when it comes to finding an apartment with favorable Feng Shui and which is conducive for home living.

The Ten Thousand Year Calendar

The Ten Thousand Year Calendar or 萬年曆 Wan Nian Li is a regular reference book and an invaluable tool used by masters, practitioners and students of Feng Shui, BaZi (Four Pillars of Destiny), Chinese Zi Wei Dou Shu Astrology (Purple Star), Yi Jing (I-Ching) and Date Selection specialists.

JOEY YAP's Ten Thousand Year Calendar provides the Gregorian (Western) dates converted into both the Chinese Solar and Lunar calendar in both the English and Chinese language.

It also includes a comprehensive set of key Feng Shui and Chinese Astrology charts and references, including Xuan Kong Nine Palace Flying Star Charts, Monthly and Daily Flying Stars, Water Dragon Formulas Reference Charts, Zi Wei Dou Shu (Purple Star) Astrology Reference Charts, BaZi (Four Pillars of Destiny) Heavenly Stems, Earthly Branches and all other related reference tables for Chinese Metaphysical Studies.

Continue Your Journey with Joey Yap's Books

Stories and Lessons on Feng Shui (English & Chinese versions)

Stories and Lessons on Feng Shui is a compilation of essays and stories written by leading Feng Shui and Chinese Astrology trainer and consultant Joey Yap about Feng Shui and Chinese Astrology.

In this heart-warming collection of easy to read stories, find out why it's a myth that you should never have Water on the right hand side of your house, the truth behind the infamous 'love' and 'wealth' corners and that the sudden death of a pet fish is really NOT due to bad luck!

More Stories and Lessons on Feng Shui

Finally, the long-awaited sequel to *Stories & Lessons on Feng Shui*!

If you've read the best-selling Stories & Lessons on Feng Shui, you won't want to miss this book. And even if you haven't read *Stories & Lessons on Feng Shui*, there's always a time to rev your Feng Shui engine up.

The time is NOW.

And the book? *More Stories & Lessons on Feng Shui* – the 2nd compilation of the most popular articles and columns penned by Joey Yap; **specially featured in national and international publications, magazines and newspapers.**

All in all, *More Stories & Lessons on Feng Shui* is a delightful chronicle of Joey's articles, thoughts and vast experience - as a professional Feng Shui consultant and instructor - that have been purposely refined, edited and expanded upon to make for a light-hearted, interesting yet educational read. And with Feng Shui, BaZi, Mian Xiang and Yi Jing all thrown into this one dish, there's something for everyone…so all you need to serve or accompany *More Stories & Lessons on Feng Shui* with is your favorite cup of tea or coffee!

Even More Stories and Lessons on Feng Shui

In this third release in the Stories and Lessons series, Joey Yap continues his exploration on the study and practice of Feng Shui in the modern age through a series of essays and personal anecdotes. Debunking superstition, offering simple and understandable "Feng Shui-It-Yourself" tips, and expounding on the history and origins of classical Feng Shui, Joey takes readers on a journey that is always refreshing and exciting.

Besides 'behind-the-scenes' revelations of actual Feng Shui audits, there are also chapters on how beginners can easily and accurately incorporate Feng Shui practice into their lives, as well as travel articles that offer proof that when it comes to Feng Shui, the Qi literally knows no boundaries.

In his trademark lucid and forthright style, Joey covers themes and topics that will strike a chord with all readers who have an interest in Feng Shui.

Mian Xiang - Discover Face Reading (English & Chinese versions)

Need to identify a suitable business partner? How about understanding your staff or superiors better? Or even choosing a suitable spouse? These mind boggling questions can be answered in Joey Yap's introductory book to Face Reading titled *Mian Xiang – Discover Face Reading*. This book will help you discover the hidden secrets in a person's face.

Mian Xiang – Discover Face Reading is comprehensive book on all areas of Face Reading, covering some of the most important facial features, including the forehead, mouth, ears and even the philtrum above your lips. This book will help you analyse not just your Destiny but help you achieve your full potential and achieve life fulfillment.

Continue Your Journey with Joey Yap's Books

BaZi - The Destiny Code (English & Chinese versions)

Leading Chinese Astrology Master Trainer Joey Yap makes it easy to learn how to unlock your Destiny through your BaZi with this book. BaZi or Four Pillars of Destiny is an ancient Chinese science which enables individuals to understand their personality, hidden talents and abilities as well as their luck cycle, simply by examining the information contained within their birth data. *The Destiny Code* is the first book that shows readers how to plot and interpret their own Destiny Charts and lays the foundation for more in-depth BaZi studies. Written in a lively entertaining style, the Destiny Code makes BaZi accessible to the layperson. Within 10 chapters, understand and appreciate more about this astoundingly accurate ancient Chinese Metaphysical science.

BaZi - The Destiny Code Revealed

In this follow up to Joey Yap's best-selling *The Destiny Code*, delve deeper into your own Destiny chart through an understanding of the key elemental relationships that affect the Heavenly Stems and Earthly Branches. Find out how Combinations, Clash, Harm, Destructions and Punishments bring new dimension to a BaZi chart. Complemented by extensive real-life examples, *The Destiny Code Revealed* takes you to the next level of BaZi, showing you how to unlock the Codes of Destiny and to take decisive action at the right time, and capitalise on the opportunities in life.

Xuan Kong: Flying Stars Feng Shui

Xuan Kong Flying Stars Feng Shui is an essential introductory book to the subject of Xuan Kong Fei Xing, a well-known and popular system of Feng Shui, written by International Feng Shui Master Trainer Joey Yap.

In his down-to-earth, entertaining and easy to read style, Joey Yap takes you through the essential basics of Classical Feng Shui, and the key concepts of Xuan Kong Fei Xing (Flying Stars). Learn how to fly the stars, plot a Flying Star chart for your home or office and interpret the stars and star combinations. Find out how to utilise the favourable areas of your home or office for maximum benefit and learn 'tricks of the trade' and 'trade secrets' used by Feng Shui practitioners to enhance and maximise Qi in your home or office.

An essential integral introduction to the subject of Classical Feng Shui and the Flying Stars System of Feng Shui!

Xuan Kong Flying Stars: Structures and Combinations

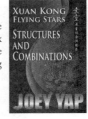

Delve deeper into Flying Stars through a greater understanding of the 81 Combinations and the influence of the Annual and Monthly Stars on the Base, Sitting and Facing Stars in this 2nd book in the Xuan Kong Feng Shui series. Learn how Structures like the Combination of 10, Up the Mountain and Down the River, Pearl and Parent String Structures are used to interpret a Flying Star chart.

(Available Soon)

Xuan Kong Flying Stars: Advanced Techniques

Take your knowledge of Xuan Kong Flying Stars to a higher level and learn how to apply complex techniques and advanced formulas such as Castle Gate Technique, Seven Star Robbery Formation, Advancing the Dragon Formation and Replacement Star technique amongst others. Joey Yap also shows you how to use the Life Palace technique to combine Gua Numbers with Flying Star numbers and utilise the predictive facets of Flying Stars Feng Shui.

(Available Soon)

Annual Releases

Chinese Astrology for 2010

This information-packed annual guide to the Chinese Astrology for 2010 goes way beyond the conventional `animal horoscope' book. To begin with, author Joey Yap includes a personalized outlook for 2010 based on the individual's BaZi Day Pillar (Jia Zi) and a 12-month micro-analysis for each of the 60 Day Pillars – in addition to the annual outlook for all 12 animal signs and the 12-month outlook for each animal sign in 2010. Find out what awaits you in 2010 from the four key aspects of Health, Wealth, Career and Relationships…with Joey Yap's **Chinese Astrology for 2010**!

Feng Shui for 2010

Maximize the Qi of the Year of the Metal Tiger for your home and office, with Joey Yap's **Feng Shui for 2010** book. Learn how to tap into the positive sectors of the year, and avoid the negative ones and those with the Annual Afflictions, as well as ascertain how the annual Flying Stars affect your property by comparing them against the Eight Mansions (Ba Zhai) for 2010. Flying Stars enthusiasts will also find this book handy, as it includes the monthly Flying Stars charts for the year, accompanied by detailed commentaries on what sectors to use and avoid – to enable you to optimize your Academic, Relationships and Wealth Luck in 2010.

Weekly Tong Shu Diary 2010

Organize your professional and personal lives with the **Tong Shu Diary 2010**, with a twist… it also allows you to determine the most suitable dates on which you can undertake important activities and endeavors throughout the year! This compact Diary integrates the Chinese Solar and Lunar Calendars with the universal lingua franca of the Gregorian Calendar.

Tong Shu Monthly Planner 2010

Tailor-made for the Feng Shui or BaZi enthusiast in you, or even professional Chinese Metaphysics consultants who want a compact planner with useful information incorporated into it. In the **Tong Shu Monthly Planner 2010**, you will find the auspicious and inauspicious dates for the year marked out for you, alongside the most suitable activities to be undertaken on each day. As a bonus, there is also a reference section containing all the monthly Flying Stars charts and Annual Afflictions for 2010.

Tong Shu Desktop Calendar 2010

Get an instant snapshot of the suitable and unsuitable activities for each day of the Year of the Earth Rat, with the icons displayed on this lightweight Desktop Calendar. Elegantly presenting the details of the Chinese Solar Calendar in the form of the standard Gregorian one, the **Tong Shu Desktop Calendar 2010** is perfect for Chinese Metaphysics enthusiasts and practitioners alike. Whether it a business launching or meeting, ground breaking ceremony, travel or house-moving that you have in mind, this Calendar is designed to fulfill your information needs.

Tong Shu Year Planner 2010

This one-piece Planner presents you all the essential information you need for significant activities or endeavors…with just a quick glance! In a nutshell, it allows you to identify the favorable and unfavorable days, which will in turn enable you to schedule your year's activities so as to make the most of good days, and avoid the ill-effects brought about by inauspicious ones.

Elevate Your Feng Shui Skills With Joey Yap's Home Study Course And Educational DVDs

Xuan Kong Vol.1
An Advanced Feng Shui Home Study Course

Learn the Xuan Kong Flying Star Feng Shui system in just 20 lessons! Joey Yap's specialised notes and course work have been written to enable distance learning without compromising on the breadth or quality of the syllabus. Learn at your own pace with the same material students in a live class would use. The most comprehensive distance learning course on Xuan Kong Flying Star Feng Shui in the market. Xuan Kong Flying Star Vol.1 comes complete with a special binder for all your course notes.

Feng Shui for Period 8 - (DVD)

Don't miss the Feng Shui Event of the next 20 years! Catch Joey Yap LIVE and find out just what Period 8 is all about. This DVD boxed set zips you through the fundamentals of Feng Shui and the impact of this important change in the Feng Shui calendar. Joey's entertaining, conversational style walks you through the key changes that Period 8 will bring and how to tap into Wealth Qi and Good Feng Shui for the next 20 years.

Xuan Kong Flying Stars Beginners Workshop - (DVD)

Take a front row seat in Joey Yap's Xuan Kong Flying Stars workshop with this unique LIVE RECORDING of Joey Yap's Xuan Kong Flying Stars Feng Shui workshop, attended by over 500 people. This DVD program provides an effective and quick introduction of Xuan Kong Feng Shui essentials for those who are just starting out in their study of classical Feng Shui. Learn to plot your own Flying Star chart in just 3 hours. Learn 'trade secret' methods, remedies and cures for Flying Stars Feng Shui. This boxed set contains 3 DVDs and 1 workbook with notes and charts for reference.

BaZi Four Pillars of Destiny Beginners Workshop - (DVD)

Ever wondered what Destiny has in store for you? Or curious to know how you can learn more about your personality and inner talents? BaZi or Four Pillars of Destiny is an ancient Chinese science that enables us to understand a person's hidden talent, inner potential, personality, health and wealth luck from just their birth data. This specially compiled DVD set of Joey Yap's BaZi Beginners Workshop provides a thorough and comprehensive introduction to BaZi. Learn how to read your own chart and understand your own luck cycle. This boxed set contains 3 DVDs and 1 workbook with notes and reference charts.

Interested in learning MORE about Feng Shui? Advance Your Feng Shui Knowledge with the Mastery Academy Courses.

Feng Shui Mastery Series™
LIVE COURSES (MODULES ONE TO FOUR)

Feng Shui Mastery – Module One
Beginners Course

Designed for students seeking an entry-level intensive program into the study of Feng Shui , Module One is an intensive foundation course that aims not only to provide you with an introduction to Feng Shui theories and formulas and equip you with the skills and judgments to begin practicing and conduct simple Feng Shui audits upon successful completion of the course. Learn all about Forms, Eight Mansions Feng Shui and Flying Star Feng Shui in just one day with a unique, structured learning program that makes learning Feng Shui quick and easy!

Feng Shui Mastery – Module Two
Practitioners Course

Building on the knowledge and foundation in classical Feng Shui theory garnered in M1, M2 provides a more advanced and in-depth understanding of Eight Mansions, Xuan Kong Flying Star and San He and introduces students to theories that are found only in the classical Chinese Feng Shui texts. This 3-Day Intensive course hones analytical and judgment skills, refines Luo Pan (Chinese Feng Shui compass) skills and reveals 'trade secret' remedies. Module Two covers advanced Forms Analysis, San He's Five Ghost Carry Treasure formula, Advanced Eight Mansions and Xuan Kong Flying Stars and equips you with the skills needed to undertake audits and consultations for residences and offices.

Feng Shui Mastery – Module Three
Advanced Practitioners Course

Module Three is designed for Professional Feng Shui Practitioners. Learn advanced topics in Feng Shui and take your skills to a cutting edge level. Be equipped with the knowledge, techniques and confidence to conduct large scale audits (like estate and resort planning). Learn how to apply different systems appropriately to remedy situations or cases deemed inauspicious by one system and reconcile conflicts in different systems of Feng Shui. Gain advanced knowledge of San He (Three Harmony) systems and San Yuan (Three Cycles) systems, advanced Luan Tou (Forms Feng Shui) and specialist Water Formulas.

Feng Shui Mastery – Module Four
Master Course

The graduating course of the Feng Shui Mastery (FSM) Series, this course takes the advanced practitioner to the Master level. Power packed M4 trains students to 'walk the mountains' and identify superior landform, superior grade structures and make qualitative evaluations of landform, structures, Water and Qi and covers advanced and exclusive topics of San He, San Yuan, Xuan Kong, Ba Zhai, Luan Tou (Advanced Forms and Water Formula) Feng Shui. Master Internal, External and Luan Tou (Landform) Feng Shui methodologies to apply Feng Shui at every level and undertake consultations of every scale and magnitude, from houses and apartments to housing estates, townships, shopping malls and commercial districts.

BaZi Mastery Series™
LIVE COURSES (MODULES ONE TO FOUR)

BaZi Mastery – Module One
Intensive Foundation Course

This Intensive One Day Foundation Course provides an introduction to the principles and fundamentals of BaZi (Four Pillars of Destiny) and Destiny Analysis methods such as Ten Gods, Useful God and Strength of Qi. Learn how to plot a BaZi chart and interpret your Destiny and your potential. Master BaZi and learn to capitalize on your strengths, minimize risks and downturns and take charge of your Destiny.

BaZi Mastery – Module Two
Practitioners Course

BaZi Module Two teaches students advanced BaZi analysis techniques and specific analysis methods for relationship luck, health evaluation, wealth potential and career potential. Students will learn to identify BaZi chart structures, sophisticated methods for applying the Ten Gods, and how to read Auxiliary Stars. Students who have completed Module Two will be able to conduct professional BaZi readings.

BaZi Mastery – Module Three
Advanced Practitioners Course

Designed for the BaZi practitioner, learn how to read complex cases and unique events in BaZi charts and perform Big and Small assessments. Discover how to analyze personalities and evaluate talents precisely, as well as special formulas and classical methodologies for BaZi from classics such as Di Tian Sui and Qiong Tong Bao Jian.

BaZi Mastery – Module Four
Master Course in BaZi

The graduating course of the BaZi Mastery Series, this course takes the advanced practitioner to the Masters' level. BaZi M4 focuses on specialized techniques of BaZi reading, unique special structures and advance methods from ancient classical texts. This program includes techniques on date selection and ancient methodologies from the Qiong Tong Bao Jian and Yuan Hai Zi Ping classics.

Xuan Kong Mastery – Module One
Advanced Foundation Course

This course is for the experienced Feng Shui professionals who wish to expand their knowledge and skills in the Xuan Kong system of Feng Shui, covering important foundation methods and techniques from the Wu Chang and Guang Dong lineages of Xuan Kong Feng Shui.

Xuan Kong Mastery – Module Two A
Advanced Xuan Kong Methodologies

Designed for Feng Shui practitioners seeking to specialise in the Xuan Kong system, this program focuses on methods of application and Joey Yap's unique Life Palace and Shifting Palace Methods, as well as methods and techniques from the Wu Chang lineage.

Xuan Kong Mastery – Module Two B
Purple White

Explore in detail and in great depth the star combinations in Xuan Kong. Learn how each different combination reacts or responds in different palaces, under different environmental circumstances and to whom in the property. Learn methods, theories and techniques extracted from ancient classics such as Xuan Kong Mi Zhi, Xuan Kong Fu, Fei Xing Fu and Zi Bai Jue.

Xuan Kong Mastery – Module Three
Advanced Xuan Kong Da Gua

This intensive course focuses solely on the Xuan Kong Da Gua system covering the theories, techniques and methods of application of this unique 64-Hexagram based system of Xuan Kong including Xuan Kong Da Gua for landform analysis.

Walk the Mountains! Learn Feng Shui in a Practical and Hands-on Program

 Feng Shui Mastery Excursion Series™ : CHINA

Learn landform (Luan Tou) Feng Shui by walking the mountains and chasing the Dragon's vein in China. This Program takes the students in a study tour to examine notable Feng Shui landmarks, mountains, hills, valleys, ancient palaces, famous mansions, houses and tombs in China. The Excursion is a 'practical' hands-on course where students are shown to perform readings using the formulas they've learnt and to recognize and read Feng Shui Landform (Luan Tou) formations.

Read about China Excursion here:
http://www.masteryacademy.com/Education/schoolfengshui/fengshuimasteryexcursion.asp

Mian Xiang Mastery Series™
LIVE COURSES (MODULES ONE AND TWO)

Mian Xiang Mastery – Module One
Basic Face Reading

A person's face is their fortune – learn more about the ancient Chinese art of Face Reading. In just one day, be equipped with techniques and skills to read a person's face and ascertain their character, luck, wealth and relationship luck.

Mian Xiang Mastery – Module Two
Practical Face Reading

Mian Xiang Module Two covers face reading techniques extracted from the ancient classics Shen Xiang Quan Pian and Shen Xiang Tie Guan Dau. Gain a greater depth and understanding of Mian Xiang and learn to recognize key structures and characteristics in a person's face.

Yi Jing Mastery Series™
LIVE COURSES (MODULES ONE AND TWO)

Yi Jing Mastery – Module One
Traditional Yi Jing

'Yi', relates to change. Change is the only constant in life and the universe, without exception to this rule. The Yi Jing is hence popularly referred to as the Book or Classic of Change. Discoursed in the language of Yin and Yang, the Yi Jing is one of the oldest Chinese classical texts surviving today. With Traditional Yi Jing, learnn how this Classic is used to divine the outcomes of virtually every facet of life; from your relationships to seeking an answer to the issues you may face in your daily life.

Yi Jing Mastery – Module Two
Plum Blossom Numerology

Shao Yong, widely regarded as one of the greatest scholars of the Sung Dynasty, developed Mei Hua Yi Shu (Plum Blossom Numerology) as a more advanced means for divination purpose using the Yi Jing. In Plum Blossom Numerology, the results of a hexagram are interpreted by referring to the Gua meanings, where the interaction and relationship between the five elements, stems, branches and time are equally taken into consideration. This divination method, properly applied, allows us to make proper decisions whenever we find ourselves in a predicament.

Ze Ri Mastery Series™
LIVE COURSES (MODULES ONE AND TWO)

Ze Ri Mastery Series Module 1
Personal and Feng Shui Date Selection

The Mastery Academy's Date Selection Mastery Series Module 1 is specifically structured to provide novice students with an exciting introduction to the Art of Date Selection. Learn the rudiments and tenets of this intriguing metaphysical science. What makes a good date, and what makes a bad date? What dates are suitable for which activities, and what dates simply aren't? And of course, the mother of all questions: WHY aren't all dates created equal. All in only one Module – Module 1!

Ze Ri Mastery Series Module 2
Xuan Kong Da Gua Date Selection

In Module 2, discover advanced Date Selection techniques that will take your knowledge of this Art to a level equivalent to that of a professional's! This is the Module where Date Selection infuses knowledge of the ancient metaphysical science of Feng Shui and BaZi (Chinese Astrology, or Four Pillars of Destiny). Feng Shui, as a means of maximizing Human Luck (i.e. our luck on Earth), is often quoted as the cure to BaZi, which allows us to decipher our Heaven (i.e. inherent) Luck. And one of the most potent ways of making the most of what life has to offer us is to understand our Destiny, know how we can use the natural energies of our environment for our environments and MOST importantly, WHEN we should use these energies and for WHAT endeavors!

You will learn specific methods on how to select suitable dates, tailored to specific activities and events. More importantly, you will also be taught how to suit dates to a person's BaZi (Chinese Astrology, or Four Pillars of Destiny), in order to maximize his or her strengths, and allow this person to surmount any challenges that lie in wait. Add in the factor of `place', and you would have satisfied the notion of `doing the right thing, at the right time and in the right place'! A basic knowledge of BaZi and Feng Shui will come in handy in this Module, although these are not pre-requisites to successfully undergo Module 2.

Feng Shui for Life

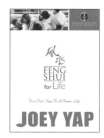

Feng Shui for life is a 5-day course designed for the Feng Shui beginner to learn how to apply practical Feng Shui in day-to-day living. It is a culmination of powerful tools and techniques that allows you to gain quick proficiency in Classical Feng Shui. Discover quick tips on analysing your own BaZi, how to apply Feng Shui solutions for your own home, how to select auspicious dates for important activities, as well as simple and useful Face Reading techniques and practical Water Formulas. This is a complete beginner's course that is suitable for anyone with an interest in applying practical, real-world Feng Shui for life! Enhance every aspect of your life – your health, wealth, and relationships – using these easy-to-apply Classical Feng Shui methods.

Mastery Academy courses are conducted around the world. Find out when will Joey Yap be in your area by visiting **www.masteryacademy.com** or call our office at **+603-2284 8080**.